The political systems that have replaced communist rule in East-Central Europe and Eurasia are closely associated with their presidents. The first democratically elected presidents of these countries – men like Yeltsin, Havel and Wałęsa – have frequently been viewed as "founding fathers" of their countries' independence. But were they successful in creating strong presidential systems in these states? Has their unquestioned personal power and charisma been institutionalized in the presidencies? Will executive power in postcommunist states remain the same when the first incumbents of the office are gone?

This book offers the first comparative analysis of the role of presidents in postcommunist states. The countries studied are Russia, Ukraine, Kazakstan among former Soviet republics, and Poland, the Czech Republic, and Hungary among Central European states. Leading specialists analyze presidential elections in these six states, including the historic 1996 election in Russia. They assess the powers of the president and describe the often-turbulent relations between presidents and parliaments in the 1990s. These experts also examine how the office has been shaped by its first incumbent and the degree to which presidents set "rules of the game" that will be in place long after they have left office.

The book also includes theoretical chapters by distinguished academics on the perils of a strong presidential system, the relevance of the separation of powers doctrine to postcommunist states, and the impact of the region's democratic breakthrough on the nature of the presidency.

Postcommunist presidents

Postcommunist presidents

Edited by
Ray Taras

CAMBRIDGE
UNIVERSITY PRESS

PUBLISHED BY THE PRESS SYNDICATE OF THE UNIVERSITY OF CAMBRIDGE
The Pitt Building, Trumpington Street, Cambridge CB2 1RP, United Kingdom

CAMBRIDGE UNIVERSITY PRESS
The Edinburgh Building, Cambridge CB2 2RU, United Kingdom
40 West 20th Street, New York, NY 10011-4211, USA
10 Stamford Road, Oakleigh, Melbourne 3166, Australia

First published 1997

Printed in the United Kingdom at the University Press, Cambridge

Typeset in Plantin 10/12 pt

A catalogue record for this book is available from the British Library

Library of Congress cataloguing in publication data

Postcommunist presidencies / edited by Ray Taras.
    p.   cm.
ISBN 0 521 58282 2. – ISBN 0 521 58765 4 (pbk)
1. Europe, Eastern – Politics and government – 1989   2. Former Soviet
republics – Politics and government.   3. Presidents – Europe, Eastern.
4. Presidents – Former Soviet republics.   5. Post-communism –
Europe, Eastern.   6. Post-communism – Former Soviet republics.
I. Taras, Ray, 1946–
DJK51.P684   1997
320.447–dc21 96–50024 CIP

ISBN 0 521 58282 2 hardback
ISBN 0 521 58765 4 paperback

VN

Contents

Notes on contributors

JON ELSTER is Robert K. Merton professor of social sciences at Columbia University. Author of numerous books on theories of social science, among recent volumes are *Constitutionalism and Democracy* (Cambridge University Press, 1993), *Political Psychology* (Cambridge University Press, 1993), and *The Roundtable Talks and the Breakdown of Communism* (University of Chicago Press, 1996).

KRZYSZTOF JASIEWICZ is professor of sociology at Washington and Lee University in Virginia, and a research fellow at the Institute of Political Studies of the Polish Academy of Sciences (ISP PAN) in Warsaw, Poland. In the 1980s he was co-author of a series of political attitudes surveys beginning with *The Poles of '80* and repeated in 1981, 1984, 1988, and 1990. From 1991 to 1993 he was director of electoral studies at ISP PAN.

JUAN J. LINZ is Sterling Professor of Political and Social Science at Yale University. The author of numerous books on democracy, he coedited volumes in the influential series *The Breakdown of Democratic Regimes* published in the 1970s. His recent books include *The Failure of Presidential Democracy* (Johns Hopkins University Press, 1994), *Between States: Interim Governments and Democratic Transitions* (Cambridge University Press, 1995), and *Problems of Democratic Transition and Consolidation: Southern Europe, South America, and Post-Communist Europe* (Johns Hopkins University Press, 1996). He holds honorary degrees from universities in Germany, Spain, and the US.

MARTHA BRILL OLCOTT is Professor of Political Science at Colgate University in New York state and Senior Associate at the Carnegie Foundation for International Peace in Washington, DC. Among her many publications on Central Asia are *The Kazakhs* (Hoover Institution Press, 1987) and *Central Asia's New States* (United States Institute of Peace Press, 1996).

PATRICK O'NEIL is assistant professor of politics and government at the University of Puget Sound, Washington. He is editor of *The Media and Global Democratization* (Frank Cass, 1997), and is also completing a book on the collapse of socialism in Hungary. His current research addresses the issue of risk management in transitional societies.

RAY TARAS has been Professor of Political Science at Tulane University in New Orleans. He has also taught at the universities of Michigan, Kentucky, and Vermont in the US, and in Canadian and British universities. His recent books include *Consolidating Democracy in Poland* (Westview Press, 1995) and *National Identities and Ethnic Minorities in Eastern Europe* (Macmillan, 1997).

STEPHEN WHITE is Professor of Politics and a member of the Institute of Russian and East European Studies at the University of Glasgow, and president of the British Association for Slavonic and East European Studies. His recent books include *After Gorbachev* (4th edn, Cambridge University Press, 1994), *Russia Goes Dry: Alcohol, State and Society* (Cambridge University Press, 1996), and *How Russia Votes* (with Richard Rose and Ian McAllister, Chatham House, 1996).

ANDREW WILSON is Senior Research Fellow at Sidney Sussex College, Cambridge University. He received his Ph.D. from London School of Economics in 1993 and has written extensively on the political transition in Ukraine. His books include *Ukraine: Perestroika to Independence* (with Taras Kuzio; Macmillan, 1994) and *Ukrainian Nationalism in the 1990s: A Minority Faith* (Cambridge University Press, 1996).

SHARON L. WOLCHIK is Director of Russian and East European Studies of the Elliot School of International Affairs at the George Washington University. She is author of *Czechoslovakia in Transition: Politics, Economics and Society* (Pinter, 1991) and editor of *Building a State: Ukraine in a Post-Soviet World* (Oxford University Press, 1996).

Introduction: some thoughts on presidentialism in postcommunist Europe

Juan J. Linz

Studying presidential systems

Since the publication of my essay "Presidential or Parliamentary Democracy: Does it Make a Difference?", from the early version to the more definitive one in my book with Arturo Valenzuela entitled *The Failure of Presidential Democracy*, I have become known as a critic of presidentialism.[1] I am, therefore, not an unbiased contributor to this volume, although the catchy title of the book was perhaps too strongly worded a revision of the more skeptical formulation contained in the title of my essay.

I have not said that presidential democracies cannot consolidate, be stable, and even function reasonably well, nor that parliamentary systems are always a guarantee of stability of democracy. The facts I myself have analyzed prove this. I have argued only that basic structural characteristics of presidential systems make it more likely that they will encounter serious difficulties and that, under certain circumstances, to be specified in each case, they might contribute to the breakdown of democracies that, with adequate parliamentary institutions, might have had a better chance to survive. The crises of parliamentary systems are crises of government, the crises in presidential systems are more likely to be crises of regime. This means that I am not predicting the imminent breakdown of the presidential regimes in the postcommunist states. I would, however, have prophesied that some of the serious crises of postcommunist democracies are related to the option exercised for presidentialism, even when they have not led to a breakdown of democratic processes. I would also argue, on the basis of the available evidence, that a significant number of the postcommunist democracies that have been consolidated or are on the way toward consolidation are parliamentary or, at the most, semi-presidential functioning largely as parliamentary democracies. I do not dare quantify this conclusion, given the ambiguity of the constitutions and the constitutional practice in many postcommunist countries, and the uncertainties about whether democracy has been consolidated or is on the way to consolidation, using the criteria Alfred Stepan and I have developed.[2]

If all this were not sufficient to make an analysis of the consequences for democracy of the constitutional options discussed in the case studies of this book and several others that have recently been published difficult,[3] there is a prior question: are we really talking about regimes that satisfy the basic definition of exhibiting the characteristics of democracy besides the holding of more or less free and fair elections? Particularly in the case of the former members of the Yugoslav Federation and of the Soviet Union – some of them now members of the Commonwealth of Independent States – very different answers to the question, of whether presidentialism or parliamentarism makes a difference, could be discovered. There is no clear consensus on which countries can be considered democracies beyond an electoralist definition. Although there is some consensus that a number of countries which were part of the Soviet Union and Yugoslavia do not satisfy any reasonable definition of democracy, it happens that a number of them have opted for presidential or semi-presidential constitutions, and that their presidents are the most powerful office-holders in those countries. Can we venture the hypothesis that the option for presidentialism was a result of prior undemocratic or anti-democratic tendencies, or that the failure to progress in a democratic direction was the result of having opted for presidentialism or semi-presidentialism? I, for one, would not like to advance an answer without a thorough analysis of the political developments in some of those countries. For my analysis, it would be convenient to argue the second answer. Using the data from the rating of twenty-six postcommunist countries on political rights and civil liberties, I could make a case for the conclusion that the option for presidentialism and/or strong presidential powers is associated with those countries located below the threshold of democracy.[4]

However, I want to insist that my analysis of the difficulties, if not failure, of presidentialism is not based on such a quantitative analysis. That is why I do not consider the continuity of democratic institutions or the formal breakdown of those institutions a test of my approach to the problem of presidentialism. I would, however, argue that the frequency and intensity of crises in the political system and the quality of democratic political processes should be related to the type of regime.

As Jon Elster writes in the concluding chapter to this book, it is easier to give answers to the question of why the political actors choose, at some point, one or another type of institutions and the calculations, correct or mistaken, influencing their decision, what he has called "the upstream question." It is much more difficult to give an answer to the question of what difference it makes. The "downstream question" is more complex in systems that only recently have enacted their constitutions, which are sometimes still in the constitution-making process, systems which provide us with only a short historical record, in which particular power constellations or particular incumbents may explain more than institutional structures do. Therefore, my comments are more questions for future scholarly work than answers to the basic question of what difference constitutions and institutions make. Even so, I do not think that the reader of this book or of other works on the constitutions and politics of postcommunist Europe will not have the feeling that some of the doubts about the advisability of presidentialism in new democracies were totally unjustified. I cannot here call attention to specific cases and events which would be relevant, I will leave this to the reader and future scholarly work. Implicit in any such analysis is the difficult question of counter-factuals: would things have been different if those states had started with parliamentary institutions? It is well known that counter-factuals cannot be proven.

Studying semi-presidential/semi-parliamentary systems comparatively, I confront the difficult question of the working of semi-parliamentary/semi-presidential regimes or, to use the terminology of Matthew Shugart and John Carey, the premier-presidential, and the even more complicated type they define as president/parliamentary.[5] There have been relatively few regimes that could be so characterized. If one ignores (as one should) the newly independent states in interwar Europe that introduced semi-presidentialism but which functioned in practice as parliamentary systems in spite of the direct election of the president and the considerable powers which, in some cases, were given to those presidents in the constitutions, it is not possible to make empirically based generalizations. Let me leave out Ireland, Iceland, the more complex case of Finland (until recent reforms), and Portugal (where the 1982 reforms to the 1976 constitution and political practice have moved the system closer to parliamentarism). Although I accept some of the objections of Giovanni Sartori[6] to the dominant thesis that the premier/presidential or semi-presidential/semi-parliamentary regimes have tended to function alternatively as presidential or parliamentary, it is difficult to evaluate systematically how those regimes have performed.

We are basically left with the two cases of the successful Fifth Republic in France after 1958, and the Weimar Republic, a case of failure, in post-World War I Germany. It is, therefore, difficult to make generalizations on the basis of previous cases of semi-presidentialism, particularly since one can debate the extent to which the transition to presidential cabinets without parliamentary support under Hindenburg in Germany represented a breakdown of democracy even before the appointment of

Hitler as chancellor. Besides, in the case of Germany, it is debatable whether the abdication by the Reichstag of its function to provide a government having parliamentary support and its toleration of the Brünning presidential government was possible thanks to Article 48 of the constitution. In any case, until we have more semi-parliamentary/semi-presidential regimes, it will be difficult to analyze systematically how they work, and to question the preference that some scholars, on the basis of the French experience, express for this type of system and the choices made in its favor by a number of postcommunist regimes.

Even so, we should not forget that semi-presidential systems share at least two of the characteristics of presidentialism: the dual democratic legitimacy of the presidency and the legislature as a result of popular election and, with some modifications, the rigidity in the time for which presidents are elected.

In addition, presidential and semi-presidential regimes share the unique personal character of the office (with the exception of Bosnia, with its three-person presidency). This again makes comparisons extremely difficult since, unless there have been several elections and different incumbents, it is not possible to distinguish the characteristics of the office from the personal idiosyncracy of the incumbents.

In my view, the postcommunist regimes did well in not choosing a complex hybrid like the new Israeli system.[7] It is a system that, despite the direct election of the prime minister, in the view of Sartori (with which I can concur), is not presidential since the prime minister is still subject to parliamentary confidence or non-confidence votes. On the other hand, he is not comparable to a prime minister having parliamentary confidence as in a semi-presidential system, since he might be tolerated while neutralized for the four years for which he is elected, with only the possibility of dissolution automatically leading to his downfall. The expectations of the designers of this system were that on the "coat-tails" of his election, the prime minister would be able to obtain a strong representation for his party or supporting coalition in the Knesset. The hope was also to weaken the minor parties that had so much blackmail potential in the formation of governments in Israel. This, at least in the first election under the new system, has not happened. Perhaps the voters, having chosen "their" premier, felt freer to vote for particular parties close to their more specific interests, in this way strengthening the minor parties. The prime minister must make do with the support or non-support given to him in the Knesset by the electorate.

Heads of state in parliamentary democracies

A number of the countries included in this study of postcommunist democracies are parliamentary republics and as such have as head of state a president indirectly elected or, in some cases, popularly elected, but apparently with very limited powers. Even in the cases in which presidents are heads of state of a parliamentary republic – not to be confused with presidents in presidential or semi-presidential regimes – they have been provided with somewhat greater powers or roles than in traditional parliamentary republics or, on account of their personality (as in the case of Havel), enjoy considerable prestige, influence and thereby potential power.

In analyzing these president-heads of state in parliamentary regimes such as in Hungary and the Czech Republic, we face the difficulty that there are few studies of heads of state in parliamentary democracies. There is no systematic analysis of the role of monarchs in long-time stable parliamentary regimes such as the United Kingdom, Scandinavia, the Benelux countries, and Spain after Franco. There is no systematic comparative study of the heads of state in parliamentary republics, although there are interesting studies and biographies of the presidents of the Federal Republic of Germany[8] and Italy that would show how different incumbents have perceived their role; there are probably comparable materials for the Third and Fourth Republics in France. We cannot compare the role of Göncz and Havel with Theodore Heuss in Germany, Luigi Einaudi or Sandro Pertini in Italy, or René Coty in France, among many others. We cannot say how similar or different in the conception of their role the presidents-heads of state in the new parliamentary democracies of postcommunist Europe are from their Western counterparts in similar periods. Such a comparison should be incorporated into the comparative study of parliamentary postcommunist states.

One of the great questions for a comparativist to ask is to what extent the United States is a paradigm to compare presidential systems, as the Fifth Republic in France is a paradigm to compare semi-presidential systems. If we would argue, as Fred Riggs does,[9] that the United States has a unique combination of institutions and political practices that have made presidentialism work, perhaps even in spite of some of the structural problems connected with presidentialism, such a comparison would be, in many ways, misleading. American exceptionalism, which includes a two-century-old constitution and a profound commitment to constitutionalism, a strong and generally respected Supreme Court, a federal system that disperses power, a distinctive two-party system of largely non-ideological and not highly disciplined parties, etc., makes it difficult to see to what extent presidential regimes in postcommunist Europe would be comparable and similar to the United States model. Even in the case of the French Fifth Republic, the politicians who created it had long experience in democratic politics under the Fourth Republic; the party system pre-dated the introduction of presidentialism, and there was a capable and, to some extent, independent bureaucracy, among many other factors.[10] It may be objected that such a focus on "my country is different" prevents comparative analysis. But there can be no question that a better understanding of the uniqueness of the models would help us understand the new democracies in which they are more or less imitated and where institutional arrangements are borrowed piecemeal. Such a focus would perhaps stimulate more systematic comparison across postcommunist presidential and semi-presidential systems.

Among the many reasons to be cautious at this point about a comparative analysis of postcommunist presidencies is the uncertainty about the emerging party system, the volatility in some of the countries of the electorate, and the possibility of changes in the electoral laws. In addition, there are uncertainties about the political articulation of nationalist, autonomist, or secessionist demands which, in many cases, should favor the introduction of proportional representation but which, as we know, is not particularly congruent with presidentialism.

Addressing the downstream question

I am somewhat frightened to travel downstream in the troubled waters of transitions and consolidations of the new presidential or semi-presidential systems in postcommunist Europe. Who is to tell whether the political process will take place within the channels generated by institutions and not overflow those channels or, in the course of events, take another way fully outside of the institutional channels being created.

Some readers might feel that, after all, neither presidentialism nor semi-presidentialism has failed in the former Soviet Union and Eastern Europe. If we define failure as not holding elections, the assumption of power by presidents without electoral legitimation, or the violent overthrow of elected presidents rather than their impeachment or resignation without a coup, this has not happened except in some of the new states in the Caucasus and Central Asia. Leaving that part of the world aside, the new systems have worked rather less well in other cases too.

I shall ignore the Gorbachev presidency of the USSR as this was *not* a democratic presidency. He had not been elected by the people of the USSR nor even by a fully democratic legislature. It therefore becomes difficult to say if the crisis of Gorbachev's authority, the disintegration of the USSR, and the coup against him were related or not to the presidential character of his office. The participation of his vice-president in the conspiracy against him shows some similarity with other cases of vice-presidents elected to balance the ticket representing a different political orientation, and ultimately coming into conflict with the president. It could be argued that the choice of a presidential regime by Gorbachev and his advisers contributed to his disinterest in using the widespread mobilization of civil society in the USSR, or at least parts of it, to build a party supporting a democratic transition to democracy. It would be interesting to analyze to what extent the introduction of the presidential model into many of the republics of the USSR, with the exception of the Baltic states, contributed to creating a personalized leadership of former secretaries-general of the party or leading nomenklatura members, who, to legitimize themselves, had to turn to nationalism. In any case, I would not like to use the failure of Gorbachev to support the thesis of the failure of presidentialism.

The case of Yeltsin provides more evidence for several of the arguments against presidentialism. First of all, the success of introducing, through a referendum, the question of creating the presidential office, the subsequent election of Yeltsin to the presidency in June 1991, and his conception of the office after his moment of glory, during the coup attempt against Gorbachev, had decisive consequences for political developments in Russia. One of them was that Yeltsin missed the opportunity to transform the democratic political forces that supported him in the election into a political party, at a time when the Communist Party had lost its prestige even though it could not be fully outlawed. By conceiving the presidency as above party and even introducing, as in other postcommunist constitutions, the principle that the president could not be the leader of the party, he missed a great opportunity. Ever since, it has been difficult to create a single block of moderate party supporters of democracy.

A second consequence was that, in exchange for support for some of his economic reforms, Yeltsin allowed the sitting Russian Soviet to continue to exist rather than calling for elections and ensuring the enactment of a constitution by a democratically elected body or at least, reform of the constitution. Swift parliamentary elections at the time of his highest popularity might have allowed him to obtain the support of a large block of deputies elected with his support. Instead, preserving the existing Soviet made possible the continuity of a diarchy, a situation which made it difficult for Yeltsin to govern. This dual power structure led to the compromise of the April 1993 referendum, which allowed Yeltsin to claim a victory in public opinion but *not* to eliminate the source of conflict between the Soviet-inherited legislature and the presidency. The festering conflict culminated in the confrontation with parliamentary speaker Ruslan Khasbulatov that ended with the bombing and assault on the White House in October 1993. In addition, the logic of presidentialism had earlier led Yeltsin to run in June 1991 on a ticket with former general Aleksandr Rutskoi who, from the beginning, did not share his views but brought to the ticket a balance and probably some voters.[11] Obviously, presidential regimes exist without vice-presidents but in an uncertain situation, such as that in 1991, vice-presidents can generate this kind of problem. A logical conclusion drawn from the 1993 crisis by several postcommunist presidential systems has been to abolish the office of vice-president. With it has been lost one of the possible advantages of presidentialism: assuring continuity for the period of the mandate of the president and the holding of elections only every few years, thanks to the device of the transfer of the office of president to the vice-president in case of death or incapacity.

A further consequence of the victory of President Yeltsin was that the constitution-making process did not take place with the participation of a deliberative body. Rather, the draft constitution would be proposed directly by the president to the people. It thereby derived all of its legitimacy from the December 1993 referendum and the relatively narrow and even dubious victory in that referendum. It could be argued that the disasters that marked the first presidency of Yeltsin seriously threatened the stability of democracy, and probably contributed to a delegitimation of new democratic political institutions among important sectors of the population. They were part of the difficulties of the transition. The coexistence of institutions, some based on the constitution and the political structure of the old regime, with the new democratically elected presidency, can be seen as part of the unfinished transition. Again one can claim this was not a failure of presidentialism.[12]

We will have to wait to see how the Russian presidency evolves after the December 1995 legislative elections and the 1996 presidential election. We will observe the forms that cohabitation takes between the Duma and the president, and a prime minister caught in conflicts between president and legislature. Will it lead to "flexible diarchy," Sartori's characterization of the working of the French system? But the problem remains of the possible divided power and dual legitimacy of the two chambers of the Russian parliament, derived from the federal character of the Russian Federation. It is therefore much too early to talk about the success or failure of the Russian constitutional system as becomes even clearer from reading Stephen White's chapter.

The presidency is a single-person office that, in the absence of a simultaneously elected vice-president, can become vacant in case of incapacity or death. The question of who is in charge in that situation is worrisome. In the Russian, as in the French constitution, the president, in case of temporary incapacity, can delegate his authority to a person of his choice. However, will such a person enjoy the same authority as the elected president? In the case of death, after an interim period elections are held to fill the office. It could be argued that in a parliamentary regime problems of transition would be less acute. Another member of the cabinet with the same parliamentary base would simply assume power. In case of death, the parliamentary majority could either confirm the same person or choose someone else.

The chapter on Poland by Krzysztof Jasiewicz shows the many problems that emerged from the confrontations between president Wałęsa, the Sejm, and the prime ministers who had support in the legislature. In spite of the fears expressed by many observers, that conflict did not lead to a breakdown of democracy in Poland. However, we have survey data showing the ambivalences of Polish citizens about their democracy and the conflict between those who favored the legitimacy of the president's powers versus those who supported the legislature.[13] It is not easy to say what legacy divided government left Polish citizens. We cannot speculate about the counterfactual that Wałęsa could have become the leader of a party which would have held together at least for some time, integrating sectors of the old Solidarity movement rather than, as happened, causing disintegration when Wałęsa ran against Mazowiecki in the 1990 presidential election. I do not think that anyone would question that the long delay in approving the constitution, which would have established clarity about the powers of all actors on the political scene and determine whether Poland would be a parliamentary or semi-presidential system, has been due largely to holding an early election for the president, rather than first enacting a constitution. Poland is now a clear case of a semi-presidential system in which the party or coalition supporting the president and the prime minister is the same and with it the potential conflicts derived from cohabitation disappear. We cannot say, on the basis of the early experience of Polish semi-presidentialism without a new constitution or with only the "little constitution," how the system will ultimately work.

A question requiring answers is to what extent in Russia and in Poland the conflicts between institutions and their incumbents, and delays in creating a well-defined institutional constitutional framework, have affected the capacity to generate, enact, and implement important policies. This question is also central in the evaluation of the political developments in Ukraine where, as Andrew Wilson notes, the type of confrontation which took place in Russia was avoided. Many observers would agree that the intensity of conflict between the elites about the institutions and the distribution of power between different offices has delayed the formulation of policies at critical junctures, with a loss of efficacy for the political system as a whole.

Bringing the party system back in

Any analysis of the functioning of semi-presidential/semi-parliamentary systems has to focus on the party system at least as much or more than in the study of presidential systems. The success of a system having a predominance of the president, or his cohabitation with a prime minister with the support of the majority in parliament, is largely dependent on the party system and the relationship between the president and the parties. The regime can only work as presidential when the president has the support of a party or a solid party coalition with a majority in parliament. The president has to identify with the party, has to work for the success of his party in the legislative elections and, in the absence of a majority for a party identified with him, work for the building of a coalition in the legislature able to support his choice of prime minister. This means that a semi-presidential/semi-parliamentary system will not work very well in a highly fragmented party system or a polarized multiparty system. The provision in many constitutions of the postcommunist democracies that the president should not be a member of a party is in contradiction, therefore, with a prerequisite for effective presidential government. Furthermore, the conception of many of the incumbents is that they want to be presidents above parties, and they often loosen their ties with them after their own election is secured.

The assumption of a degree of alternation between presidential and parliamentary type of government in semi-presidential regimes assumes that there is a legislature able to give support to a prime minister of a different party or coalition than the one that has elected the president. It assumes that the legislature is able to provide that prime minister with a majority. Should this not be possible due to the fragmentation of the party system or a multiparty system that is polarized and unable to provide a majority coalition, the system is not likely to function with a prime minister resting on a parliamentary base. Power reverts to a president who will have to choose his prime minister from among the contenders, attempt to form a coalition supporting him/her, or at least prevent a negative majority from blocking his/her choice of prime minister through a vote of no-confidence. This last alternative can prove unstable and difficult, even when the prime minister is given some protection by restricting the legislature's ability to vote no-confidence or by sanctioning a legislature if it does so, such as through its dissolution.

Werner Kaltefleiter[14] has highlighted these different situations by distinguishing structured, unstructured, and stalemated party systems. In the first case, the president can be either the leader of a party, an influential leader in his party, or lacking significant influence in the party. The Fifth Republic of France, in which de Gaulle and Mitterand were simultaneously presidents and party leaders, is an example. Kaltefleiter mentions President Schärf of Austria as a president with influence in his party; most other Austrian presidents were presidents without particular influence in a party. It should be remembered that many authors consider that the Austrian system, in spite of its semi-presidential/semi-parliamentary constitution, does not fit their definition of that type of regime.

The role of the president in an unstructured party system, or at least a relatively unstructured one, also varies in terms of the relationship of the president with the parties. Kaltefleiter gives examples of presidents as leaders of a party: Ebert, the social democratic leader and first president of the Weimar Republic, and Kekkonen in Finland. As presidents with influence in their party, he mentions the second presidency of Ebert and the majority of Finnish presidents. Finally, as an example of a president without strong influence in a party, in an unstructured party system, he cites the first presidency of Hindenburg in the Weimar Republic.

The most difficult situation arises in a stalemated party system in which there is a very unstable or no majority in the legislature and the president cannot have either support or influence on a party or party coalition, as was the case in the second presidency of Hindenburg. In such a situation the president might turn to extra-parliamentary leaders to provide support in forming a government, or to a shadow government of persons with access to him or her. The temptation to govern without or against the legislature, to dissolve it and seek a new majority and, in case of failure, even to disband the legislature thereby turning to an *autogolpe* strategy, cannot be excluded.

The postcommunist semi-presidential/semi-parliamentary democracies, at least in the first period, cannot rest upon well-structured party systems, either because parties did not form and had no representation in the legislatures inherited from the pre-democratic period, or because of a high level of electoral volatility. The idea that presidents should be above party, not members of a party and not actively engaged in campaigning for any party or party coalition, means that the most successful and stable type of president who is at the same time a party leader, did not develop in many postcommunist, semi-presidential/semi-parliamentary systems, with the exception of some in the Caucasus and Central Asian former Soviet Republics. In other cases, as in Kazakstan, we see the president making efforts to exercise influence on a party and even to encourage the creation of a party to support him. Or perhaps the Kazak system, as described by Martha Brill Olcott, is even moving toward a kind of sultanism.[15]

Our emphasis on the linkage between the type of party system and the functioning of semi-presidential and semi-parliamentary regimes would be incomplete without further analysis of the electoral laws that contribute to one or another party system, a well-researched topic.

It would be interesting to see to what extent Russia, after the December 1995 legislative elections and the June 1996 presidential election, is closer to the last of the situations analyzed by Kaltefleiter, the stalemated system. Perhaps this explains the complexity of the presidential government of Yeltsin, the multiple power structures surrounding the president, the shifting roles played by the government and its prime minister, and the forced reliance on the support of a previous outsider, General Alexander Lebed, leader of an unsuccessful party but pivotal in swinging support to Yeltsin in the second round of the presidential election.

It would be tempting to analyze the presidency by distinguishing periods after legislative elections in the different postcommunist, semi-presidential/semi-parliamentary systems, a task beyond my scope here.

I want to emphasize that the typology of Kaltefleiter is not applicable to presidents/heads of state in parliamentary republics. In fact, since they do not formulate national policy, do not exercise executive authority, and have only a limited and indirect influence on the formation of governments, even in multiparty situations, they should proceed and act with considerable neutrality toward parties. Even when they are elected with the support of a particular party coalition or individual party, they should not identify with it. Indeed, the identification of a head of state in a parliamentary system with distinct partisan positions is likely to weaken his authority and legitimacy and has sometimes led to serious political crises. A head of state is able to exercise his influence on public opinion and on the politicians above all when he is perceived as being above partisan conflicts, concerned with the defense of the constitution and democracy, or articulating widely shared values. As may be seen from the chapters by Sharon Wolchik and Patrick O'Neil, perhaps Havel and Göncz owe their prestige, standing, and influence, as well as popular approval, to having conceived their role in this way.

Presidents in systems that constitutionally are semi-presidential/semi-parliamentary can choose this role for themselves. The fact that successive presidents have done so has contributed to what could be called the material constitution of those states to develop into parliamentary systems. Iceland, Ireland, to a large extent Austria and probably, since the presidency of Mario Soares, Portugal, are examples. However, it does not seem likely that all presidents in the semi-presidential/semi-parliamentary systems of postcommunist Europe will conceive their role in this way or that, given the pressing demands on them, particularly in unstructured or stalemated party systems, this would be possible.

NOTES

1 Juan J. Linz, "Presidential or Parliamentary Democracy: Does it Make a Difference?" in J. Linz and Arturo Valenzuela (eds.), *The Failure of Presidential Democracy* (Baltimore: Johns Hopkins University Press, 1994), pp. 3–87.

2 Juan J. Linz and Alfred Stepan, *Problems of Democratic Transition and Consolidation. Southern Europe, South America and Post-Communist Europe* (Baltimore: Johns Hopkins University Press, 1996), ch. 1.

3 "The Postcommunist Presidency," *East European Constitutional Review*, 2, 4 (Fall 1993); 3, 1 (Winter 1994); Irena Grudzinska Gross (ed.), *Constitutionalism and Politics, International Symposium*, Bratislava, 11–14 November 1993, published by the Slovak Committee of the European Cultural Foundation; Carlos Flores Juberias (ed.), "The New Political Institutions of Eastern Europe" (unpublished manuscript); Arend Lijphart and Carlos Waisman (eds.), *Institutional Design in New Democracies. Eastern Europe and Latin America* (Boulder, CO: Westview Press, 1996).

4 See: Linz and Stepan, *Problems of Democratic Transition and Consolidation*, pp. 442–449.

5 Matthew Soberg Shugart and John M. Casey, *Presidents and Assemblies: Constitutional Design and Electoral Dynamics* (Cambridge: Cambridge University Press, 1992).

6 Giovanni Sartori, *Comparative Constitutional Engineering. An Inquiry into Structures, Incentives and Outcomes* (New York: New York University Press, 1994), pp. 121–140.

7 Vernon Bogdanor, "Electoral System, Government and Democracy," in Ehud Sprinzak and Larry Diamond (eds.), *Israeli Democracy Under Stress* (Boulder, CO: Lynne Rienner, 1993), pp. 83–106, see especially pp. 96–100. In the same volume see Arend Lijphart, "Israeli Democracy and Democratic Reform in Comparative Perspective," pp. 107–123, especially pp. 119–121. For Sartori's critique, see *Comparative Constitutional Engineering*, pp. 115–116, pp. 126–127. Maurice Duverger, "A New Political Model: Semi-presidential government," *European Journal of Political Research*, 8 (1980), p. 166.

8 See Alfred Grosser, *Das Deutschland im Westen. Eine Bilanz nach 40 Jahren* (Munich: Carl Hansen, 1983), pp. 118–122, on the different conceptions of the role of presidents of the Federal Republic of Germany.

9 Fred W. Riggs, "The Survival of Presidentialism in America: Para-Constitutional Practices," *International Political Science Review*, 9, 4 (1988), pp. 247–278.

10 Sylvia von Steinsdorff, "Die Verfassungsgesetz der Zweiten Russischen und der Fünften Französischen Republik im Vergleich," *Zeitschrift für Parlamentsfragen*, 3 (1995), pp. 486–504; Ellen Boss, "Verfassunggebungsprozess und Regierungssystem im Russland," in Wolfgang Merket et al. (eds.), *System-*

wechsel Die Institutionalisierung der Demokratie (Opladen: Westdeutscher Verlag, 1996), pp. 179–209.

11 Yitzhak M. Brudny, "Ruslan Khasbulatov, Aleksandr Ruskoi, and Intraelite Conflict in Postcommunist Russia, 1991–1994," in Timothy J. Colton and Robert C. Tucker (eds.), *Patterns in Post-Soviet Leadership* (Boulder, CO: Westview Press 1995), pp. 75–101; also Brudny, "The Dynamics of Democratic Russia, 1990–1993," *Post-Soviet Affairs*, 9 (April–June 1993), pp. 141–170.

12 For an analysis of the choices made in the transition to democracy in Russia, see Linz and Stepan, *Democratic Transition and Consolidation*, pp. 388–400; Margareta Mommsen, "Wohin Freibt Russland?" *Eine Grossmacht zwischen Anarchie und Demokratie* (Munich: Piper, 1996).

13 See public opinion data quoted in chapter 16 on Poland in Linz and Stepan, *Democratic Transition and Consolidation*, pp. 255–292.

14 Werner Kaltefleiter, *Die Funktionen des Staatsoberhauptes in der Parlamentarischen Demokratie* (Cologne: Westdeutscher Verlag, 1970).

15 On sultanism, see my forthcoming volume with H. E. Chehabi, also, Linz and Stepan, *Problems of Democratic Transition*, pp. 51–54.

1   Separating power: keeping presidents in check

Raymond Taras

Democratic consolidation and form of government: are they connected?

Many factors contribute to the consolidation of democracy in a country shedding its authoritarian past. The collapse of communist systems generated a new wave, often involving old thinking, of inquiry into what makes democracies endure. Huntington[1] referred to pre-existing democratic traditions and Putnam[2] spoke of pre-existing civic virtue. Karl and Schmitter[3] stressed the nature of the democratic transition itself while Offe[4] and Przeworski[5] highlighted elite management of change. Following de Tocqueville, the existence of intermediary or voluntary organizations[6] and the level of economic development[7] are widely recognized as consolidating factors. A country's geopolitical position, its experience as a colony of a democratic state, or its exposure to the influence of Protestantism are other factors said to contribute to the consolidation of democracy.[8] Sartori[9] pointed to the "taming" of politics whereby political elites no longer perceived it as warlike, and earlier he had stressed the importance of well-developed party systems to democratic stability.[10] For Linz and Stepan[11] democracy is consolidated, finally, when it becomes "the only game in town," accepted in behavioral, attitudinal, and constitutional terms.

Among this catalogue of factors making for democracy is the choice of political institutions decided upon after authoritarianism has collapsed. How power is distributed among institutions is a central concern of democratizers. Specialists have, therefore, carefully weighed the relative merits of presidential versus parliamentary system of government,[12] executive-legislative relations[13] and, underpinning institutional configurations, the separation of powers doctrine, all of which we examine below.[14]

In the process of institution-building, postcommunist states have been concerned with achieving such enduring and universal objectives as institutionalizing the rule of law, creating a balance among political institutions, ensuring accountability of elected officials, and enhancing the efficiency of government. In a few states of the postcommunist world leaders may have held out for alternatives to existing systems found in the West or East; indeed, after the democratic breakthroughs in Eastern Europe and Soviet Union between 1989 and 1991 there were opportunities for institutional innovation and experimentation, deemed by Nobel prize-winning economist Douglass North to be crucial to future political and economic development.[15] But in many countries the "new institutions" soon turned out to be a rediscovery of the "old institutions" of liberal democracy. The separation of powers doctrine, which often served as a guidepost in achieving the objectives identified above, once again became a focus of attention.

In post-authoritarian states such as those emerging from communist rule, there has tended to be a drift toward, rather than a decision in favor of, a particular type of political system. Whether a presidential or parliamentary system has become dominant in a country has depended to a great extent on the relations between the first democratically elected president and the legislature, on the political ambitions of members of the new elite ensconced in different branches of government, and on the prevailing consensus about the desirability of strong leadership or of checks and balances.

As suggested by other studies, in Russia and most of the other new states in the region presidents stand at the apex of political systems. In much of Central and Eastern Europe outside the Balkans, presidents are at the top of either semi-presidential systems modelled on the French Fifth Republic, or they have been eclipsed by prime ministerial or cabinet government. Intriguingly, the attraction of the Fifth Republic model may lie precisely in its ability to switch from being a presidential system to a parliamentary one – as occurred when "cohabitation" took place between 1986 and 1988 between socialist president Mitterand and a conservative-dominated National Assembly led by Prime Minister Jacques Chirac, who enhanced the power of his office during this interregnum. The cases examined in this book shed further light on the type of system favored in different parts of the postcommunist world and the consequences that have followed.

To date, research on leadership in the postcommunist states has tended to focus on individuals rather than institutions (though Huskey's volume on the USSR is an exception),[16] and on the social composition of elites rather than the powers they have acquired. Thus, three scholars concerned with elite theory have tried to make sense of the continuity of political elites in Central Europe and the western states of the former Soviet Union. John Higley, Judith Kullberg, and Jan Pakulski drew paradoxical conclusions about the reasons for and consequences of elite continuity. "Although perceived by many observers both inside and outside the region as a troubling indicator of the lack of change in postcommunist regimes, or as evidence of the continuing legacy of communism, the generally high degree of elite continuity is better understood as a consequence of how elites were evolving before communism's collapse."[17] The authors continued: "Although it seems perverse, the essential continuity of elites is one reason why democracy has been able to progress in Central and Eastern Europe: democracy has not constituted a dire threat to most established elites."[18] However, this trend was not perceptible in other regions of the postcommunist world: "In the southern countries of Central Europe and across the vast sweep of the former Soviet Union, very high degrees of elite continuity have gone hand-in-hand with postcommunist regimes that hide the substance of authoritarianism behind a veneer of democratic forms." The authors concluded: "Moderate degrees of elite continuity are compatible with, and apparently conducive to, democratic politics in the postcommunist period; really high degrees of continuity are associated with serious shortcomings in democracy."[19] In this view, then, "new" political leaders like Wałęsa in Poland, Klaus in the Czech Republic, Antall in Hungary, and Yavlinsky in Russia have contributed to building democratic regimes.

Postcommunist presidents have served as foci of research mainly in terms of biographical studies.[20] Comparative research on this subject is scarce: Alfred Stepan and Cindy Skach's work, discussed below, is an exception.[21] Likewise, Thomas Baylis carried out an important preliminary comparative inquiry that pointed out how "In general, there is a discrepancy between the visibility and popularity of most East European presidents and their circumscribed constitutional powers. They have not been able to translate the former into a sustained expansion of their actual influence, although most have sought to do so."[22] But he noted that the discrepancy is logical: "The greater popularity of presidents as compared with prime ministers undoubtedly owes something to the very limits placed on their governmental powers. They are not closely associated with unpopular economic measures or with the day-to-day partisan squabbling in parliament; in fact, their positions allow them to act as spokesmen for popular discontents."[23] Most postcommunist presidents, Baylis discovered, have disassociated themselves from a single party and, in the much-admired Gaullist manner, have projected themselves to be above party politics.

The early popularity of men such as Wałęsa, Havel, Göncz (in Hungary), Zhelev (in Bulgaria), Landsbergis (in Lithuania), and Meri (in Estonia) stemmed from their reputation as political dissidents in the late communist era and propelled them to become presidents in the postcommunist one. This attribute did not ensure success over the longer term as Wałęsa, Zhelev, and Landsbergis failed to obtain a second popular mandate (being elected indirectly, Havel, Göncz and Meri did not have to test electoral waters). Yeltsin and Kravchuk (in Ukraine) engaged in daring political risk-taking before the USSR collapsed, securing for themselves initial legitimacy and popularity. By contrast, the power base built up in the communist period by Soviet republic leaders such as Nazarbaev (in Kazakstan), Niiazov (in Turkmenistan), Karimov (Uzbekistan), Aliev (in Azerbaijan), and Shevardnadze (in Georgia), and by Balkan leaders like Milosevic (in the new Yugoslavia) though not Iliescu (in Romania), guaranteed that they would win "popular" elections and referenda for some time into the future. Being "above party politics" had nothing to do with their success; being former Communist Party apparatchiks had everything to do with it. What nearly all these men (there were no women presidents) had in common was what in Western democracies is referred to as name recognition, regardless of whether it was in a flattering light.

Postcommunist prime ministers, on the other hand, have tended to come from the more mundane world of economists, lawyers, technocrats, and scholars of the late communist era. While vested with considerable constitutional power in some East European states, their primary tasks of putting together viable if often shaky parliamentary coalitions, formulating (more often than not) unpopular policies, and becoming involved in seemingly inevitable conflicts with presidents, have produced a high attrition rate among these office-holders, greater turnover among incumbents and, consequently, overall diminuition of their perceived standing. A contributory factor requiring prime ministers to struggle for primacy in the new political system is the fact that this office was assigned the role of second violin during decades of Communist Party rule. Nevertheless, if postcommunist presidents enjoy a higher profile, as Baylis has suggested, this does not necessarily translate into the emergence of a presidential system – one where the powers and prerogatives of the office of president are expansive.

Relations between presidents and prime ministers have differed over time and space. In Central Europe it is the latter who seem to have enjoyed the upper hand in conflicts over policy. But in the six cases studied in this book, the presidents of Russia, Ukraine, Kazakstan, and Poland have managed to remove at least one prime minister each, while no prime minister has been able to undermine a president. Among states not considered here, Slovak Prime Minister Mečiar may have tried hardest to depose his country's president, Kovac, but he did not succeed, while Belarus's first president, Shushkevich, may have proved an exception in having been removed by parliament. Paradoxically, however, and unlike in the newly independent republics of the former Soviet Union, in Central Europe "the popularity of most of the present [presidential] incumbents and public frustration with both governments and parliaments [has not] led anywhere to broadly based demands for a drift from a parliamentary to a presidential system."[24] Here parliaments have served as the locus of power, deciding who will rule and what policies will be pursued, or at the very least the source of power, choosing from among its members a prime minister and ministers of government (or cabinet) who exercise power but remain accountable to parliament.

Determining whether presidents or legislatures hold greater power can be measured in absolute or relative terms, and it can involve analysis of their formal or informal authority. While a necessary starting point, examining the formal powers of presidents[25] cannot fully capture the changed reality of political power in post-authoritarian systems. Accordingly, this book focuses on the exercise of power of postcommunist presidencies. Descriptive case studies can best indicate which institution has established itself as more powerful in a particular country. When we include a number of cases, it is possible to go on to the next question: whether postcommunist presidencies, parliamentarism, or some hybrid form of prime ministerialism[26] or semi-presidentialism[27] contributes most to democratic development.

Several studies have tested the proposition that choice of system indeed affects democratic development by treating parliaments as, in effect, the independent variable. For example, Remington, as well as Olson and Norton,[28] centered on the role played by legislatures in the democratic transition in Eurasia and Europe. In a similar way, Kornberg and Musolf[29] earlier assessed the impact of legislatures on the process of political development in postcolonial states. In his study of postcommunist parliaments' relations with presidencies in Central Europe and the former USSR, Remington concluded that "all sides in the debate can find confirmation of their positions."[30] By contrast, data have been aggregated from around the world indicating democracies adopting a parliamentary system have been somewhat less prone to collapse than those employing a presidential one.[31] Linz has been the leading theoretical critic of presidentialism, though with caveats he notes in the previous chapter.[32]

Officially none of the democratizing states that comprised the former Soviet bloc has become undemocratic, so our cross-national study cannot substantiate whether this finding holds for the postcommunist world. Focusing on presidencies – that is, treating them as a variable explaining systemic development – may not provide conclusive evidence as to which system institutionalizes democracy most effectively. But it does offer a better idea about what consequences follow from concentrating power in the presidency or from separating the powers of different branches of government. By analyzing how presidents have exercised power in six states, we can discover whether they have been responsive to the views of the majority, abided by political outcomes determined by fixed rules, accepted political pluralism and, in these ways, promoted democratic development. We may also be able to verify with greater precision the proposition developed by Stepan and Skach in their comparative research on parliamentarianism and presidentialism:

The analytically separable propensities of parliamentarianism interact to form a mutually supporting system. This system, qua system, increases the degrees of freedom politicians have as they attempt to consolidate democracy. The analytically separable propensities of presidentialism also form a highly interactive system, but they work to impede democratic consolidation.[33]

Related to questions concerning the construction of authoritative institutions is the more fundamental nature of leadership in post-authoritarian societies. In Colton and Tucker's comparative study of post-Soviet leaders, "The first and most elementary theme concerned individual character and values."[34] Contributors to that volume examined changes in rulers' mentality, their new perceptions, and the new opportunities for political action. In this book authors consider how the "character and values" of incumbents of the executive branch of government have affected the political system. Whether they are constitutionally weak as in Central Europe or enjoy extensive powers as in the former Soviet republics, it is evident that, as Baylis observed, "the imprint on their offices left by the performance of East Central Europe's current group of presidents will be felt in their countries' political systems for decades to come."[35] For these reasons, then, the first postcommunist presidents merit particular scrutiny. Before we consider their roles further, let us examine the theoretical rationale behind this form of government.

Changing interpretations of separation of powers

There has been a natural tendency among scholars to "leap" into a discussion of the relative merits and demerits of presidential and parliamentary systems. However it seems important to trace the origins of the two systems since they are the products of long-term processes of doctrinal evolution and institutional experimentation dating from the founding of Western liberal democracy. Before we get into the "new institutionalism" – hardly new as it emerged in the mid-1980s but indeed new for studying postcommunist states – it seems advisable to recall the "old institutionalism" that sparked interest in the subject in the first place. Understanding presidential power has a long scholarly tradition that students of the recent postcommunist systems would be remiss to ignore. Doctrinal themes embedded in this tradition are the evolution of the notion of *executive power* and, closely related, the *separation of powers*. The doctrine of separation of powers has been assigned special importance by the framers of the new constitutions of the postcommunist states in Central Europe and Eurasia, just as the fathers of the US political system gave it top priority. The doctrine lurks in the background in debates over the relative merits of presidential versus parliamentary systems of government, so let us review these first principles.

Surprising as it may seem, there is relatively little comparative research on executives and their power. As Anthony King has written:

there are any number of textbooks on the American presidency and a certain number of studies of the British cabinet. But there is hardly anything on the executives of most other countries and almost nothing by way of a genuinely comparative literature . . . Moreover, small though it is, the volume of literature on executives is not matched by an equal volume of what can reasonably be called research.[36]

The modern view of government as consisting of a "holy trinity" of three functions – legislative, executive, and judicial – arose between 1650 and 1750 and was most apparent in the writings of Locke and Montesquieu. As one specialist noted, however, this tripartite classification "had in itself little to do with an analysis of the essential nature of government: it was concerned more with the desire, by delimiting certain functional areas, to be able to restrict a ruler to a particular aspect of government and so to exercise limits on his power."[37] This consideration was reflected in the work of James Madison who, in *The Federalist No. 47*, asserted: "The accumulation of all powers legislative, executive, and judiciary in the same hands, whether of one, a few or many, and whether hereditary, self-appointed, or elective, may justly be pronounced the very definition of tyranny."[38] In postcommunist countries with such different political histories and cultures as Russia, Kazakstan, Poland, and the Czech lands, the trade-off between tyranny and strong personal leadership has been subject to differing interpretations. Not unexpectedly, the separation of powers doctrine has not, therefore, received a uniformly enthusiastic reception.

A relatively minor doctrine in the English political system that first emerged in the seventeenth century, the separation of powers concept flourished in the formative years of the United States. Seeking to avoid replicating the top-heavy structure of power of the British monarchy, the founding fathers' overriding concern was to put checks on what was perceived as the most dangerous branch of government, the executive. The checks-and-balances idea swiftly insinuated itself at the core of the nascent American democratic system. Praised and popularized by Montesquieu, modern democratic systems seemed unimaginable without as their starting point a clear demarcation of powers between government branches.

Yet it is important to put the doctrine into a broader context. Just as we noted the different ways that writers have contended that democratization can be consolidated, so democracy has other defining qualities – such as assuring representative and responsible government – as well. William Gwyn, a specialist on the doctrine, called attention to the multiplicity of factors other than institutional ones in ensuring good government: "Since there are other principles of governmental organization of equal or greater importance . . . it does not follow that the greater the degree of independence of the legislative, executive, and judicial branches, the better the governmental system."[39]

Having signalled this crucial caveat – that there are many ways that democracy can be institutionally constructed and secured – let us consider the nature of separation of powers more closely. Two central questions are raised by the doctrine. The first concerns specifying the values that are to be maximized by separating powers. The second entails identifying the institutional architecture that might best embody the separation of powers doctrine. Let us examine each in turn.

From Madison's understanding of tyranny it is clear that one negative function performed by the doctrine is to eliminate tyranny. A broad definition of a system of tyranny is where government is self-interested and corrupt even if not necessarily inefficient. Arbitrary power stemming from unlimited government is likely to be abused, the logic holds, hence the need to place institutional checks on it. The positive values promoted by the doctrine are more self-evident: the consolidation of constitutionalism and of liberty, the promotion of the public interest and of the common good, and the application of the rule-of-law. Leaders of postcommunist states have expressed their concern that both the negative and positive functions identified here be carried out.

In postcommunist states it is difficult today not to be an advocate of separation of powers since the discredited antecedent regime had stressed the fusion and indivisibility of power in the hands of workers and their representatives. It is important to remember, therefore, that traditionally separation of powers theorists placed different emphasis on the objectives the doctrine could attain. Gwyn arrived at a synthesis of five different versions of the separation of powers. Four were concerned with achieving liberty and one with ensuring efficiency. The first was the *rule-of-law* version. It was based on the difference between making and applying law, which was the original distinction between legislative and executive branches of government. This version asserted that, "What is required is that discretionary actions be taken and legal rules made by the executive within limits set by more general known laws made by a legislature not subject to the will of the executive."[40]

A second way that separation of powers has been understood is in terms of *accountability*. Positing the need for an independent judicial branch of government, this version stressed how an institution like the legislature (as well as the judiciary, of course) should be able to hold officials, above all, those in the executive branch, accountable for their actions. Third, the *common interest* version held that no single group in the legislature should be able to determine decisions or have disproportionate influence on the political system. Separation of powers could help eliminate the powerful group bias of governmental officials, or bureaucrats. It could also keep in check what have become known as the "iron triangles" that emerge when a government ministry or agency, a group of legislators, and an interest group combine forces to push for a policy that might not be in the public interest.

The fourth version, called *balancing*, is familiar to most students of constitutionalism and is often treated as identical with the separation of powers doctrine. It simply states that the three branches of government are all empowered to check the exercise of the function of the others. Finally, the *efficiency* version was originally dictated by the need to create a streamlined executive branch of government that could implement laws with the necessary "secrecy and dispatch" that the larger, more cumbersome legislative body could not.

For emergent postcommunist democracies, the rule-of-law and balancing versions have particular resonance in the aftermath of their experience with centralized one-party rule. A popular slogan in many countries in the postcommunist period has been the need to construct a *Rechtstaat*, or state governed by the rule-of-law. In a less universal way, balancing the powers of branches of government is regarded as a fundamental principle of political organization. Certainly the need for an independent judiciary is subscribed to by all major political actors, whereas putting checks on the executive branch so that there would be no return to the period of communist dictatorship is more of a priority in some countries – in general, those in Central Europe – than in others – the former Soviet republics.

It should be noted, too, that the executive branch is not synonymous with the presidency in a number of postcommunist states. As our individual case studies will indicate, some constitutions regard both president and prime minister as part of the executive branch. So the issue of checks *on* the executive branch in these states becomes secondary to that of reciprocal checks *within* the constituent parts of the executive branch – president and prime minister.

As evidenced by this conception of the executive, which is alien to most Western scholars, if the rationale behind the separation of powers doctrine is clear and widely endorsed, there is much less agreement about the institutional arrangements that follow. Indeed in *The Federalist No. 47* Madison recognized that a large variety of institutional arrangements can satisfy the separation of powers norm. The difficulty in institutionally implementing the separation of powers doctrine goes beyond the issue of choice. The very meaning of executive and legislative powers has changed. In eighteenth-century England executive power had a residuary character – that power falling to the monarch. As Herman Finer put it, the executive was "the residuary legatee in government after other claimants like Parliament and the law courts have taken their share."[41] Similarly, from the initial attributes of legislative power – to pass laws – the notion was expanded to entail multifunctional aspects: to make laws, impose taxation, authorize government spending, create new governmental bodies, to name only a few. Given this evolution in the various branches of government, Gwyn concluded that, "one cannot find historical or geographical agreement among those articulating the doctrine about what the terms 'legislative,' 'executive,' and 'judicial' power mean, let alone how much of an 'intrusion' one branch of the government can make into the power of another without violating the prescribed separation."[42]

Some hints about the institutions needed to fulfill the separation of powers principle come from the distinction Gwyn drew between the formalist and functionalist approaches to the doctrine. "The former are inclined to limit each branch of government to the exercise of a power assigned to it by the Constitution, unless that document has explicitly permitted an exception. The latter are inclined to take a flexible approach, emphasizing the need for a blending as well as a separation of powers."[43] In postcommunist states, formalists have tended to be those defending the expansive enumerated powers of the president, such as Yeltsin's supporters who invoke the 1993 constitution that broadened presidential powers. Functionalists have been more in evidence in Eastern Europe, where a pragmatic approach to the power balance between executives and legislatures has taken hold.

Both schools share a legalist approach to separation of powers, and Gwyn suggested that greater political realism had to be used to resolve disputes between branches of government. Tugs-of-war between presidents and parliaments, for example, should not be regarded in exclusively constitutional terms but also in political ones. Frequently they could best be solved through negotiations between the branches themselves, a method Gwyn felt was, in the case of the United States, more in keeping with the spirit of the framers anyway.[44] This approach appears even more appealing in conditions where the modern state has expanded, making it even more difficult to distinguish different branches of government, to demarcate their powers, and to manage conflicts between them.

A further refinement of separation of powers, advanced by a Central European constitutional specialist, was to stress its holistic nature. The doctrine ought not to dwell on the purely negative aspect of limiting power of another branch of government, such as through the commonly employed device of a presidential veto over legislation. For Pawel Sarnecki, it also possessed a positive aspect: "inspiring the influence of one power on the performance of the function of the second."[45] This was exemplified by the introduction of bills in the legislature by the president, his nomination of candidates for cabinet positions, and parliamentary control over the executive through special budgetary powers. All of these procedures are familiar to students of Western political systems. For Sarnecki the important point was to understand separation of powers as offering an opportunity structure for postcommunist states to "custom design" their governmental system.

Given the expanded functions of the state in the twentieth century, a tripartite understanding of power seemed anachronistic and simplistic. Sarnecki argued that the state – especially that previously constructed by the communist regime – was much more than a "night watchman" and was involved in many other activities in addition to law-making, administration, and adjudication. Executive power itself had a broader meaning: not only to execute laws but to administer, manage, and govern. The executive branch not only ensured compliance with legislation passed by parliament but also congruence with the more general interests of the state as interpreted by the executive power – a role eagerly embraced by the majority of postcommunist presidents regardless how circumscribed their formal powers were. There was an expanded role for parliaments, too. In order to perform its expanded functions, the state had to be enabled in new ways. Legislatures' broader law-making powers involved not only drafting legal acts but also giving legal status to new political entities (a function known as *Massnahmengesetze* in German) such as quasi-governmental organizations. For Sarnecki, the many new activities undertaken by the state and the accompanying proliferation of institutions eroded the meaning of the term "power." A more accurate characterization of the political system postcommunist societies needed to construct was in terms of a "division of responsibilities" rather than of a separation of powers.[46]

In our discussion of the separation of powers doctrine so far, we have taken note of specialists who support organizing government on this principle. But separation of powers is not without its critics. The most general criticism of what is often treated as a sacrosanct doctrine is that the separation of powers fragments government, providing for inconsistent, incoherent, inchoate policy. The leaders of the different fragments of government become enmeshed in a constant struggle for power, each trying to take over a piece from the other. While many contemporary examples of such conflict can be found, from the US to Russia and from Peru to Zaire, the case studies included in this volume underscore how frequent an occurrence presidential–legislative showdowns have been in the postcommunist democracies.

Arguably the most detailed account of the shortcomings produced by the application of the separation of powers doctrine was provided by Charles Hardin. He identified eight dysfunctions of the doctrine as it was embodied in the US constitution:

1 The inability quickly and legitimately to replace a failed or discredited president.
2 Increasingly grievous ills caused by fixed calendar elections.
3 The distortion of the presidency arising out of the alternative excesses of acclaim and denigration.
4 The disruption of the legislative process; its progressive fragmentation; the fostering of quasi-independent iron triangles.
5 The unremitting vilification of the legislature.
6 The impossible conception of the people as the omniscient, omnipotent, and infallibly correct arbiter of all questions – at the expense of trivializing the one practical and necessary function of the people to create by its vote a government and an opposition.
7 The progressive weakening of political parties, the only known instruments capable of organizing the parts of government into a working whole.
8 The failure sufficiently to examine the essential concepts of democratic government, including majority rule, the loyal opposition, accountability and responsibility, and the mandate.[47]

Some scholars before Hardin had already criticized the exaggerated importance attached to the doctrine. In 1940 Charles McIlwain proposed rejecting the separation of powers doctrine altogether. For him, power had to be concentrated so as to be accountable, otherwise a diffusion of power centers bred irresponsibility and, with it, corruption. Accepting the interpretation described above that separation of powers grew haphazardly from an initially insignificant to an eventually overriding organizational principle, he inveighed how "These political balances were unknown before the eighteenth century, were almost untried before the nineteenth, and have been disastrous wherever they have been tried since."[48]

Moreover, the separation of powers doctrine may or may not be relevant to crafting a democratic system. As Gwyn noted, "In some cases, whether a function is given either to the legislative or to the executive branch probably has no bearing on the quality of government. In other cases, however, the allocation of an activity to one branch of government rather than to another could be critical to maintaining the rule of law, the accountability of officials, and the efficiency of government."[49]

In a similar vein, in addressing the question of how political power should be organized, the distinguished British political scientist Harold Laski offered a revealing, if prosaic, metaphor half a century ago: "A system of government is very like a pair of shoes; it grows to the use of the feet to which it is fitted." He quickly added that "the shoes must be suited to the journey it is proposed to take."[50] Put another way, no single formula or set of institutions – whether a powerful presidency or a weak one – can be regarded as assuring political development, but one system may be more suited to some countries than to others. Consequently, institutional arrangements, derived generally from the separation of powers principle, ought to allow for a great degree of flexibility and experimentation, as North envisaged any efficient system would embody.[51] What attributes of the presidency, then, offer opportunities for postcommunist states to build in responsible, representative, and effective government into their new system?

The debate on presidentialism and parliamentarism

In the past decade there has been a resurgence of interest in the institutions of government. Among other research subjects, neo-institutionalism has conducted studies of the respective merits and drawbacks of presidential and parliamentary systems. The chapters that follow reflect many of the arguments advanced by leading political scientists participating in the debate. But, as in the case of the separation of powers doctrine, in these writings neo-institutionalists do not always demonstrate familiarity with earlier debates on institutions carried on by political scientists. Let me review the most salient issues figuring in these debates on systems of government in order to illuminate the institutional dilemmas faced by postcommunist states.

The generally accepted starting point for comparing presidential and parliamentary systems has been Walter Bagehot's *The English Constitution*, published in 1867. His praise for the British system of parliamentary, or cabinet, government emanated from what he viewed as the "fusion of powers" in this system. The cabinet, made up of the prime minister and chief ministers, was portrayed as both legislating and executing: it was "the committee which unites the law-making power to the law-executing power."[52] If for Bagehot the fusion of powers provided responsible and effective government in Britain, then the US presidential system, with its separation of powers, was held to engender unaccountable and inefficient government.

There has been disagreement whether Bagehot intended to distinguish fusion from separation of powers, and parliamentary from presidential systems, as distinctly as has been imputed to him. But one political leader influenced by Bagehot's favorable account of parliamentary government was future US president Woodrow Wilson. In *Congressional Government* he wrote how the parliamentary system provided both immediate political responsibility and sufficient power for the executive to balance special interests and develop a coherent national policy.[53] Wilson found this system preferable to the presidential one which encouraged continual squabbles between the executive branch and Congress. Another American proponent of the parliamentary system was Walter Lippmann.[54]

In 1943–44 a celebrated discussion of the respective merits of presidential and parliamentary systems of government was conducted in the journal *Public Administration Review*. The classic argument in favor of each system was put forward by an American and a British specialist. Don Price defended the US system and contended that the British system had converged with it: "The British in effect did to the House of Commons what the Americans did much earlier to their Electoral College: they made it an automatic machine for registering the vote of the people, as organized into parties, for a Prime Minister."[55] Not only had the House of Commons become relegated to a creature of the party system, it increasingly took on the function of political theatre: "The parliamentary system, the effective system of Bagehot's day, has now become one of the 'theatrical elements' of the British constitution, like the monarchy itself."[56]

While parliament could theoretically remove the cabinet, it was effectively controlled by party machines and could do nothing against their dictate.[57] British writers such as Sidney Low in 1914[58] and William Sharp McKechnie in 1912[59] had already noted this tendency and a former

prime minister, Lloyd George, admitted as much when he bluntly stated
in 1931 that "Parliament has really no control over the Executive; it is a
pure fiction."[60] In the British system, then, the executive now controlled
the legislature rather than the other way around; Winston Churchill's war
cabinet was only a further step in asserting the primacy of the executive
branch. As Price remarked, "The British have been pretty enterprising
since the war began in discarding the dogmas of the parliamentary
system. In their peculiar informal way, they seem to be putting into effect
something more like the presidential system. At least their political issues
now revolve around a single chief executive."[61]

The same author contended that adherence to the separation of powers
doctrine had provided the US with more responsible government. In a
presidential system there was dual control of the executive branch: "the
people elect the President and the President holds his appointees responsible, retaining the power to discharge them at his discretion; and the
people elect the Congress, which controls the executive by statutes, by
appropriations, and by investigations."[62]

Of course presidential leadership embodied its own virtues. A directly
elected president came to office with a political program – even a political
vision – that he sought to realize. Accordingly he was invested with
executive power that, if employed skillfully, would allow him to make
good on this vision. In a variant of the presidential system, such as the
French Fifth Republic, the president was also empowered with an "arbitrage," or mediating, function in relation to other institutions of government (Article 5 of the 1958 constitution). Initially interpreted as a
"neutral power" allowing the French president to protect the interests of
the state, it was later interpreted more broadly to signify his power to
"harmonize" the functioning of institutions so that they could enable him
to carry out the presidential program. It was the potential for providing
exceptional leadership that was most appealing about the presidential
system.

Finally, Price singled out an aspect of the parliamentary system that
made it susceptible to undemocratic practices:

Civil servants under a parliamentary system of democracy remain anonymous
and deferential to the legislature as a matter of principle; it is almost essential for
them to have permanent tenure of office, and a set of permanent officials at the top
of the administrative hierarchy would seriously imbalance the democratic process
if it took a leading role in the public discussion of politics.[63]

The advocate for the parliamentary system was Harold Laski. He
reiterated the importance of the idiosyncracies of each country in determining the suitability of one system over the other: "each seems to me to

have its own special merits, and neither is likely to be capable of transference to another environment, where alien traditions are deep-rooted, without becoming something very different from what it was in the country of its origin."[64]

For Laski the function of the parliamentary system was not just to legislate but to "ventilate grievance and thereby scrutinize the executive's policy." He added that "it must so discuss the principles upon which the government of the day proposes to proceed that the virtues and defects are fully known to the electorate."[65] But Laski was not conceding a mere amplificatory or theatrical role for parliament. He rejected the criticism that party discipline had turned the House into a creature of the party machines, and highlighted instead how the individual member of parliament was concerned with his constituents and with local interests that the national party was not concerned with. Furthermore, he stressed the "selective function" of parliament that could, under certain circumstances, produce a vote of no confidence in the government, thereby forcing its resignation. As Hardin was to put it, parliamentary government "can quickly, expeditiously, and legitimately replace leaders who have been found inadequate to the occasion."[66] Such a mechanism of changing inadequate leaders in midstream was unknown to the US presidential system where terms in office were fixed and unalterable, regardless of the quality of leadership displayed.

As the parliamentary system's greatest virtue, Laski pointed to its provision of "coherence of policy." Indeed, "It is difficult to think of a legislative object that is more important in a modern community."[67] Coherence of policy followed from the roles that a government minister had to play. Not only was he a legislative leader, he also had to develop ideas, create an effective team for carrying out those ideas, and secure support for them in parliament so that they could become law. Much like executive power, then, a legislative leader had to possess political vision and see it carried out in practice.

If Price had hinted at the undemocratic role that top civil servants could play in the British parliamentary system, Laski pointed to the inherent defects of a system where there were many centers of power. Anticipating the arguments of later critics of the US system, notably Theodore Lowi,[68] he warned about "the quite special influence it offers to pressure groups by reason of the separation of powers."[69] Congress encouraged lobbying by special interests, thereby giving them disproportionate influence in politics. Laski went further to stress how separation of powers applied at the local level compounded this problem. It produced parochialism and, often, "an underworld of politics which breeds corruption wherever its influence extends . . . the result is the far more mischievous consequence that the politician and the businessman are engaged either in joint corruption or in mutual conflict at the expense of the common welfare."[70]

These classic arguments about the advantages and disadvantages of the two systems have been complemented in the past decade by analysis influenced by rational choice. From this perspective, presidential regimes are more likely to foster antagonism between the executive and legislative branches of government and, consequently, cause gridlock in government. They set up a zero-sum game in which parties and their leaders concentrate overwhelmingly on capturing the presidential office. One party's victory in the presidential contest is the others' loss, and this for the duration of the presidential term. Hypotheses put forward by detractors of presidential systems also include how winners of the presidency have few incentives to make amends with losers, and losers have little reason to cooperate with winners. Have postcommunist systems sought to insulate themselves from such dangers, either by opting outright for parliamentarism or by imposing extensive checks on presidencies?

Postcommunist choices

We are now familiar with the long-standing debate on the merits of presidential and parliamentary systems, and those of the separation and concentration of powers. The constitutional issues that postcommunist states have grappled with during the 1990s are not unprecedented or novel. What is rather unique is the abbreviated time frame within which institutional choices have had to be made. Many of these nations have existed for centuries in the shadow of the Russian empire, and they are acutely aware of the unparalleled historic opportunity that they have been presented with in the 1990s to construct political systems of their own choosing.

Yet, to varying degrees, institutional choices have been hamstrung by the abrupt appearance of a conflict of interests between different branches of government, as Jon Elster points out in chapter 8. Deciding on a presidential or parliamentary system, and on the separation or fusion of powers, has not been a mere matter of preference, whether for the new ruling elite or the electorate. Elster emphasizes that bargaining among political interests, such as at the roundtable talks that ushered in the democratic transition in the region in 1989, was crucial to subsequent development. Unlike Brazil in 1992, no open-ended referenda were conducted in any of these countries to determine which system voters prefer. The case studies indicate that in certain postcommunist states, clearcut decisions, determined by vested institutional interests, were taken favoring one system. Others have been characterized by institutional drift, the product of the intransigence of key political actors and the standoffs that resulted.

In order to contrast institutional development in postcommunist states, this volume includes three case studies of nations that, until 1991, formed part of the Soviet Union, and three that were East European satellites. This mix of cases allows us to test the often-stated proposition that more authoritarian systems, now taking the form of powerful presidencies, have evolved in the former Soviet republics, whereas greater political pluralism, power-sharing, and democracy, in the form of parliamentary systems, have emerged in what we now refer to as Central Europe. Indeed, in the chapter on Russia, Stephen White demonstrates how the presidency has defined the character of the entire political system. He notes how Yeltsin interpreted the results of the April 1993 referendum on confidence in institutions as a mandate for a presidential republic. The December 1993 constitution became the basis for a "superpresidential republic," and the power of the presidential apparatus that resulted led one Yeltsin opponent, Ruslan Khasbulatov, to speak of "a collective Rasputin" that now ruled Russia. Using the presidency as an example, White considers how democratic institutions engender a democratic political culture, not the reverse causality. Finally, he analyzes how Yeltsin created a power base during his first term and was able, in spite of his personal unpopularity, to win reelection in July 1996.

In the case of Ukraine, Andrew Wilson describes how, until the promulgation of a new constitution in June 1996, there had been stalemate between the presidency and parliament, which converted into uncertainty in many policy areas. Helped by the fact that there was no readily identifiable presidential party, the Ukrainian parliament contested the powers of both Kravchuk and Kuchma even as each attempted a step-by-step institutionalization of a strong presidency. How Kuchma pulled off his constitutional coup that instituted a presidential type of system is carefully assessed. Wilson also considers how nationalists and communists in Ukraine each had an interest at one time in setting up a strong presidential system, and he points to the danger of a winner-take-all presidential system under conditions of ethno-linguistic division.

More than in most other postcommunist states, Kazakstan's political development was affected by events in Russia. Yeltsin's election as president in June 1991 induced Nazarbaev to set up a similar institution in this Central Asian republic. However, as Martha Brill Olcott makes clear, Nazarbaev faced many constraints in creating a strong presidency, a chief one being the emergence of a feisty parliament in 1994–95, eventually closed down by a constitutional court ruling. In addition, the Kazak president faced challenges from ethnic, clan, and regional groups that required use of all his political skills. Olcott challenges the belief that, like strongmen in other Central Asian states, the Kazak presidency is an all-powerful institution that necessarily impedes democratic development. But she identifies evidence, such as the prolongation of Nazarbaev's term in office and his own undemocratic instincts, that indicate how the process of democratization has been curtailed.

Turning to Central European cases, Krzysztof Jasiewicz focuses on Wałęsa's efforts to expand the powers of his office and his failure to secure the authority he desired and, ultimately, even be reelected. Already the 1990 presidential election won by the Solidarity leader presaged future political alignments that came to stymie his institutional vision for Poland. Jasiewicz makes the intriguing argument that by pushing so hard for additional presidential powers, almost to the point of threatening democracy itself, Wałęsa inadvertently promoted the consolidation of a parliamentary system. Indeed, the author explains the political realignment that allowed Kwaśniewski to win the December 1995 presidential election by a slim margin and, subsequently, to act largely as a passive president, all the while stressing that his few interventions were to defend national interests.

Arguably the most respected president in the postcommunist world has been Havel. It is curious, then, that this often-touted philosopher king was elected to the presidency not by the electorate but indirectly, by parliament, on two occasions, in the former Czechoslovak Federation in 1989 and in the new Czech Republic that emerged from it. Sharon Wolchik describes the evolution of Havel's presidencies from largely powerless, primarily symbolic, offices to a more assertive one, reflected in his own personal wish to have real power. As a symbol, Havel assured political stability and democratic growth at a time when a new state was created and a party system had still to crystallize. Wolchik documents Havel's growing assertiveness and his role in seeking a resolution to the political impasse caused by the hung parliament elected in summer 1996.

The greatest success story in enhancing the office of the president may well be that of Göncz in Hungary. Elected initially by the Hungarian parliament as a transitional figure, Göncz's skills both as political broker and elder statesman assured him a second term in office. In his chapter Patrick O'Neil argues how, paradoxically, Göncz was implored by many political leaders in parliament to become more powerful. At the outset the Hungarian presidency was a piecemeal arrangement. Conflict between Göncz and the prime minister was as much political as institutional. O'Neil recapitulates the theoretical arguments for and against powerful presidencies and suggests that, while far from constituting a presidential system, the Hungarian case shows how even parliaments have need for an alternative source of authority and a method of guaranteeing continuity when changes in the balance of power in the legislature and turnover of leadership in cabinet government occur.

We suggested earlier that evidence from our case studies pointing to the inherent superiority of one democratic system of government over another is unlikely to be conclusive. But this has been so since modern political systems emerged in the eighteenth century. Our objective in this book is different, then. Studying institutional development in postcommunist states by way of the most visible of all political institutions – the presidency – can provide insight into the strength and pervasiveness of the democratic ethos in nations that not long ago made up the Soviet bloc.

NOTES

1 Samuel P. Huntington, *The Third Wave: Democratization in the Late Twentieth Century* (Norman, OK: University of Oklahoma Press, 1991).
2 Robert D. Putnam, *Making Democracy Work: Civic Traditions in Modern Italy* (Princeton, NJ: Princeton University Press, 1993).
3 Terry Lynn Karl and Phillipe C. Schmitter, "Modes of Transition in Latin America, Southern and Eastern Europe," *International Social Science Journal*, 128 (1991), pp. 269–284.
4 Claus Offe, "Capitalism by Democratic Design? Democratic Theory Facing the Triple Transition in East Central Europe," *Social Research*, 58 (Winter 1991), pp. 865–892.
5 Adam Przeworski, *Democracy and the Market: Political and Economic Reforms in Eastern Europe and Latin America* (Cambridge: Cambridge University Press, 1992).
6 Alexis de Tocqueville, *Democracy in America* (Garden City, NY: Doubleday, 1969); Phillipe C. Schmitter, *Trends Toward Corporatist Intermediation* (Beverly Hills, CA: Sage, 1979); Peter L. Berger and Richard J. Neuhaus, *To Empower People: the Role of Mediating Structures in Public Policy* (Washington, DC: American Enterprise Institute, 1977);
7 Samuel P. Huntington, "Democracy for the Long Haul," *Journal of Democracy*, 7, 2 (April 1996), pp. 3–13.
8 See Huntington, *The Third Wave*, pp. 38–39.
9 Giovanni Sartori, "How Far Can Free Government Travel?" *Journal of Democracy*, 6, 3 (July 1995), pp. 101–111.
10 Giovanni Sartori, *Parties and Party Systems: A Framework for Analysis*, vol. I (Cambridge: Cambridge University Press, 1976).
11 Juan Linz and Alfred Stepan, *Problems of Democratic Transition and Consolidation: Southern Europe, South America, and Postcommunist Europe* (Baltimore, MD: Johns Hopkins University Press, 1996).
12 Juan Linz, "Presidential or Parliamentary Democracy: Does it Make a Difference?" in Linz and Arturo Valenzuela (eds.), *The Failure of Presidential Democracy*, vol. I (Baltimore, MD: Johns Hopkins University Press, 1994); Matthew

Shugart and John M. Carey, *Presidents and Assemblies* (Cambridge: Cambridge University Press, 1992); Douglas V. Verney, *The Analysis of Political Systems* (London: Routledge and Kegan Paul, 1979).

13 Arend Lijphart (ed.), *Parliamentary Versus Presidential Government* (New York: Oxford University Press, 1992); Harold J. Laski, "The Parliamentary and Presidential Systems," *Public Administration Review*, 4, 4 (Autumn 1944), pp. 347–359.

14 M. J. C. Vile, *Constitutionalism and the Separation of Powers* (Oxford: Clarendon Press, 1967).

15 Douglass C. North, *Institutions, Institutional Change, and Economic Performance* (Cambridge: Cambridge University Press, 1992).

16 Eugene Huskey (ed.), *Executive Power and Soviet Politics: The Rise and Decline of the Soviet State* (Armonk, NY: M. E. Sharpe, 1992).

17 John Higley, Judith Kullberg, and Jan Pakulski, "The Persistence of Postcommunist Elites," *Journal of Democracy*, 7, 2 (April 1996), p. 136.

18 Ibid., p. 138.

19 Ibid., p. 138.

20 Havel, Wałęsa, and Yeltsin have attracted greatest interest among biographers. This seems to be more a result of their colorful personalities than their performance as presidents.

21 Alfred Stepan and Cindy Skach, "Constitutional Frameworks and Democratic Consolidation: Parliamentarianism versus Presidentialism," *World Politics*, 46, 1 (October 1996), pp. 1–22.

22 Thomas A. Baylis, "Presidents Versus Prime Ministers: Shaping Executive Authority in Eastern Europe." *World Politics*, 48, 3 (April 1996), pp. 302–303.

23 Ibid., p. 304.

24 Ibid., p. 319.

25 On this, see the special issue of *East European Constitutional Review*, "The Postcommunist Presidency," 2, 4 and 3, 1 (Fall 1993, Winter 1994).

26 Sergio Fabbrini, "Presidents, Parliaments, and Good Government," *Journal of Democracy*, 6, 3 (July 1995), pp. 128–138; Anthony King (ed.), *The British Prime Minister* (London: Macmillan, 1969).

27 Maurice Duverger, "A New Political System Model: Semi-Presidential Government," *European Journal of Political Research*, 8, 2 (June 1980), pp. 165–187.

28 David M. Olson and Philip Norton (eds.), *The New Parliaments of Central and Eastern Europe* (London: Frank Cass, 1996).

29 Allan Kornberg and Lloyd D. Musolf, *Legislatures in Developmental Perspective* (Durham, NC: Duke University Press, 1970).

30 Thomas Remington (ed.), *Parliaments in Transition: The New Legislative Politics in the Former USSR and Eastern Europe* (Boulder, CO: Westview Press, 1994), p. 21.

31 See Shugart and Carey, *Presidents and Assemblies*.

32 See especially the results reported in Linz's two-volume work with Valenzuela, *The Failure of Presidential Democracy*.

33 Stepan and Skach, "Constitutional Frameworks and Democratic Consolidation," p. 22.

34 Timothy J. Colton and Robert C. Tucker (eds.), *Patterns in Post-Soviet Leadership* (Boulder, CO: Westview Press, 1995), p. 3.
35 Baylis, "Presidents Versus Prime Ministers," p. 322.
36 Anthony King, "Executives," in Fred I. Greenstein and Nelson W. Polsby (eds.), *Handbook of Political Science: Governmental Institutions and Processes*, vol. 5 (Menlo Park, CA: Addison-Wesley, 1975), p. 173.
37 Vile, *Constitutionalism and the Separation of Powers*, pp. 316–317.
38 James Madison, *The Federalist No. 47*, in Alexander Hamilton, John Jay, and Madison, *The Federalist: a Commentary on the Constitution of the United States*, J. Cooke (ed.) (New York: Random House, 1961), p. 324.
39 William B. Gwyn, "The Separation of Powers and Modern Forms of Democratic Government," in Robert A. Goldwin and Art Kaufman (eds.), *Separation of Powers – Does It Still Work?* (Washington, DC: American Enterprise Institute for Public Policy Research, 1986), p. 83.
40 Ibid., p. 68.
41 Herman Finer, *The Theory and Practice of Modern Government* (New York: Holt, 1949), p. 575.
42 William B. Gwyn, "The Indeterminacy of the Separation of Powers and the Federal Courts," *George Washington Law Review*, 57, 3 (January 1989), p. 503.
43 Ibid., pp. 474–475.
44 Ibid., p. 505.
45 Pawel Sarnecki, "Wspolczesne rozumienie podzialu wladzy," in Karol B. Jankowski (ed.), *Nowa Konstytucja RP: Wartosc, Jednostka, Instytucje* (Torun: Wydawnictwo Adam Marszalek, 1995), p. 28.
46 Ibid., p. 25.
47 Charles M. Hardin, *Constitutional Reform in America: Essays on the Separation of Powers* (Ames, IA: Iowa State University Press, 1989), p. 100.
48 Charles H. McIlwain, *Constitutionalism: Ancient and Modern* (Ithaca, NY: Great Seal Books, 1940 and 1958), p. 143.
49 William B. Gwyn, "The Indeterminacy of the Separation of Powers in the Age of the Framers," *William and Mary Law Review*, 30, 2 (Winter 1989), p. 267.
50 Harold J. Laski, "The Parliamentary and Presidential Systems," *Public Administration Review*, 4, 4 (Autumn 1944), p. 358.
51 North, *Institutions*.
52 Walter Bagehot, *The English Constitution* (London: Oxford University Press, 1928), p. 201.
53 Woodrow Wilson, *Congressional Government: A Study in American Politics* (New York: Meridian Books, 1885 and 1956).
54 Walter Lippmann, *The Essential Lippmann: A Political Philosophy for Liberal Democracy* (New York: Random House, 1963).
55 Don K. Price, "The Parliamentary and Presidential Systems," *Public Administration Review*, 3, 1 (Winter 1943), p. 319.
56 Ibid., p. 331.
57 For a more recent analysis, see Michael Laver and Kenneth A. Shepsle, *Cabinet Ministers and Parliamentary Government* (Cambridge: Cambridge University Press, 1994).
58 Sidney Low, *The Governance of England* (London: Ernest Benn, 1914).

59 William Sharp McKechnie, *The New Democracy and the Constitution* (London: John Murray, 1912).
60 Cited by Price, "The Parliamentary and Presidential Systems," p. 320.
61 Ibid., p. 333.
62 Ibid., p. 326.
63 Ibid., pp. 325–326.
64 Harold J. Laski, "The Parliamentary and Presidential Systems," *Public Administration Review*, 4, 4 (Autumn 1944), p. 347.
65 Ibid., p. 347.
66 Hardin, *Constitutional Reform in America*, p. 54.
67 Laski, "The Parliamentary and Presidential Systems," p. 349.
68 Theodore Lowi, *The End of Liberalism: the Second Republic of the United States* (New York: W. W. Norton, 1979).
69 Laski, "The Parliamentary and Presidential Systems," p. 357.
70 Ibid., p. 358.

2   Russia: Presidential leadership under Yeltsin

Stephen White

Presidential government in Russia is of recent origin. Mikhail Gorbachev was elected the first head of state of the USSR in March 1990; Russia elected its first president a year later, in June 1991. Some of the other republics and lower levels of government had begun to adopt presidential forms of government even earlier, as had most members of the United Nations.[1] The presidency, it was established by this time, was normally an elective office, and it was a position of executive authority: neither Gorbachev nor Boris Yeltsin, as former prime minister, Nikolai Ryzhkov, remarked, liked the idea of "reigning like the Queen of England."[2] Indeed in Russia, after December 1993, it was the presidency that defined the character of the political system, as Yeltsin used his ascendancy after the dissolution of parliament to secure the adoption of a constitution that extended his already considerable powers.

A strongly personalist political leadership was of course a longstanding Russian tradition, extended into the Soviet period by the dominance of the general secretary of the Communist Party. Gorbachev, when he became party leader in 1985, was (as he put it) more powerful than any of the other leaders he confronted on the world stage: the virtually unchallengeable leader of a party that could not itself be challenged through the ballot box, the media or the courts of law.[3] And yet, even in the Soviet period, there were countervailing forces. Leadership, after Stalin, was increasingly collective. The general secretaryship had been separated from the position of prime minister after 1964 to avoid an excessive concentration of power in the hands of a single person. The state system itself was strengthened, through the reform of local government and an expanded committee system within the USSR Supreme Soviet. Indeed effective authority had begun to migrate from party to state, even during the late communist years, as Gorbachev was elected first to the chairmanship of the Supreme Soviet Presidium in 1988, then to a newly established chairmanship of the Supreme Soviet in 1989, and then to the presidency itself in 1990.

Developments in Russia were part of a wider trend toward executive presidencies, not only in the former Soviet republics but throughout the postcommunist world. Turkmenia had been the first to institute a presidency of this kind, in 1990; in 1994, with the adoption of a new constitution, Belarus became the last to do so. Most of Eastern Europe had moved toward an executive presidency by this time, with the Czech Republic, Hungary, and Slovakia the main exceptions.[4] At the same time the late 1980s had seen the development of a body of scholarship that "took institutions seriously," and there were many indications, in this literature, that an executive presidency was unlikely to contribute toward the formation of a party system or political stability more generally.[5] Did the Russian experience, by the mid-1990s, bear out these gloomy forecasts? Had a working balance been found between an elected president, the government that he appointed, and a parliament that was also directly elected? And how did the institution of presidential government relate to a society that had rediscovered mass politics but become disillusioned by it within a few short years?

The emergence of presidential government

The creation of the new presidency had been among the radical proposals announced by Gorbachev at the Central Committee plenum in February 1990 at which the constitutionally guaranteed "leading role" had been relinquished.[6] The idea of a Soviet presidency, in fact, was a good deal older than this. It had been under discussion at the time of the adoption of the 1936 Constitution; Stalin, however, declared against a presidency that could challenge the newly established Supreme Soviet and the idea made no further progress.[7] A presidency was considered again in 1964 when Khrushchev proposed it to the commission that was preparing a new constitution; a chapter was drafted accordingly, but the discussion lapsed when Khrushchev himself was forced out of office later in the year.[8] In 1985, after Gorbachev had become general secretary, the idea was put forward once more by two senior members of the leadership, Georgii Shakhnazarov and Vadim Medvedev. Gorbachev, however, was still committed to a system of elected soviets, and in a system of this kind there was "no place for a presidency."[9]

The idea of presidential government was discussed again before and during the nineteenth Party Conference in the summer of 1988. Some, Gorbachev told delegates, had argued for a return to the practice of Lenin's day, when the party leader was also the head of government; others wanted to separate party and government entirely; others still favored the introduction of a Soviet presidency. But a presidency, Gorbachev argued, would "concentrate too much power in the hands of a single person," and in the end it was decided to introduce a different position, a chairmanship of the Supreme Soviet or, in effect, a parliamentary speakership.[10] The new position, however, proved an unhappy compromise and the discussion continued, with the radical Inter-Regional Group increasingly influential among the advocates of a fully-fledged system of presidential government. Andrei Sakharov, released from his exile in Gorky, suggested the direct election of the chairman of the Supreme Soviet in his election address in the spring of 1989; and in the draft constitution that he proposed later in the year he included a "President of the Union of Soviet Republics of Europe and Asia," who would be elected by the population every five years and would "hold supreme power in the country, not sharing it with the leading bodies of any party."[11]

It was already clear to Gorbachev's associates that they would have to recapture the initiative on political reform, and in late 1989 a discussion began within a limited group of his advisors about the introduction of a presidency as part of a larger series of changes in the structure of government. The Politburo was not involved in these discussions, as many of its members regarded Gorbachev's activities (Medvedev later recalled) "with considerable anxiety."[12] Gorbachev, it appears, was finally convinced of the need to move to a presidential system at a discussion with his closest advisers that took place after the Second Congress of People's Deputies in December 1989. The discussion was based upon a memorandum prepared by Medvedev and Shakhnazarov, which was very close to the proposals that were put into effect early the following year.[13]

As Medvedev and Shakhnazarov explained, the new state system was working badly. The chairman of the Supreme Soviet was fully engaged in the management of parliamentary proceedings and had no means of enforcing his own decisions. The Soviet government was busy defending its position in the committees and commissions of the new parliament; and parliament was itself holding up the implementation of important state decisions. Medvedev and Shakhnazarov proposed a rather different system, based upon a directly elected president who would head a Cabinet of Ministers. The CPSU would propose its own general secretary for the position; he would preside over meetings of the Politburo in his presidential capacity, and the general secretaryship as such would be abolished. It was agreed that, in the first instance, the president would be elected by the Congress of People's Deputies and not by the population at large. "There was no time", Medvedev recalled; in any case a direct election would have raised procedural difficulties – the president would have needed the support of a majority of the republics, not just of voters, and this made it possible that a decision might be deadlocked indefinitely.[14]

The first steps were taken to sound out the opinions of deputies at an informal meeting on 13 February 1990. Fedor Burlatsky, one of the hundred who attended, began the proceedings by stating the case for a system of presidential government; he was already a well-known advocate of constitutional changes that would allow the promotion of a reform agenda that bypassed the party bureaucracy.[15] Other deputies were concerned that a presidential system would strengthen the party leadership by adding to the already considerable powers of the general secretary. And wasn't there a danger that the president, as a CPSU member, would simply become the executant of the instructions of the Central Committee? But, for others again, the attraction of an elected presidency was precisely that it would allow Gorbachev to develop a political base that was independent of his more orthodox colleagues in the party leadership. Deputies were also interested in the possible extension of a presidential system to the republics. What, it was asked, would be the relationship among the fifteen presidents that might emerge as a result? Shakhnazarov urged Gorbachev to ensure that there was just a single president in such circumstances; Gorbachev, in a fateful decision, preferred to allow the institution to develop more widely, with "30–40 presidents" at lower levels of government.[16]

Following the discussion, it was agreed to place the question of a presidency on the agenda of the Supreme Soviet; and after the Supreme Soviet had approved the introduction of a presidency by a very large majority, the issue was placed before a specially convened session of the Congress of People's Deputies. Anatolii Luk'yanov, who presented the proposals, argued that a presidency would encourage dialogue among the various sociopolitical movements that had been brought into being by perestroika, and help to develop a political consensus. The president would also be able to act quickly in the event of public disorders or other emergencies, and an executive agency of this kind would help to resolve the impasse that had developed between the Soviet government and the Congress and Supreme Soviet. Nor was there any reason to fear that the presidency would lead to a new form of authoritarian rule: there was an "entire system of safeguards" against this, including limits on age and tenure and the ability of Congress – if a sufficiently large majority decided accordingly – to recall the president and overrule his decisions.[17] As jurist Boris Lazarev explained, laws were adopted but rarely put into practical effect; and there was often a need to take decisions quickly, in a way that even the Supreme Soviet Presidium had not found possible.[18] In short, it was "either a presidency, or chaos," as sources "close to the government" told *Pravda* shortly after the vote had been taken.[19]

Understandably, perhaps, some deputies were concerned that an elected presidency of the kind that had been proposed would encourage a slide back to personal dictatorship. The radical historian Yuri Afanas'ev, for instance, agreed with a presidency in principle but argued that the proposals were premature: the first step should have been the adoption of a new constitution. Another deputy pointed to the danger that the idea of a "little father" would become increasingly popular as their difficulties deepened. What would protect them from a "tsarist-style socialism" under such circumstances? Many of the republican leaders were concerned about the possible exercise of presidential power to suspend the operation of their own parliaments; and there was a majority, though not a sufficiently large one, in favor of a formal separation between the presidency and the party leadership.[20] Other speakers, however, accepted the proposals as a means of ending what was described as a "vacuum of power," and in the end the establishment of the presidency was approved by 1817 votes to 133, with 61 abstentions.[21] Gorbachev was the only candidate when elections to the new post took place on 14 March, and he was sworn in the following day as the first (and last) president of the USSR with the support of 71 percent of the deputies who voted.[22]

Any citizen aged between 35 and 65 could be elected to the presidency of the USSR for a maximum of two five-year terms. The president would normally be elected by universal, equal, and direct suffrage, although it was agreed that Gorbachev – exceptionally – would be elected by the Congress itself (the "father of the house," literary scholar Dmitrii Likhachev, carried the day on this point with an impassioned warning that if they did not elect a president without further delay – and he was old enough to have experienced the revolution of 1917 – there was a real danger of civil war).[23] The president, under the terms of the legislation, was to report annually to the Congress of People's Deputies and would brief the Supreme Soviet on the "most important questions of the USSR's domestic and foreign policy." He would propose candidates for the premiership and other leading state positions, he had a suspensory veto over legislation, and he could dissolve the government and suspend its directives. He could also declare a state of emergency, and introduce direct presidential rule. The president headed a new Council of the Federation, consisting of the presidents of the fifteen union republics; he also headed a Presidential Council, which was responsible for the "main directions of the USSR's foreign and domestic policy."[24]

A further law to "protect the President's honor and dignity" was adopted in May; and in September 1990 these already impressive powers were extended by parliamentary vote, giving Gorbachev the right to institute emergency measures to "stabilise the country's sociopolitical life" for a period of eighteen months.[25] Several further changes were made by the Fourth Congress of People's Deputies in December 1990, completing the move to a fully presidential administration. The Council of Ministers was replaced by a more limited "Cabinet", headed by a prime minister who would be nominated by the president and accountable to him. The president meanwhile became head of a new Security Council with overall responsibility for defence and public order; and he appointed a vice-president, responsible for carrying out the functions that were entrusted to him (Gennadii Yanaev, a member of the party Secretariat who had formerly worked in the trade union movement, was elected to this position after Gorbachev had intervened on his behalf).[26] The Presidential Council disappeared entirely, and a reconstituted Council of the Federation headed by the president became, in effect, the supreme state decision-making body.[27]

Formally, at least, these were greater powers than any Stalin had commanded, and they deepened the concern of deputies and of Gorbachev's opponents outside parliament that they could open the way to a further period of dictatorial rule. For the Inter-Regional Group, once again, the new presidency represented an "usurpation of power," leaving too much authority in the hands of a single person. Boris Yeltsin went still further, complaining that the central authorities were "seeking to constitutionalise an absolutist and authoritarian regime which could ultimately be used to provide a legal pretext for any high-handed act."[28] Gorbachev himself drew attention to a cartoon in which he had been shown with a tsar's crown in his hands, trying it on for size.[29] There were, in fact, considerable limitations upon the powers of the new president, extensive though they undoubtedly were. He could be impeached by a two-thirds vote of the Congress of People's Deputies; his ministerial nominations required the approval of the Supreme Soviet, which could force the resignation of the Cabinet as a whole if it voted accordingly; and he had himself to report annually to the Congress of People's Deputies upon the exercise of his responsibilities. In any case, as Gorbachev told a gathering of miners in April 1991, he had voluntarily surrendered the extraordinary powers that he possessed as general secretary of the CPSU. Would he have done so if he had been seeking unlimited personal authority?[30]

From the Soviet to the Russian presidency

There was, in fact, an attempt to dismiss Gorbachev as president at the Fourth Congress of People's Deputies in December 1990; and his powers had already been undermined by the increasing reluctance of the union republics to accept the decisions of what they came to describe as "the Centre." The republics were led by Russia, where Boris Yeltsin had been

Table 2.1 *The Russian presidential election, 12 June 1991*

	Votes	Percent of electorate	Percent of valid vote
Yeltsin, Boris	45,552,041	42.8	59.7
Ryzhkov, Nikolai	13,395,335	12.6	17.6
Zhirinovsky, Vladimir	6,211,007	5.8	8.1
Tuleev, Aman-Gel'dy	5,417,464	5.1	7.1
Makashev, Al'bert	2,969,511	2.8	3.9
Bakatin, Vadim	2,719,757	2.6	3.6
Total valid votes	76,265,115	71.6	100.0
Invalid votes	3,242,167	3.1	
Non-voters	26,977,236	25.3	
Electorate	106,484,518	100.0	
(Turnout 74.7 per cent)			

Source: Communiqué of the Central Electoral Commission, reported in *Pravda*, 20 June 1991, p. 1.

elected parliamentary chairman in May 1990 following elections in which radicals in "Democratic Russia" had secured more than 20 per cent of the seats available.[31] In March 1991, as the wider population was taking part in a referendum on the future of the USSR as a "renewed federation," voters in Russia were being asked in addition if they would support the institution of a directly elected presidency. They declared overwhelmingly in favor; and at the election that subsequently took place, in June 1991, Yeltsin was a clear winner on the first ballot (Table 2.1). By the end of the year most of the other republics had moved in the same direction, towards a presidential system with an elected chief executive. The Russian presidential election was accordingly a decisive moment: in shifting legitimacy from the USSR to its republics, from Gorbachev and the CPSU towards Yeltsin and the radical democrats who provided his most active supporters, and from parliaments to presidents.

The decision to create the office of Russian president had not originally been controversial.[32] At the first Russian Congress of People's Deputies, in May and June 1990, the proposal had the support of deputies from all of the parliamentary factions. But once Yeltsin had become parliamentary chairman and (in July 1990) resigned from the CPSU, the issue of the presidency became more partisan and the question of who might fill the position became a bitterly contested one. At the Second Russian Congress of People's Deputies, in December 1990, all that was agreed was that the Supreme Soviet and its constitutional committee should consider appropriate amendments to the Russian constitution.[33] As a constitutional amendment would require a two-thirds majority in the Congress of Deputies, Yeltsin's hardline opponents seemed well placed to resist any change that would be to their disadvantage. The decision to call a referendum on the future of the USSR, however, altered the position once again. On 25 January 1991 the Presidium of the Russian Supreme Soviet proposed an additional question on the establishment of a directly elected presidency; its proposal was approved by the Supreme Soviet; and then Russia's voters were asked to express their views. On a 75.1 percent turnout a resounding 69.9 percent approved the change.[34]

The Congress of People's Deputies had originally been called by deputies anxious to condemn the Russian president. The outcome of the referendum, and the open expression of public support throughout the republic, influenced the Congress in a different direction and on 5 April it was resolved that a presidential election would be held on 12 June 1991. The Supreme Soviet, meanwhile, was asked to prepare a law on the presidency as well as any amendments that might be necessary to the Russian constitution.[35] The changes concerned were duly approved on 24 April and by the full Congress on 22 May. It was agreed that candidates for the Russian presidency must be citizens aged between 35 and 65, and that they could hold the office for no more than two five-years terms. Nominations could be made by political parties, trade unions and public organisations, or by other groupings that were able to collect 100,000 signatures in their support. The president, for his part, could not be a deputy or a member of a political party; he enjoyed the right of legislative initiative, reported to the Congress once a year, and appointed the premier with the consent of the Supreme Soviet.[36] Yeltsin's own standing was strengthened further when he headed the resistance to the attempted coup of August 1991 (Gorbachev, meanwhile, lost his extraordinary powers), and in the discussions that took place later in the year to negotiate a looser association of sovereign republics it was the Russian president who was the dominant figure.

Yeltsin owed much of his authority to the fact that he had been directly elected, unlike Gorbachev who had been chosen – in the first instance – by Soviet parliamentarians. At the same time he had to govern through a Congress of People's Deputies that had also been chosen by a popular vote, and which was able to claim the same right to represent the will of the electorate. The Congress had initially been supportive, electing Yeltsin its chairman, approving a declaration of Russian sovereignty in June 1991, and then granting him emergency powers the following November. Yeltsin, however, used his position to launch a program of radical economic reform under the guidance of Yegor Gaidar, who was acting prime

minister from June 1991; and parliamentary resistance strengthened as
the consequences of those reforms became clearer. Gaidar was forced to
stand down at the Seventh Congress in December 1992. At the Eighth
Congress, in March 1993, the president was stripped of his emergency
powers and ordered to act in accordance with the constitution, in terms of
which the Congress was itself the "supreme body of state power" and the
president merely the "chief official."[37] Yeltsin's supporters had already
talked of "emergency measures," and on 20 March the president called
publicly for a "special form of administration" under which the Congress
would continue to meet but would be unable to challenge his decrees.
The Congress, hurriedly convened for an emergency session, voted to
impeach the president but not by the necessary two-thirds majority; the
outcome was an agreement that a referendum, originally approved the
previous December, would be held on 25 April 1993 to decide "who rules
Russia."[38]

The referendum, in the event, did little to resolve a continuing impasse.
Voters were asked if they "had confidence" in Yeltsin as Russian president, and if they approved the policies that president and government had
been pursuing; they were also asked if they favored early presidential or
parliamentary elections. The turnout was a respectable 64 percent. Of
those who voted, 58.7 percent supported the president and 53.1 percent
approved his policies; 49.5 percent favored early presidential elections
and a much more substantial 67.2 percent early parliamentary elections,
but in both cases this fell short of the majority of the electorate that was
necessary for constitutional changes.[39] For Yeltsin and his supporters this
was a verdict that justified pressing ahead with a constitution that provided for a presidential republic with a much more limited legislature,
and by the end of the year they had attained their objective. It was
"inevitable," Yeltsin reflected later, that at the end of the Soviet period
there would be a conflict between "two systems of power."[40] The Congress, he complained, tended "just to reject, just to destroy." Too many
deputies engaged in "cheap populism and open demagoguery . . . and in
the final analysis, the restoration of a totalitarian Soviet-Communist
system."[41]

For parliamentarians and their speaker, Ruslan Khasbulatov, the issue
was a rather different one: whether government should be accountable to
elected representatives, and whether a broadly representative parliament
should be allowed to act as a counterbalance to what would otherwise be
an overwhelmingly powerful executive. For Khasbulatov, Russian history, and then Marxism–Leninism had combined to exaggerate the power
of a single "tsar." It was essential, in these circumstances, to establish a
secure division of powers and then to develop the role of parliament as a
"representative organ" of the whole society. Parliament, in particular,

could serve as a "counterweight" to the executive, exercising its influence over public spending, legislation, and the composition of government as parliaments did in other countries.[42] Opening the Russian parliament in March 1992, Khasbulatov accused the government of an "attack on democracy" and complained that individual ministers had a dismissive attitude toward representative institutions in general.[43] He insisted that government should be accountable to the Congress and Supreme Soviet rather than to the "collective Rasputin" that surrounded the president.[44] And he argued more generally that a presidential republic was not appropriate to the particular circumstances of postcommunist Russia, with its need to maximise consensus and public understanding.[45]

These differences, in the end, were resolved by force, when parliament was dissolved by presidential decree on 21 September 1993 and then seized by the Russian army on 4 October following an attempt by parliamentary supporters to occupy the Kremlin and establish their own authority. Yeltsin had produced his own draft of a new constitution in April 1993, on the eve of the referendum, and a constitutional conference which met in June and July with a number of deputies in attendance produced another version that was in Yeltsin's view "neither presidential nor parliamentary." Yeltsin had however predicted a "decisive battle" between the supporters and opponents of his program of reforms, and in the different circumstances that obtained after the suppression of what he described as a parliamentary insurrection it was a rather more centralist draft that was published in November 1993 and approved at a referendum the following month. There was, in fact, some doubt if the constitution was itself constitutional: under the law on the referendum a majority of the electorate, not just of voters, had to indicate their support, and there was some evidence that the turnout had in any case fallen below 50 per cent, which was the level Yeltsin had specified in his decree.[46] It was difficult, however, to alter any of the provisions of the document that had now become Russia's first postcommunist constitution, and it appeared to have shifted Russian politics decisively toward what an *Izvestiya* journalist described as a "superpresidential republic."[47]

Yeltsin and the Russian presidency

The man who now exercised these far-reaching powers had been born in the village of Butko in the Sverdlovsk region of western Siberia in 1931, the son of peasant parents. According to his autobiography, Yeltsin was lucky to be alive at all: the priest nearly drowned him when he was being baptised, remarking calmly, "Well, if he can survive such an ordeal it means he's a good tough lad." Both his father and his uncle were

---

The Russian presidency, December 1993

Under the December 1993 Constitution, the President of the Russian Federation is:
head of state (Art. 80:1);

the guarantor of the Constitution (Art. 80:2), to which he swears an oath (Art. 82:1);

he "defines the basic directions of the domestic and foreign policy of the state" (Art. 80:3) and represents the Russian Federation domestically and internationally (Art. 80:4);

he is elected for four years by direct, equal and secret ballot (Art. 81:1); he must be at least 35 years old, and have lived in the Russian Federation for at least ten years (Art. 81:2), and may not be elected for more than two consecutive terms (Art. 81:3);

he "appoints with the agreement of the State Duma the Chairman of the Government of the Russian Federation," has the right to preside at government meetings and "takes decisions on the resignation of the Government of the Russian Federation"; he nominates candidates for the Chairmanship of the State Bank; on the recommendation of the prime minister, he appoints and dismisses deputy premiers and federal ministers; he nominates candidates for the Constitutional Court, the Supreme Court and the Procuracy General; he forms and heads the Security Council, appoints and dismisses his plenipotentiary representatives in the regions as well as the high command of the armed forces and diplomatic representatives in foreign states and international organisations (Art. 83); additionally, he calls elections to the State Duma, dissolves the Duma in appropriate circumstances, calls referenda, initiates legislation, and reports annually to the Federal Assembly on "the situation in the country" and the "main directions of the domestic and foreign policy of the state" (Art. 84);

he is commander in chief and can declare a state of war (Art. 87) as well as a state of emergency (Art. 88); he declares amnesties (Art. 89) and issues decrees that have the force of law throughout the territory of the Federation (Art. 90).

Based upon *Konstitutsiya Rossiiskoi Federatsii. Prinyata vsenarodnym golosovaniem 12 dekabrya 1993 g.* (Moscow: Yuridicheskaya literatura, 1993).

---

persecuted in 1934 when they fell foul of the campaign against kulaks, who were rich or simply more efficient farmers. They were accused of conducting anti-Soviet agitation and, though they protested their innocence, given three months' hard labor; Yeltsin himself, though only three, remembered the "horror and fear" years later.[48] Yeltsin's childhood was the time of the famine that followed agricultural collectivization: there were always shortages of food, and the family might not have survived the war but for the milk and sometimes the warmth of their nanny-goat.

Yeltsin lost two fingers in an accident; he broke his nose and contracted typhoid fever; his father, a harsh disciplinarian, beat him regularly. But he did well at school and graduated as an engineer at the Urals Polytechnical Institute, where he perfected his volleyball technique and met his future wife.[49]

After completing his studies, Yeltsin worked as a construction engineer managing a large state enterprise that specialized in prefabricated housing. In 1961 he joined the CPSU, becoming a full-time party functionary in 1968 and in 1976 first secretary of the Sverdlovsk regional party organization. He joined the Central Committee, as befitted his rank, at the next Party Congress in 1981, and as a full member. One of Yeltsin's decisions as party first secretary was to order the destruction of the Ipat'ev house in which the tsar's family had been shot in 1918, and which had become a place of pilgrimage. The decision, he explained later, had been taken secretly by the Politburo and there was no alternative but to carry it out, although he knew that "sooner or later" they would all be ashamed of what they had done.[50] Yeltsin's managerial qualities – he had, on his own account, become "steeped in command-administrative methods" by this time[51] – caught the attention of the central leadership, and early in 1985 he was invited to Moscow to take up a position in the party apparatus as head of its construction department. In December 1985, after Gorbachev had taken office, he transferred to the position of first secretary of the Moscow city party organization in succession to a disgraced Brezhnevite, Viktor Grishin.

Yeltsin's outspoken comments soon attracted attention. His speech at the Twenty-Seventh Party Congress in early 1986 began with references to the "Bolshevik spirit" and "Leninist optimism" that prevailed at their deliberations, but went on to ask why over so many years the party had failed to eliminate social injustice and the abuse of official position.[52] Then in October 1987 – according to those who were present, almost by accident[53] – he was called to speak to the Central Committee plenum that was considering Gorbachev's draft report on the seventieth anniversary of the revolution. Yeltsin wanted, he wrote later, to "screw up [his] courage and say what [he] had to say"; his speech was no more than a few headings on a sheet of paper. It was nonetheless the decisive moment in his political career. There had been no changes in the way the party secretariat operated, Yeltsin told the delegates, or in the conduct of its head, Yegor Ligachev. More and more instructions were being issued, but they were receiving less and less attention. Meanwhile in the Politburo there had been a "noticeable increase" in what he "could only call adulation of the general secretary." In seventy years, he declared in another version of the speech, they had failed to feed and clothe the people they claimed to represent, while providing for themselves abundantly. And there were criticisms of the general secretary's wife, who was being paid for what was thought to be voluntary work and was in danger of acquiring her own "cult of personality."[54]

Yeltsin knew what would happen next: he would be "slaughtered, in an organised, methodical manner, and . . . almost with pleasure and enjoyment."[55] The plenum itself described his speech as "politically mistaken" and called for his dismissal as Moscow party secretary.[56] Gorbachev, "almost hysterical," denounced him at the Politburo and complained that everything in the Soviet capital was "going badly."[57] The Moscow party organization, when it met in November, dragged a "barely conscious" Yeltsin out of a hospital bed to listen to a series of charges of incompetence and even Bonapartism in what was the political equivalent of a Stalinist show trial, and then voted to remove him from his post.[58] He was dropped from the Party Politburo in February 1988 and urged to retire, but in the end moved to a junior ministerial position at the State Construction Committee. A "political outcast, surrounded by a vacuum,"[59] Yeltsin's political career seemed at an end; even his membership of the CPSU was in doubt as the Central Committee, in a decision without postwar precedent, voted to investigate his increasingly outspoken views to determine if they were compatible with party policies.[60]

But the more Yeltsin was attacked by the party leadership, the more he came to be seen as a champion of ordinary citizens against an overpowerful, often corrupt establishment; and the introduction of competitive elections at the same time as his disgrace allowed him to turn this popular following to his advantage. In March 1989, standing for the Moscow national-territorial constituency, he won over 89 per cent of the vote against a party-approved competitor;[61] his winning margin, over 5 million votes, was so large it entered the Guinness Book of Records, and it contrasted sharply with Gorbachev's decision to take one of the 100 seats that were reserved for the CPSU and for which 100 candidates were nominated, avoiding a direct appeal to the electorate and still more so a direct confrontation with his leading opponent. A year later, in elections to the Russian parliament, Yeltsin won another popular mandate when he took over 80 percent of the vote in his native Sverdlovsk;[62] and he began to use his position, once he had been elected parliamentary chairman at the end of May 1990, to advance the claims of the republics and especially of Russia against the central state and its ruling party.

Yeltsin's appeal was based on his open opposition to the party-state bureaucracy, but he also advanced more specific proposals. Speaking to the Central Committee in February 1990 he called for the private ownership of land, independence for the republics, financial autonomy for factories and farms, freedom of political association, and freedom of conscience.[63] Asked in the summer of 1990 if he was still a socialist, Yeltsin turned the question round: what was meant by socialism? It could mean the "developed socialism" that the USSR itself had experienced under Brezhnev, or Pol Pot socialism. In Hitler's Germany there had been national socialism; and there were many different kinds of capitalism too. What was the point of arguing about definitions?[64] His models, he told interviewers, were Peter the Great and Yaroslav the Wise, grand duke of Kievan Rus in the early eleventh century;[65] but in general, he confessed, he was happy to rely on his intuition.[66] A study of his speeches by three academics found that the Russian president was "predictable in only one respect – his unpredictability."[67]

Yeltsin admitted in the memoirs he published in 1994 that he relied on his self-image as a "wilful, determined, strong politician." But he also confessed that he was easily influenced by the opinions of people he respected; and sometimes his ideas were changed completely by "a word said in passing or a line in a newspaper article." There was, it seems, a decisive moment in this intellectual trajectory, in late 1989, when Yeltsin visited a Moscow bathhouse. He found himself surrounded by a crowd of about forty naked men, all urging him to keep up his challenge to the leadership. It was, he recalled, "quite a sight." And it was at this moment in the *banya*, with everything reduced to its essentials, that he had "changed [his] world view, realised that [he] was a communist by Soviet tradition, by inertia, by education, but not by conviction."[68] Yeltsin was also influenced by a visit to the United States in September 1989, his first to a capitalist country. Amazed by the array of foodstuffs that was readily available in a Houston supermarket, he commented that this disproved the "fairy tales" about the superiority of socialism. In the view of Lev Sukhanov, one of his closest aides, it was at this time Yeltsin decided to leave the ranks of the CPSU.[69]

Once Yeltsin had been elected and, in 1993, secured greatly enhanced powers, the struggle for political influence shifted from the Russian parliament and came to focus around the presidential administration – in effect, a supra-government – and the varying influence of Yeltsin's immediate advisers. As of 1996, when it was reorganized, the presidential administration had six main divisions: (i) the Main Administration for the Constitutional Rights of Citizens, which dealt with the president's correspondence, with citizenship and state awards; (ii) the Main Administration for Internal and Foreign Policy, which handled relations with the regions, with political parties and movements, and with parliament; and (iii) the Main Administration for the State Service, which dealt with official appointments. There was also (iv) a Main Analytical Administration, which dealt with research and documentation; (v) a Main Administration for the president's Special Programmes; and (vi) a Main Legal Administration.[70] The total number of staff that worked in the presidential administration, up to the introduction of these new arrangements, was about 2,000; other estimates suggested much larger figures, and certainly more than the number that had been employed by the central party bureaucracy in the years before 1991.[71]

Rather more important, in terms of policy formulation, was a series of other bodies with powers that were at best loosely defined by the constitution. These included the Security Council, headed by Alexander Lebed after the 1996 presidential elections and likened by some to a "Politburo." It was the Security Council, for instance, that directed the war in Chechnya after December 1994, and the Security Council that was convened to discuss "Black Tuesday" in October 1994 when the ruble suddenly crashed on the foreign exchanges.[72] A Presidential Council was less influential: it consisted of figures from the cultural and industrial worlds together with a few trusted politicians, and met infrequently.[73] The president's press service was of more significance, at least when it was headed, up to 1994, by Vyacheslav Kostikov.[74] The president's chief of staff, from 1996 Anatolii Chubais, was a still more important figure, particularly where appointments were concerned.[75] In particular spheres of policy the president's staff of counsellors also enjoyed a great deal of influence: Alexander Livshits, for instance, advised him on economic policy, Yuri Baturin on national security, and Dmitrii Ryurikov on international affairs. Viktor Ilyushin had the most powerful position of all as first counsellor or chief presidential aide (in August 1996 both Livshits and Ilyushenko joined the government itself).[76]

In the end, these formal positions mattered less than the shifting patterns of influence that focused around the president himself, and the struggles for influence that intensified whenever the president was indisposed. The president's security chief, for instance, until 1996 Alexander Korzhakov, held a position of no constitutional significance. But he saw the president daily, and played tennis with him regularly (making sure to lose more often than he won); he commanded a security service of about 20,000 men, and began to offer views on current politics that were assumed to carry considerable weight at the very center of the administration.[77] When Korzhakov sought to bring his influence to bear upon the role that foreign companies should play in energy policy *Izvestiya* was moved to ask in a front page headline: "Who rules Russia: Yeltsin, Chernomyrdin or General Korzhakov?"[78] And there was intensive speculation when Korzhakov, in an interview with the London *Observer*, suggested publicly that the 1996 presidential elections should be postponed or called off altogether, even though these views were immediately disowned by the president.[79]

The result was a system of "court politics," involving struggles for advantage between official advisers, cronies, and intimates. As an overburdened president, Yeltsin was in danger of having staff take decisions in his name in the belief that by arrogating this power to themselves they were "protecting" the president from distractions and difficulties. His former press spokesman, Vyacheslav Kostikov, remarked later that a common expression among Yeltsin staff was, "It is no business of the Tsar," that is, aides rather than the president himself would make the decision.[80] This meant that it could often be very difficult to sort out the relationships among the various structures that were responsible for drafting presidential decisions; the best way to achieve one's objectives, in these circumstances, was to "gain a personal audience with the president."[81] Meanwhile there was constant competition among the president's associates "for which of the 'closest' persons is the closest of all," just as Politburo members had jostled for the central positions above the Lenin Mausoleum for the parade on the anniversary of the revolution.[82] And while the president was ill or elsewhere, as was often the case, his entourage was free to engage in "palace intrigues with far-reaching consequences."[83]

The struggle for influence within the presidency took place against a steady fall in the public standing of the president himself. Yeltsin had clearly overtaken Gorbachev in public support before he became Russian president: in 1989 it was the Soviet president who was "man of the year," and by a wide margin, but by 1990 Yeltsin (with 32 percent) came first, ahead of Gorbachev with 19 percent.[84] Indeed Yeltsin, in one survey at this time, came first among all Russian leaders of the twentieth century, ahead of Lenin, Gorbachev, and (by a wide margin) Nicholas II.[85] Yeltsin, in more qualitative terms, was seen as "open and straightforward" (34 percent), "ambitious" (26 percent), but also "resolute" (24 percent). Gorbachev, by contrast, was "hypocritical" (28 percent), "weak and lacking in self-confidence" (20 percent), and "indifferent to human suffering" (19 percent), although he was also "flexible and capable of adapting to change" (18 percent); just 7 percent saw him as "decisive."[86] According to the All-Russian Centre for the Study of Public Opinion, it was in the summer of 1990 that Yeltsin's popular support overtook that of the Soviet president; the peak of his popularity, with an approval rating of 80 percent, was at the end of May 1990 when he was elected chairman of the Russian parliament. His support rose again, to 74 percent, at the time of the attempted coup in August 1991.[87]

Once in office, however, Yeltsin's support declined rapidly. It had fallen to about 50 percent at the time of the collapse of the USSR at the end of 1991, and fell more sharply from the start of 1992 as Gaidar's economic policies began to bite. The president's popularity recovered a little at the time of the April 1993 referendum, and again during the conflict with the Russian parliament in September and October 1993, but then resumed its earlier decline. In July 1991 about 71 percent of Russians were Yeltsin supporters and 18 percent were opponents; by the end of 1994 the positions were almost reversed, with 22 percent of the population his supporters but 59 percent his declared opponents.[88] It was at this point, in December 1994, that Yeltsin sent Russian forces into Chechnya to restore federal authority and perhaps to recover his personal standing in what was expected to be a "short, victorious war."[89] If this was the intention, it came badly unstuck. Chechen resistance proved unexpectedly stubborn; the Russian campaign was incompetently conducted, particularly at the outset; and losses were heavy, up to 30,000 within the first year. Yeltsin's support, in the event, plunged still further, a majority holding him personally responsible for the war and just 5.8 percent prepared to support him in the event of an early presidential election.[90]

Yeltsin had a number of positive features, according to surveys that were conducted in March 1996. He was, for some, a leader who was "continuing democratic reforms" (21 percent took this view). He "guaranteed some kind of public order" for 14 percent; and he was "able, when it was necessary, to act decisively" for another 13 percent. A rather larger proportion, however, thought the Russian president had "no positive features at all" (30 percent) or were unable to respond (22 percent). There were fewer difficulties in identifying Yeltsin's negative features: most (31 percent) pointed to the "crisis in the economy"; others pointed to the "mistakes of recent years" (27 percent), to Yeltsin's "responsibility for the war in Chechyna" (24 percent), or to his "lack of a program for getting the country out of its crisis" (20 percent). In addition, the president was seen as "not concerned about the social wellbeing of the population" (19 percent), and as "remote from the people" (12 percent). Only 5 percent had no criticism to offer; and a majority (52 percent), in response to a different question, thought he should resign.[91]

The Duma election of December 1995 made it still clearer that the president was a remote and isolated figure. He was not identified directly with any of the competing parties; but the grouping that was formed by Prime Minister Chernomyrdin in the spring of 1995, Our Home is Russia, was clearly intended as a means by which he could hope to sustain his policies in the new Duma and then develop a successful campaign for the presidency when his term expired in the summer of 1996. In the event, his opponents were much more successful: the Communist Party of the Russian Federation took 22.3 percent of the party-list vote and about a third of all the 450 seats and Vladimir Zhirinovsky's Liberal Democrats came second in the party-list vote with 11.2 percent, ahead of Our Home is Russia with 10.1. Yeltsin professed to regard the result as "not a tragedy,"[92] and it had no direct bearing on the composition or conduct of the government that he appointed; but it was a result that, together with his own approval rating, gave few grounds for believing that he would be able to recover sufficiently to mount a credible challenge for a second term as president. Indeed, given his health and the apparent opposition of his wife, it was far from clear he would even attempt to do so.

Yeltsin, in the end, declared his candidacy on 15 February 1996 and then mounted a remarkable campaign which carried him to victory in the two rounds that took place in June and July. It was a victory that owed a good deal to his use of the prerogatives of the presidency itself. Yeltsin made full use of his influence over the state media, and particularly television. He invited the head of Russia's newly established independent television service, which had been critical of his policies in Chechnya, to join his campaign staff. He committed public funds with increasing abandon: to small businesses and the Academy of Science, to pensioners and those who had lost their savings. An end was declared to the conscription in the armed forces, and troops were allowed to avoid compulsory duty in Chechnya or other hot spots.[93] Perhaps as much as $500m was spent on his campaign, rather than the $3m allowed by the electoral law.[94] But most important of all, Yeltsin campaigned with increasing confidence, traveling the country with an energy that belied his 65 years, and presenting himself as the only serious alternative to a return to the Soviet system. The changes in his behavior were so extraordinary that ordinary Russians began to believe he had been connected to a battery; another view, put about by a financier involved in his campaign, was that "At key points in his life, Yeltsin wakes up."[95]

The outcome in the first presidential ballot, on 16 June 1996, was a narrow plurality (see Table 2.2). But within a few days Yeltsin had received the third-placed candidate, former general Alexander Lebed, and offered him a place in his administration as secretary of the Security Council with particular responsibility for public order. Gennadii Zyuganov, the communist candidate, found himself unable to broaden his coalition of supporters between the two rounds, despite a series of attempts to form a broadly based "government of national confidence"; and Yeltsin, in the second round, won a clear victory with most of Lebed's voters behind him as well as the overwhelming majority of the voters that had backed liberal reformers like Grigorii Yavlinsky.[96] It was a striking

Table 2.2 *The Russian presidential election, June–July 1996*

	Votes	Percentages
(i) The first round, 16 June 1996		
Bryntsalov, Vladimir	123,065	(0.2)
Vlasov, Yuri	151,282	(0.2)
Gorbachev, Mikhail	386,069	(0.5)
Yeltsin, Boris	26,665,495	(35.3)
Zhirinovsky, Vladimir	4,311,479	(5.7)
Zyuganov, Gennadii	24,211,686	(32.0)
Lebed, Alexander	10,974,736	(14.5)
Fedorov, Svyatoslav	699,158	(0.9)
Shakkum, Martin	277,068	(0.4)
Yavlinsky, Grigorii	5,550,752	(7.3)
Tuleev, Aman-Gel'dy	308[a]	(0.0)
Against all	1,163,921	(1.5)

Electorate: 108,495,023
Total vote: 75,587,139 (69.7 percent of the electorate)
Total valid vote: 74,515,019

	Votes	Percentages
(ii) The second round, 3 July 1996		
Yeltsin, Boris	40,203,948	(53.8)
Zyuganov, Gennadii	30,102,288	(40.3)
Against both	3,604,462	(4.8)

Electorate: 108,589,050
Total vote: 74,691,290 (68.8 percent of the electorate)
Total valid vote: 73,910,698

[a] Votes cast before Tuleev's withdrawal of his candidacy.
Source: Communique of the Central Electorate Commission: reported in *Vestnik Tsentral'noi izbiratel'noi komissii Rossiiskoi Federatsii* 15 (1996), pp. 40–1 for (i); and ibid., 17 (1996), pp. 8–9 and 24–5, which corrected the results originally announced, for (ii).

success; yet it also made clear that Yeltsin's committed supporters were only a quarter of the electorate, a smaller share than non-voters, and a much smaller number than had been prepared to support him in June 1991 and again in the April 1993 referendum. The distribution of support for pro-Yeltsin reformers and for communists and their allies scarcely changed between the December 1995 Duma election and the first round of the presidential contest in June 1996.

The causes and consequences of Russian presidentialism

The experience of Russian presidentialism in its early years suggested a number of points that were general to presidential systems, but also a number of features that were distinctively Russian. One of the strengths of a presidential system was that it had given Russia at least a temporary stability. Yeltsin represented a clear choice in favor of "reform," even democracy, even if the president was not always true to such values himself, and in this sense he had allowed Russians to choose the political future that corresponded to their wishes. The old Soviet system had found it necessary to identify a single figure, normally the CPSU general secretary, who could represent it in international dealings, and the Russian president fulfilled this role. The Russian presidency reflected the long-standing tradition of a single ruler, a "tsar." But it also reflected the particular circumstances of early postcommunist Russia, and the search for some form of public order. Yeltsin, in this sense, was the guarantor of incumbent elites, who had largely survived the transition from communist rule;[97] and he represented security for those who had acquired property, from the state or (less often) from their own activities. A return to communist rule in 1996 might have threatened many of these groups with a public trial, and not simply the loss of their position.

The likely consequences of a Russian presidency were a little more remote, but they provided further evidence of the "perils of presidentialism." The existence of an elected president with an exceptionally wide range of powers, in conjunction with an elected parliament, exposed at least three serious difficulties in this connection.

1. All presidential systems depend heavily upon the person of the president. The Russian system depends more than many others, and in terms not simply of the president's policy choices but also of his physical health and personality. The 1993 constitution added to these concerns by abolishing the position of vice-president (in the postcommunist world only Bulgaria, Korea, Kazakstan and Kirgizia retained a position of this kind).[98] Under the constitution, the president relinquishes office ahead of time in the event of his resignation, impeachment or "inability to perform the duties of his office for reasons of health." In these circumstances the powers of the president pass on a temporary basis to the prime minister, and new elections have to be called within three months (Article 92). But who, asked commentators, was to decide if the president was "totally unable to exercise his powers? The patient himself, by signing a decree? Or the prime minister? Or a special conference of doctors? Including whom? Or, perhaps, a presidential assistant – but which one?" As long as there were no answers to such questions, there was a "real possibility" that the president could be isolated from power and the country governed "in his name" by "powerful 'backstage figures.'"[99]

Yeltsin himself complained that "as soon as [he went] on holiday, speculation [began] about [his] health."[100] But there were many such absences, and several occasions on which the president's health was acknowledged to be the reason; and it was not surprising that every visit to the hospital was accompanied by "arguments and rumors that undermine[d] his authority."[101] In 1993 Yeltsin was confined to hospital with a nerve disease, radiculitis, that could require strong sedation. In December 1994 he underwent an operation on his nose. In April 1995 a spring holiday was extended by a further week because of the president's high blood pressure, and in July he was rushed to hospital complaining of acute chest pains; appointments were cancelled and a scheduled visit to Norway had to be postponed. In October 1995 there was a recurrence of the same cardiac difficulties; he was in hospital for more than a month and did not return to his Kremlin desk until the end of December. There were further rumors when Yeltsin disappeared from public view between the two rounds of the presidential election in 1996, and a wooden television appeal on the eve of the decisive vote was not reassuring. The president had become a "painted mummy," complained one of Zyuganov's supporters; "they're suggesting we vote for a living corpse."[102]

Concerns about the presidential role were not allayed by repeated reports of alcoholism. The president himself admitted, in an interview in 1993, that he "sometimes" allowed himself a glass of cognac on a Sunday evening with his family, or some beer after visiting the bathhouse.[103] His parliamentary critics were more forthcoming. "It's time to stop the public drunkenness of our President," a communist deputy demanded after an unsteady performance during the president's first visit to the United States. "When he's shown on television, he can't stand up without support."[104] There was further criticism in early 1993 when the president, defending himself against impeachment, spoke uncertainly before the Russian parliament and had to be assisted from the hall (deputies agreed he had "created a strange impression"), and later in the year when Russian troops withdrawing from Germany were treated to a "stirring rendition of Kalinka" under the impromptu conductorship of the president.[105] A number of advisers who expressed their concern at his performance while in Germany were simply left at home on the president's next foreign trip, which concluded with his controversial non-appearance at Shannon airport to take part in discussions with the Irish prime minister. Yeltsin, his staff explained, had simply overslept; his political opponents took a less charitable view and accused him subsequently of being in a "permanent state of visiting Ireland."[106]

2. The complex and unsatisfactory relationship between president and parliament was a much more general feature of presidential systems. The December constitution had been intended to resolve any tensions of this

kind in favor of the president. It certainly endowed him with extensive powers to nominate the prime minister and government, to dissolve the Duma if it repeatedly refused to endorse his choices, and to issue his own decrees with the force of law. In 1994 and 1995 alone Yeltsin put more than a hundred draft laws to parliament, and vetoed more than a third of the draft laws that were submitted for his signature after the Federal Assembly had approved them.[107] Indeed the president's frequent recourse to decrees, appeals, constitutional messages, and statements in the mass media made him appear a source of legislation in his own right, a clear violation of the principle of a separation of powers. Some of his decrees, moreover, including those on the basis of which he launched the war in Chechnya, were issued in secret and outside the knowledge let alone the capacity to scrutinize them of the Russian parliament (it was for reasons such as this that the US Congress in 1973 had adopted the War Powers Act, restricting the power of the president to commit US troops abroad).

At the same time, there was no guarantee that the government the president nominated would reflect majority opinion in the Federal Assembly, or that its decisions would find favor with the deputies of either house. The Duma, for its part, could adopt decisions entirely at odds with presidential policies, as it did in February 1994 when the conspirators of August 1991 and the parliamentary leaders of September–October 1993 were amnestied. The Duma could also pass a vote of no confidence in the government, as it did (but not by a sufficiently large majority) in October 1994. Under the provisions of Article 117 this led either to the dismissal of the government by the president, or to the dissolution of the Duma itself. But there was, again, no guarantee that future elections would resolve the crisis, and no reason for the president to accept their outcome; and there could in any case be no dissolution of the Duma on this basis within the first year of its election (Art. 109(3)). The president, unlike his American counterpart, spent little time in meetings with parliamentary leaders and factions; the result was often a compromise, as in the successive budgets that were agreed by both sides, but the outcome could also be a "cold war" between president and parliament, a deadlock that reflected the powers they had respectively been allocated under the constitution.[108]

One of the ways in which presidents and parliaments were associated in other nations was through the party system. And this, again, was a weakness in the postcommunist system, at least in Russia. President Yeltsin had left the CPSU in July 1990 at the Twenty-eighth Congress; later he took the view that, as an elected Russian president, he should remain independent of party affiliation. There was talk, before the

December 1993 election, that he might form a "party or movement" to promote his views; but there was no serious attempt to do so, and in the event Yeltsin stood above the contest, as did the prime minister, Chernomyrdin. He did so again in the Duma election of December 1995, although an eve of poll broadcast attempted to persuade voters against choosing the communists. Parties themselves remained notoriously weak, with limited memberships, a constant tendency to divide, and a focus on leadership intrigue; just 3 percent of adults were members of any of the parties, movements or political organizations that had come into being by 1994.[109] The consequence was that there was no wider framework that might have bound president and parliament to a single set of policies, and normally one that had been approved at a national election.

3. Government itself was left in a difficult situation by the presidential system. The prime minister, wholly dependent upon the president's favor, could find his position usurped by other members of the presidential entourage, or by his own deputy (as when first deputy premier, Soskovets, not Chernomyrdin, accompanied Yeltsin on his October 1994 visit to the USA and then negotiated on his behalf with the Irish government during the controversial stopover). Presidential nominations, in their turn, required parliamentary approval; but this was not likely to be forthcoming so long as president and parliament represented different political philosophies. As a result, ministers and even prime ministers could spend a considerable time in an "acting" capacity, nominated by the president (like Gaidar in June 1992) but not yet approved by the parliament (Gaidar, in the end, withdrew his own candidature after failing to secure parliamentary backing in December). There was no new finance minister for many months after the resignation of Boris Fedorov in January 1994, and the minister dismissed after "black Tuesday," Sergei Dubinin, was simply acting in that capacity and had not yet been formally appointed (he later became governor of the State Bank).

There were particular difficulties with the role of the prime minister, or (as the constitution described him) "Chairman of the Government of the Russian Federation." Nominated by the president, he nonetheless required a measure of support within the Duma: if a presidential nomination was turned down three times there were new parliamentary elections, and if the Duma passed a vote of no confidence in the government twice within three months the president had to accept its resignation or call elections (Articles 111, 117). Viktor Chernomyrdin, prime minister from the end of 1992, was generally the second-rated politician according to surveys of public opinion; and he was able to display some independent initiative at various times, opening talks (for instance) with local church leaders in an attempt to resolve the Chechen crisis. There was no basis here for the protracted struggle for influence that had taken place in some of the East European countries, particularly Poland and Slovakia;[110] and Chernomyrdin, a former gas minister and member of the CPSU Central Committee, was a figure of some personal authority. But there was some potential for constitutional difficulties in the role that the prime minister had to perform in the event of presidential incapacity; and a deeper division on the lines of Eastern Europe was possible if (for instance) the prime minister was openly associated with a party or alliance that had won a majority in the Duma, but one whose policies were unacceptable to the president.

The Soviet system had maintained an effective form of government by monopolizing political power in the hands of the Communist Party and, within the party, by concentrating authority in the hands of the leadership. The partly reformed system that existed after 1988 was an uneasy combination of party direction "from above" and electoral control "from below," a tension that was eventually resolved in favor of the voters. The postcommunist system, however, introduced a new source of tension with the separate election of an executive president and a working parliament. The tension between the two led to a governmental impasse throughout 1992 and 1993; but the constitution that was introduced in December 1993 provided no long-term solution, and there were continued calls for constitutional amendment and perhaps for the abolition of the presidency altogether.[111] A workable system, it seemed clear, would require a move to quasi-presidentialism: toward a system more like the French, in which the president enjoyed a popular mandate but the government required a parliamentary majority. The Russian tradition was strong in its attention to centralized direction; its future was likely to depend upon the extent to which it could incorporate other, more Western traditions of accountability and popular consent.

NOTES

1 N. A. Sakharov, *Institut prezidentstva v sovremennom mire* (Moscow: Yuridicheskaya literatura, 1994), notes that 130 of the United Nations' 183 members in 1993 had a presidential form of government (p. 3).

2 M. F. Nenashev, *Poslednee pravitel'stvo SSSR* (Moscow: Krom, 1993), p. 26.

3 *Izvestiya*, 6 April 1991, p. 1.

4 The classification adopted here is based on Sakharov, *Institut prezidentstva*; see also James McGregor, "The Presidency in Eastern Europe," *RFE/RL Research Report*, 3, 2 (14 January 1994), pp. 23–31. Of the Baltic republics, Estonia and Latvia had parliamentary rather than presidential systems;

Lithuania had a directly elected executive presidency, and in 1996 attempts were being made to extend its powers still further.

5 For a representative selection of views, see, for instance, Arend Lijphart (ed.), *Parliamentary versus Presidential Government* (Oxford: Oxford University Press, 1992); Giovanni Sartori, *Comparative Constitutional Engineering* (London: Macmillan, 1994), Part 2; and Juan J. Linz and Arturo Valenzuela (eds.), *The Failure of Presidential Democracy: Comparative Perspectives* (Baltimore: Johns Hopkins University Press, 1994), particularly the chapters by Linz (which is the origin of the contemporary discussion) and Stepan and Skach.

6 *Materialy Plenuma Tsentral'nogo komiteta KPSS 5–7 fevralya 1990 goda* (Moscow: Politizdat, 1990), p. 19. Speaking to a working group on 19 February 1990 Gorbachev argued similarly for a "power which can react rapidly" and for a "strong executive mechanism": *Democratizatsiya*, 2, 2 (Spring 1994), p. 331.

7 I. V. Stalin, *Sochineniya*, vol. I (14) (Stanford: Hoover Institution, 1967), p. 177 (the Supreme Soviet, in his view, could be regarded as a "collective presidency").

8 *Sovetskoe gosudarstvo i pravo*, 7 (1990), p. 4. The institution of a presidency was also briefly considered during discussion of the 1977 "Brezhnev" constitution.

9 Gorbachev as quoted by Vadim Medvedev in E. L. Kuznetsov, "Iz istorii sozdaniya instituta Prezidenta SSSR," *Gosudarstvo i pravo*, 5 (1996), p. 95.

10 *XIX Vsesoyuznaya konferentsiya Kommunisticheskoi partii Sovetskogo Soyuza, 28 iyunya – 1 iyulya 1988 g.: Stenograficheskii otchet*, 2 vols. (Moscow: Politizdat, 1988), vol. I, p. 59 (Gorbachev) and vol. II, pp. 129 ("undue concentration") and 138 (resolution).

11 See A. D. Sakharov, *Trevoga i nadezhda* (Moscow: Interverso, 1990), pp. 258–259, 272, 274. Proposals for a "firm hand" at the top in any transition from totalitarian to democratic rule had a similar logic: see, for instance, A. Migranyan in *Novyi mir*, 7 (1990), pp. 166–184, and Migranyan and I. Klyamkin in *Literaturnaya gazeta*, 16 August 1989, p. 10.

12 See Kuznetsov, "Iz istorii," p. 96.

13 Ibid.; Medvedev and Shakhnazarov's memorandum of 29 November 1989 appears with other documents in *Demokratizatsiya*, 2, 2 (Spring 1994), pp. 317–322.

14 Kuznetsov, "Iz istorii," pp. 97, 104. Medvedev also warned of the element of unpredictability in any such election that arose from the rapidly increasing influence of Boris Yeltsin; and there was at this time no legislation to define the procedures that should be followed (*Sovetskoe gosudarstvo i pravo*, 7 (1990), no. 7).

15 Burlatsky was identified as the author of a Soviet presidency by Boris Kurashvili, *Strana na pereput'e* (Moscow: Yurudicheskaya literatura, 1990), p. 105; and also in Dusko Doder and Louise Branson, *Gorbachev: Heretic in the Kremlin* (New York: Viking, 1990), pp. 279–280.

16 Kuznetsov, "Iz istorii," p. 98.

17 *Vneocherednoi tretii s"ezd narodnykh deputatov SSSR 12–15 marta 1990 g. Stenograficheskii otchet*, 3 vols. (Moscow: Izvestiya, 1990), vol. I, pp. 17–18.

18 *Pravda*, 10 March 1990, p. 2.
19 Ibid., 1 April 1990, p. 2.
20 *Vneocherednoi tretii s"ezd*, vol. I, pp. 45–6 (Afanas'ev), 126 (N. T. Dabizha), 58–61 (Gumbaridze, one of those who advanced republican arguments), and 395–396 (vote).
21 Ibid., p. 193.
22 Ibid., vol. III, p. 55.
23 Ibid., vol. II, pp. 385–386.
24 For the text of the law see *Vedomosti S"ezda narodnykh deputatov SSSR i Verkhovnogo Soveta SSSR*, 12 (1990), item 189.
25 Ibid., 22, item 487; and 40, item 802.
26 Ibid., 1 (1991), art. 18. The position of vice-president disappeared later in the year: ibid., 37, item 1082.
27 For the text of the constitutional changes see ibid., 1, item 3.
28 *Pravda*, 16 December 1990, p. 2.
29 Ibid., 1 December 1990, p. 4.
30 *Izvestiya*, 6 April 1991, p. 1.
31 *Pravda*, 26 March 1990, p. 2 (Vorotnikov's estimate).
32 On these developments see Michael E. Urban, "Boris El'tsin, Democratic Russia and the campaign for the Russian presidency," *Soviet Studies*, 44, 2 (1991), pp. 187–208; and B. Eliseev, *Institut prezidentstva v Rossiiskoi Federatsii* (Moscow: Yuridicheskaya literatura, 1992).
33 Urban, "Boris El'tsin," p. 188.
34 *Izvestiya*, 26 March 1991, p. 2.
35 Ibid., 6 April 1991, pp. 1, 3.
36 For the text of the law see *Vedomosti S"ezda narodnykh deputatov RSFSR i Verkhovnogo Soveta RSFSR*, 17 (1991), item 512.
37 *Rossiiskaya gazeta*, 13 March 1993, p. 1.
38 For these developments see Stephen White, Richard Rose, and Ian McAllister, *How Russia Votes* (Chatham House, 1997), chapter 4.
39 *Rossiiskaya gazeta*, 6 May 1993, p. 1.
40 *Izvestiya*, 10 December 1994, p. 1.
41 Ibid., 10 December 1992, p. 1.
42 *Narodnyi deputat*, 12 (1992), pp. 7–8, 13–14, and 13 (1992), pp. 7–8. For an extended statement of his views see R. I. Khasbulatov, *Vybor sud'by* (Moscow: Respublika, 1993); and Khasbulatov, *Velikaya rossiiskaya tragediya*, 2 vols. (Moscow: SIMS, 1994).
43 *Izvestiya*, 12 March 1993, p. 1.
44 Ibid., 9 February 1993, p. 1, and (for the "collective Rasputin") 10 April 1993, p. 1.
45 Ibid., 5 June 1993, pp. 1–2; similarly, *Rossiiskaya gazeta*, 2 June 1993, pp. 3–4.
46 For doubts about the validity of the reported results see, for instance, *Moskovskii komsomolets*, 11 January 1994, p. 1.
47 *Izvestiya*, 12 October 1994, p. 4.
48 Ibid., 28 September 1993, p. 4; the incident was also reported in B. N. Yeltsin, *Zapiski prezidenta* (Moscow: Ogonek, 1994), pp. 121–125.

49 B. N. Yeltsin, *Ispoved' na zadannuyu temu* (Leningrad: Chas pik, 1990), pp. 17–18 (baptism) and elsewhere. For biographical accounts see John Morrison, *Boris Yeltsin: From Bolshevik to Democrat* (Harmondsworth: Penguin, 1991); and Timothy J. Colton, "Boris Yeltsin: Russia's all-thumbs democrat," in Colton and Robert C. Tucker (eds.), *Patterns in Post-Soviet Leadership* (Boulder, CO: Westview, 1995), pp. 49–74.

50 Yeltsin, *Ispoved'*, p. 58.

51 Ibid., p. 63.

52 *XXVII S"ezd Kommunisticheskoi partii Sovetskogo Soyuza 25 fevralya – 6 marta 1986 goda. Stenograficheskii otchet*, 3 vols. (Moscow: Politizdat, 1986), vol. I, pp. 140–5.

53 V. I. Vorotnikov, *A bylo eto tak . . . Iz dnevnika chlena Politbyuro TsK KPSS* (Moscow: Sovet veteranov knigoizdaniya, 1995), p. 167.

54 *Izvestiya Tsentral'nogo komiteta KPSS*, 2 (1989), pp. 239–241; for the unauthorised version see *Le monde*, 2 February 1988, p. 6. Yeltsin referred to his preparation for the speech in *Ispoved'*, p. 134.

55 Yeltsin, *Ispoved'*, p. 137.

56 *Izvestiya Tsentral'nogo komiteta KPSS*, 2 (1989), p. 287.

57 Yeltsin, *Ispoved'*, p. 99.

58 Ibid., p. 143 ("barely conscious"); *Pravda*, 13 November 1987, pp. 1–3.

59 Yeltsin, *Ispoved'*, p. 175.

60 *Materialy Plenuma Tsentral'nogo komiteta KPSDS 15–16 marta 1989 goda* (Moscow: Politizdat, 1989), pp. 5–6.

61 *Moskovskaya pravda*, 28 March 1989, p. 2.

62 *Izvestiya*, 5 March 1990, p. 2.

63 *Materialy Plenuma Tsentral'nogo komiteta KPSS 5–7 fevralya 1990 goda*, pp. 68–9.

64 *Argumenty i fakty*, 22 (1990), p. 3.

65 *Rossiiskaya gazeta*, 4 November 1993, p. 4; Yeltsin referred again to Peter the Great in his interview in *Argumenty i fakty*, 16 (1993), pp. 1, 3.

66 *Izvestiya*, 11 June 1992, p. 3.

67 *Pravda*, 10 June 1991, p. 2.

68 Yeltsin, *Zapiski Prezidenta*, p. 181.

69 Lev Sukhanov, *Tri goda s Yel'tsinym* (Riga: Vaga, 1992), pp. 143–150.

70 L. A. Okun'kov, *Prezident Rossiiskoi Federatsii: Konstitutsiya i politicheskaya praktika* (Moscow: Infra-M/Norma, 1996), pp. 116–119.

71 *Izvestiya*, 26 March 1996, p. 1 (it was expected that these numbers would be reduced to 1,500 following the reorganization); for a larger estimate – of about 40,000 – see *Rossiya*, 41 (1994), p. 4.

72 On the Security Council see, for instance, *Moskovskie novosti*, 38 (1993), p. 2.

73 Okun'kov, *Prezident*, pp. 143–145.

74 Kostikov resigned in December 1994; he was replaced by Sergei Medvedev (*Izvestiya*, 15 March 1995, p. 1); Kostikov's memoirs were excerpted in *Argumenty i fakty*, 3 (1996), p. 3, and 5 (1996), p. 3.

75 Yeltsin's first chief of staff, Sergei Filatov, reflected on his position in his *Na puti k demokratii* (Moscow: Moskovskii rabochii, 1995), esp. pp. 433–453; another tennis player (p. 442), he had been obliged, with Viktor

Ilyushin, to create a presidential administration "practically from nothing" (p. 437).

76 Ilyushin was interviewed in *Argumenty i fakty*, 52 (1995), p. 3.
77 See, for instance, ibid., 3 (1995), p. 3, and 44 (1995), p. 1.
78 *Izvestiya*, 22 December 1995, p. 1; Korzhakov replied in ibid., 28 December 1995, p. 2.
79 See ibid., 6 May 1996, p. 1.
80 Quoted in *The Times*, 6 February 1996, p. 13.
81 *Kommersant-daily*, 8 June 1995, p. 4.
82 Ibid., 4 November 1995, p. 1.
83 *Izvestiya*, 1 November 1995, p. 2.
84 *Nezavisimaya gazeta*, 28 February 1991, p. 2.
85 *Sem's plyusom*, 12 (March 1991), p. 4.
86 *Nezavisimaya gazeta*, 28 February 1991, p. 2; similarly *Moscow News*, 15 (1991), p. 10.
87 *Argumenty i fakty*, 38 (1993), p. 2.
88 *Ekonomicheskie i sotsial'nye peremeny: monitoring obshchestvennogo mneniya*, 1 (1995), p. 5.
89 *Izvestiya*, 14 December 1994, p. 3.
90 *Kommersant-daily*, 10 March 1995, p. 3.
91 *Ekonomicheskie i sotsial'nye peremeny: monitoring obshchestvennogo mneniya*, 23 (1996), pp. 10, 43 (resignation).
92 *Moskovskaya pravda*, 21 December 1995, p. 1. For the election results see *Vestnik Tsentral'noi izbiratel'noi komissii Rossiiskoi Federatsii*, 1 (1996), pp. 48–51.
93 *Izvestiya*, 18 May 1996, pp. 1–2.
94 *International Herald Tribune*, 8 July 1996, p. 1.
95 *Argumenty i fakty*, 22 (1996), p. 1; *International Herald Tribune*, 8 July 1996, p. 1.
96 *Argumenty i fakty*, 28 (1996), p. 2.
97 See Olga Kryshtanovskaya and Stephen White, "From Soviet nomenklatura to Russian elite," *Europe-Asia Studies*, 48, 5 (July 1996), pp. 711–734.
98 Sakharov, *Institut prezidentstva*, p. 89.
99 *Moskovskie novosti*, 75 (1995), p. 5.
100 *Izvestiya*, 26 March 1994, p. 1.
101 Ibid., 5 July 1996, p. 2.
102 Stanislav Govorukhin quoted in the *Guardian* (London), 2 July 1996, p. 2.
103 *Argumenty i fakty*, 16 (1993), p. 3.
104 *Nezavisimaya gazeta*, 16 May 1992, p. 2.
105 *Guardian* (London), 29 March 1993, p. 18, and 9 September 1994, p. 12.
106 *Lipetskaya gazeta*, 2 March 1995, p. 2. Yeltsin told voters during the 1996 presidential election that he could "take a drink" but didn't "go too far" (*Izvestiya*, 22 May 1996, p. 2).
107 Okun'kov, *Prezident*, pp. 64, 74.
108 Ibid., p. 75.
109 *Obshchaya gazeta*, 40 (1994), p. 8.
110 See Thomas A. Baylis, "Presidents versus prime ministers: shaping execu

tive authority in Eastern Europe," *World Politics*, 48, 3 (April 1996), pp. 297–323.

111 Former prime minister, Nikolai Ryzhkov, for instance, called for the abolition of the presidency in *Pravda*, 8 February 1995, p. 1.

3   Ukraine: two presidents and their powers

Andrew Wilson

Introduction

Despite continuous discussion since October 1990, Ukraine only adopted a new, post-Soviet constitution in June 1996.[1] Therefore, after the institution of the presidency was established by the law of July 1991 as an amendment to the 1978 constitution, Ukrainian presidents were forced to operate in an uncertain environment for five years. Powers and responsibilities were constantly being redefined as much by actual day-to-day practice and the ebb and flow of political struggle as by each successive draft of the new constitution. Moreover, unlike Russia, Ukraine never experienced the kind of cathartic crisis provided by the Moscow events of October 1993, which at least could have more precisely defined the functions of the various branches of state and the manner in which they related to one another.

Ukraine has had two presidents since independence; Leonid Kravchuk (December 1991 to July 1994) and Leonid Kuchma (July 1994–). Both became frustrated with the lack of a clear definition of their powers and sought to arrogate more authority to themselves. Kravchuk was unsuccessful; Kuchma was able to force through the 1996 constitution which belatedly introduced some much-needed clarity to certain areas but left other problems unresolved. It is therefore somewhat premature to attempt a definitive classification of a system in evolution. Nevertheless, of all ideal-types Ukraine has evolved closest to the "president-parliamentary"[2] model through four distinct phases of development; firstly, the introduction of a presidency in July 1991 as a move in the Soviet endgame; secondly the conversion of the president into a proper head of state in early 1992 (the first year of Ukrainian independence); thirdly, a period of institutional stalemate and political drift after Autumn 1992; and finally Leonid Kuchma's renewed attempt to consolidate presidential power after July 1994 culminating in the adoption of the 1996 constitution. This chapter first describes these developments and then moves on to an overall assessment of the Ukrainian system.

The law of July 1991

The law that established the institution of a Ukrainian presidency in July 1991 must be understood in the context of the time.[3] Leonid Kravchuk was then chairman of the Supreme Soviet/Council (*Verkhovna Rada*) of the Ukrainian SSR, during the period of Ukraine's prolonged struggle with Moscow over Mikhail Gorbachev's proposed new Union Treaty. Ukrainian nationalists were strongly opposed to the Treaty, the Communist Party of Ukraine (CPU), led by Stanislav Hurenko, strongly in favor. In the *Rada* the nationalist Democratic Block controlled 122 out of 450 seats; 385 deputies were originally members of the Communist Party, but were increasingly divided between Hurenko's hardline "Group of 239" and Kravchuk's "national" or "sovereign" communists who tended to side with the nationalists.[4] This was demonstrated in June 1991, when 345 deputies voted to delay any discussion of the Union Treaty until September, in other words, after Gorbachev's proposed signing ceremony on 19 August.[5]

At the same time, in the constitutional commission chaired by Kravchuk that had been meeting periodically since October 1990 to consider the overhaul of Ukraine's Soviet-era constitution,[6] the case for and against the introduction of a Ukrainian presidency soon became the main topic of debate.[7] Most nationalists, aware that the 1990 Ukrainian elections had demonstrated their minority position, were prepared to cooperate with Kravchuk and extend him extra powers. Yurii Badz'o, leader of the opposition Democratic Party of Ukraine defined their strategy as "searching for a split between [Kravchuk and Hurenko] and widening it," and encouraging nationally minded communists to side with the opposition.[8] Levko Luk"ianenko, leader of the Ukrainian Republican Party, justified his support for Kravchuk by quoting the Ukrainian philosopher and historian V"iacheslav Lypyns'kyi to argue that at such a crucial time of transition presidential rule was necessary to overcome Ukrainians' natural tendency toward excessive emotion and anarchic individuality.[9]

Communist Party conservatives, on the other hand, opposed the introduction of a presidential system as an affront to the whole Soviet constitutional order, as a Trojan Horse for the extension of nationalist influence, and as a potential spur to conflict between Ukraine and Russia.[10] Neutrals, however, were increasingly swayed by the argument that "Ukraine needed leadership and strong government (*Hetmanstvo*),"[11] and that a popularly elected president would have a stronger hand in negotiations with Moscow, especially as Gorbachev was steadily increasing his own nominal power.[12] Finally, decisive momentum toward the creation of a

Ukrainian presidency was given by the example of Russia, where 70 percent of voters accepted Boris Yeltsin's proposal for the direct election of an executive president in the March 1991 referendum, and by Yeltsin's triumphant victory the following June.

Significantly, therefore, the 1991 Ukrainian Law on the Presidency emphasized the defense of Ukrainian sovereignty against Moscow, and was less precise on the president's powers with respect to domestic political institutions (the developing alliance between Kravchuk and the nationalist opposition was not yet strong enough to impose a fully presidential model against the protests of CPU conservatives).[13] The law clearly stated that the president had the right "to suspend the action of decisions of the executive power of the USSR on the territory of the Ukrainian SSR, if they contradict the constitution and the laws of the Ukrainian SSR" (Article 7). The "president of the Ukrainian SSR" was described as "the highest figure in the Ukrainian state and the head of the executive power" (Article 1), and given the right "to take part in sittings of the Supreme Council," to "return legislation to the Supreme Council with his objections for renewed consideration and voting" (Article 5), to "create necessary administrative and consultative structures" (Article 6), "to issue decrees (*ukazy*) in areas of his competence" (Article 7), and "to cancel decisions and instructions (*rozporiadzhennia*) of the cabinet of ministers of the Ukrainian SSR, the government of the Crimean ASSR, acts of ministers of the Ukrainian SSR, other organs responsible to them, and executive committees of local councils . . . if they contravened the law or constitution of the Ukrainian SSR" (Article 7). Any citizen of the Ukrainian SSR over the age of 35 could become president, but the president could not be a deputy, or "occupy any post in state organs or private associations, or in other organisations engaging in commercial activity."

A president could serve for a maximum of "two consecutive terms" (Article 2). The separate Law on the Election of the President of the Ukrainian SSR, also passed on 5 July, fixed the term at five years (Article 1).[14] The Law on Election also added the stipulation that candidates for president had to have "lived on the territory of the Ukrainian SSR no less than ten years and use (*volodiie*) the state language," i.e., Ukrainian (Article 1). A candidate would have to collect 100,000 signatures of support to place his name on the ballot paper (Article 10). First elections were set for 1 December 1991.

What was absent from the above list of powers is as illuminating as what was present. The law itself was very short (nearly all significant points have been quoted above). There was no mention of how the president might fulfill his functions as "head of the executive power," and no detailed explanation of how he or she might interact with the other branches of state authority. In contrast to his counterpart in Russia or France, the Ukrainian president had no power to dissolve parliament, nor any effective veto power over legislation. The power to "return legislation to the Supreme Council for renewed consideration" was not a full veto, only the power to delay legislation for a single session.[15] With renewed confirmation by a simple majority "the law would be considered passed" (Article 5). The president had no pocket veto, and the proposal to create a vice-presidency was defeated.

The 1991 presidential election

Whatever the original intentions of Ukraine's law-makers, the political context for the scheduled presidential election was changed utterly by the failure of the August 1991 coup attempt in Moscow, and the consequent declaration of Ukrainian independence and dissolution of the CPU. Moreover, the election was now to be conducted simultaneously with the campaign to confirm the declaration of independence in the referendum that was also to be held on 1 December 1991.

Kravchuk was now the indispensable centrist, with no (declared) enemies on his left and relatively few on the right. His prevarication during the three days for which the outcome of events in Moscow remained uncertain could have left him dangerously exposed if events had proceeded differently,[16] but he was now backed by most of the old elite, who either swapped communism for nationalism or calculated that they would be better able to preserve their positions in an independent Ukraine. Although a successor party to the CPU, the Socialist Party of Ukraine, appeared as early as October 1991, Kravchuk was careful to campaign on the left and ensure that only the most die-hard communist could oppose him. His relatively cautious program concentrated on the predicted economic benefits of independence and the importance of maintaining "continuity" and pragmatic expertise in government, as did his campaign slogan stressing the "5 Ds" (*Derzhavnist', demokratiia, dostatok, dukhovnist, dovir"ia* – statehood, democracy, prosperity, spirituality, and trust). Welfare and job security for all would be preserved.[17]

After careful thought the Socialist Party leader Oleksandr Moroz backed out of a challenge, and a maverick left-wing candidate, Agriculture Minister Oleksandr Tkachenko, eventually withdrew in Kravchuk's favor.[18] The only challenge to Kravchuk's monopoly of the center-left came from the deputy chairman of parliament, Volodymyr Hryn'ov, who broke ranks on the national issue to champion the rights of fellow Russian-speakers in Ukraine.[19]

Kravchuk also tried to achieve consensus with the right. The official candidate of the main opposition group *Rukh* was V"iacheslav Chornovil, veteran dissident and leader of L'viv oblast council, the nationalist stronghold in western Ukraine, who argued that a continued anti-communist crusade was as important as national independence. However, many other nationalists were appreciative of the role Kravchuk's "national communists" had played in securing independence, and their opposition to him was decidedly half-hearted.[20] Therefore Luk"ianenko and Ihor Yukhnovs'kyi, the head of the opposition in parliament, also stood in opposition to Chornovil, and in favor of building bridges with Kravchuk.

The natural polarity between right and left was therefore partly submerged in Ukraine's first-ever presidential election, results for which are shown in Figures 3.1, 3.2, 3.3 below, and in Table 3.1 in the appendix. Kravchuk won comfortably with 61.6 percent of the vote on an 84.2 percent turnout. The nationalist trio won 29.5 percent, with Chornovil taking the lion's share of 23.3 percent (Luk"ianenko won 4.5 percent and Yukhnovs'kyi 1.7 percent). Hryn'ov was supported by 4.2 percent. A sixth candidate, Leopol'd Taburians'kyi, leader of the tiny People's Party of Ukraine, received a mere 0.6 percent of the vote.

The geographical distribution of the vote between the three main camps was sharply skewed, although the divisions amongst the nationalists and Hryn'ov's candidature created something of a multipolar contest and the breadth of Kravchuk's support helped to mask underlying divisions. As in earlier elections in 1990 and 1991, nationalist support was concentrated in the west, especially in Galicia and Volhynia, and in urban areas of central Ukraine.[21] On the other hand, by positioning himself in the center-left, Kravchuk swept the board not only in the east and south, but also in the conservative Ukrainian countryside outside of the west. Hryn'ov siphoned off some of Kravchuk's support in Russophone areas of the east and south, winning 10.9 percent of the vote in his native Kharkiv and 11 percent in Donets'k.

The fact that Kravchuk's coalition of support overlapped substantially with the center-left electorate that had supported the CPU in March 1990 (and voted in favor of retaining the USSR in Gorbachev's March 1991 referendum) should be kept in mind when analyzing Kravchuk's failure to press home his "more recent mandate" in early 1992.[22] Kravchuk's natural caution, and his inability to dissolve parliament (both important differences with Yeltsin), played a part in his prudent behavior after December 1991,[23] but so did the fact that his mandate, although "more recent" than that of the conservative majority in parliament, was to all intents and purposes from the same portion of the Ukrainian electorate. In economic issues at least, Kravchuk never really sought to challenge the conservative majority in parliament, and the

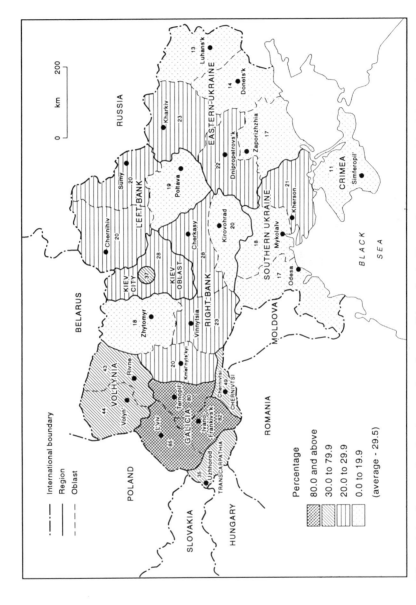

Figure 3.1 Support for the three nationalist candidates in the December 1991 presidential election

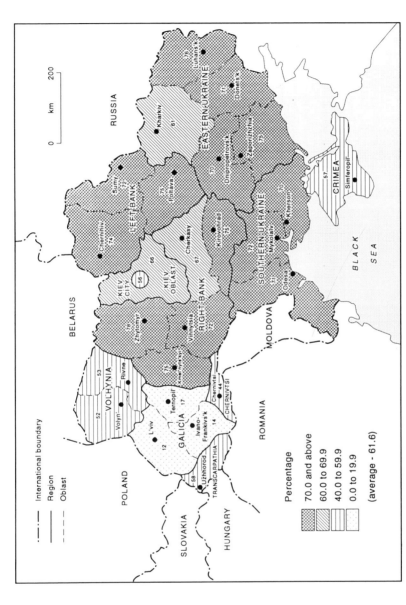

Figure 3.2   Support for Leonid Kravchuk in the December 1991 presidential election

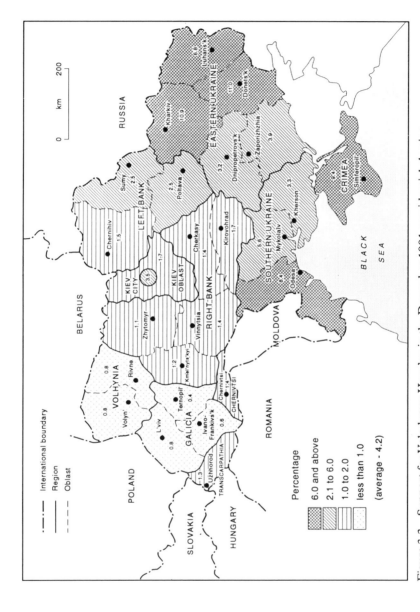

Figure 3.3   Support for Volodymyr Hryn'ov in the December 1991 presidential election

"dual mandates" of president and parliament never conflicted as sharply as in Russia, although confrontation began to increase as Kravchuk moved to the right on the national issue.

Spring 1992: the presidency receives substantial extra powers

Although Kravchuk's vote in December 1991 came mainly from the center-left where most of the Ukrainian electorate was grouped,[24] the dynamics of his support coalition soon began to change, given the political vacuum on the left after the dissolution of the CPU and the growing desire of many nationalists to close ranks with the man who had, after all, guided Ukraine towards independence. The alliance between nationalists and national communists that had been developing throughout 1991 was therefore consummated in early 1992. Rukh leader Ivan Drach declared that "he who supports Ukrainian statehood must support the president,"[25] although Chornovil's continued opposition meant that nationalist support could not be delivered wholesale. The left remained weak until the Communist Party was revived in June 1993.

Kravchuk himself, now head of an independent state, moved quickly toward an appropriate consolidation of his position. In December 1991 he named himself as commander-in-chief of the new Ukrainian armed forces,[26] and the following February persuaded parliament to support a substantial redefinition of his constitutional position.[27] The president was now declared to be both "head of state and head of the executive power in Ukraine," and would "realise the leadership of and direct the executive activity of the cabinet" (Articles 114–1 and 114–5 of the revised constitution). The president now had the power "to propose for the confirmation of the Supreme Council of Ukraine a candidate for prime minister" and seven other leading ministers of state (foreign affairs, defense, finance, justice, internal affairs, and the heads of the committees for customs and the defense of state borders), also "subject to parliamentary confirmation." The president could "bring before the Supreme Council of Ukraine a proposition" to relieve the prime minister from his post, and had the right to fire at least the seven ministers listed above. The position of lesser ministers was less clear. The cabinet of ministers was described as "subordinate to (*pidporiadkovuiet'sia*) the president of Ukraine" (Article 117), who was entitled to "make himself a member of the cabinet of ministers and other central organs of state executive power" (Article 116).

The president's responsibilities were widened to include "defending the rights and freedoms of citizens, the state sovereignty of Ukraine, and the observance of the constitution and laws of Ukraine," preserving "the military preparedness, national security and territorial indivisibility of Ukraine" (Article 114–5), and looking after the interests of Ukrainians abroad. The president was required "to place before the Supreme Council of Ukraine the project of the national budget and a report on its out-turn" and to "give a yearly report" to the Supreme Council, which would include details of "the situation in Ukraine and a program of internal and external political activity for the president and government of Ukraine" (Article 114–5). In other words, it was envisaged that the president would have a substantive legislative program to introduce, rather than just making a general address. Lastly, the president was granted the power "in the period before the adoption of a new Ukrainian constitution to issue decrees (*ukazy*) on questions of economic reform, not regulated by Ukrainian law, subject to subsequent confirmation by the Supreme Council" (Article 114–5).

A subsequent decree in February 1992 reorganized the cabinet of ministers to make it more amenable to Kravchuk's control. The system was streamlined (although it remained unwieldy), the position of minister of state was abolished, and Kravchuk created new positions of deputy prime minister and minister of the cabinet, which he proceeded to staff with his supporters.[28]

These changes alone would have substantially increased the powers of the presidency, but two further reforms were also passed in Spring 1992; the creation by decree of a presidential advisory council (*Duma*),[29] and the establishment of a system of presidential prefects (*predstavnyky*) in the Ukrainian provinces.[30] The Duma had four sections; humanitarian, science-technical, legal, and economic, with each grouping having a dozen or more "advisers" to the president. Leading members of the president's staff initially indicated that it would only have a consultative role,[31] but Oleksandr Yemets', the head of the legal section, openly called for it to usurp the functions of the cabinet of ministers.[32] All other state organs were obliged to consider the Duma's decisions.[33]

Although, as mentioned above, the 1991 Law on the President gave Kravchuk the right "to create necessary administrative and consultative structures," the Duma was soon being denounced, particularly on the left, as unelected, unconstitutional, and unaccountable. The left was also annoyed that the Duma was disproportionately staffed by prominent members of the former nationalist opposition.[34] Moreover, Kravchuk soon created several similar unelected bodies by decree, namely a council of industrialists and businessmen in May 1992,[35] a national security council in July and a short-lived coordination council for economic reform in August.[36] The process reflected Kravchuk's characteristic preference for *ad hoc* and *ad hominem* reorganization rather than the development of a clear and public system of presidential control. When parliament forced the abolition of several of these institutions (see below) he shifted most of his leading advisers into shadowy "presidential commissions."[37]

The system of prefects was equally controversial. The prefects, all presidential appointees, were declared to be "the highest organs of state executive power" (Article 1 of the Law on Prefects) in their region, and their decisions were "binding for all organs of local administration, industry, organizations and institutions, and civil associations" (Article 14). They were granted the power to remove any office-holder, or halt the activity of any association, whose activity they deemed to contradict the constitution or the president's decrees (Article 6). Moreover, the president could grant the prefects "additional powers" during states of emergency (Article 15). They were only accountable upwards to higher prefects or to the president, or to judicial process. Although the prefects were originally supposed to stick to a "control and coordination function," they soon began trying to usurp the role of local councils,[38] who were correspondingly downgraded from "organs of state power" to "systems of local self-rule" (*samovriaduvannia*), and their real loci of power, the executive branch or *vykonkom*, transferred to the prefect's direct control.[39]

The prefects were therefore increasingly seen as instruments of Kravchuk's personal rule. However, initial expectations amongst nationalists and liberals that they would serve as a means of circumventing entrenched local conservatives and implementing reforms were soon disappointed. Kravchuk chose not to offend local sensibilities too much by appointing already well-established local figures (nationalists in Galicia, former apparatchiki in the east and south). Of the twenty-six leading prefects in each of Ukraine's oblasts, twenty were former heads or deputy heads of oblast or city councils or their *vykonkomy* (or both).[40] Inevitably, however, the prefects and the local soviets were soon at loggerheads, and the president's *de facto* control over local affairs was always tenuous. The experiment was abandoned in Spring 1994.

The draft of the proposed new constitution finally published in July 1992 marked the high water mark of the trend toward heightened presidential power.[41] The changes of February–March 1992 were incorporated into the text, and the president was explicitly described as leading the cabinet of ministers, rather than merely presiding at its sittings. However, at the same time as ratifying a significant increase in his powers, the draft also reflected Kravchuk's tendency to see his political role as a bridge between all parties, and his preference for consensus over conflict.[42] Article 175 stated that "during the period of fulfilling his functions, the president suspends any party or trade union affiliation," although in the long term it was difficult to see how the president was supposed to fulfil his duties without close political allies in parliament, government, and elsewhere.

The contradictions in Kravchuk's position were gradually exposed over the Summer of 1992. He had been granted an impressive array of powers, but was reluctant to use them in case he alienated any elements in his delicate coalition of support. Having pressed to become "head of the executive power" as well as head of state, Kravchuk was still acting like the latter alone.[43] In particular, he was reluctant to move to dismiss the government of Vitol'd Fokin, in office since October 1990 and outstandingly unpopular, even after it narrowly survived a parliamentary vote of no confidence by only 139 votes to 135 in July 1992.[44] Nor did Kravchuk use his decree powers in the economic sphere decisively, in marked contrast to Yegor Gaidar's reform program in Russia. Although a series of privatization laws was passed in March–February 1992, Kravchuk did not press for their implementation. Mindful that his support in December 1991 came mainly from the center-left, many of his decrees were in fact decidedly anti-market in spirit.[45]

Kravchuk's political base therefore began to narrow surprisingly rapidly. The opposition movement Rukh split after its third congress in Spring 1992, and Kravchuk's supporters were forced to create the rival Congress of National-Democratic Forces. Moreover, the disoriented left began to revive and fight a strong campaign against the prefect system and in favor of the restoration of "soviet power" from their local redoubts in eastern and southern Ukraine. Kravchuk's failure to embrace radical economic reform alienated centrists and liberals, particularly after he dismissed the pro-market minister for economics, Volodymyr Lanovyi, in July 1992 and replaced him with Valentyn Symonenko, an open advocate of a return to *dirigisme*.[46]

Kuchma appointed prime minister, Kravchuk loses powers

The governmental crisis postponed in July 1992 came to a head at the end of September. Fokin's government fell, and he was replaced as prime minister by Leonid Kuchma, despite Kravchuk's initial preference for Symonenko and Rukh's support for the economist Volodymyr Cherniak. As an industrialist who had kept his head down in 1990–92, Kuchma initially received support from all quarters, including liberals and nationalists, who for the first time were granted a significant minority of positions in the cabinet of ministers. After the stagnation of the Fokin era and

Kravchuk's neglect of his powers, Kuchma's initial impression of dynamism created a bandwagon of support that forced Kravchuk increasingly to take a back seat. Moreover, as Fokin had never really been more than chairman of the cabinet of ministers, Ukraine now had a proper prime minister for the first time and conflict between premier and president became endemic.[47]

Kuchma asked for, and obtained, the abolition of the Duma and the economic reform council, the transfer of Kravchuk's emergency decree powers to regulate the economy to himself for a six-month period, and in December secured the amendment of the law on presidential prefects to provide for a system of dual accountability, to the president in "political" matters, and to the cabinet of ministers in economic affairs. A revised draft of the proposed new constitution that appeared in January 1993 confirmed these changes.[48] The president was no longer described as "head of the executive power," but only as "head of state" (Article 144), and the powers of the cabinet of ministers strengthened accordingly. On the other hand, it was proposed to grant the president the right to dissolve parliament (Article 148).

Although the tide was now flowing against Kravchuk, he attempted to regain the initiative once Kuchma's own reform efforts ran out of steam. Kuchma's centralizing tendencies alienated liberals and nationalists grew disillusioned with his pragmatic emphasis on rebuilding economic ties with Russia. Parliament refused to extend the prime minister's six-month emergency powers when they ran out in May 1993. However, although it had no constructive alternative to offer of its own, the Rada was now much less favorably disposed to Kravchuk than it had been in early 1992, especially as a strong left-wing revival was leading to the resurrection of old loyalties and political relationships amongst the former CPU majority. The existing Socialist and Agrarian Parties were joined by a rejuvenated CPU after it held a revival congress in Donets'k in June 1993 (the party was officially registered in October), and, as in Russia, the united left led a campaign to cut the presidency down to size and restore the system of "soviet rule." Oleksandr Moroz, leader of the Socialist Party, argued that the president should in future be elected by an assembly of councils, not by direct popular vote,[49] the CPU that the post should be abolished altogether.

Parliament therefore refused to accept either Kuchma's resignation or Kravchuk's request for a return of emergency powers to the presidency, the abolition of the post of prime minister and the replacement of the cabinet of ministers with a presidential council (only ninety deputies voted to support the latter proposal). The deadlock was again apparent at the parliamentary session on the new draft constitution called on 2 June against a backdrop of public protests calling for early elections for both parliament and president. No proposal on the division of powers between president and prime minister received the necessary constitutional majority (two-thirds of 450, i.e. 300). The largest number of votes, 269, was for both president and prime minister to be "jointly responsible" for the exercise of executive power. Kravchuk attempted to break the deadlock on 16 June by issuing a decree to split the cabinet of ministers in two, with a special economic commission under Kuchma's control, and a commission of the "power ministries" (interior, justice, the security services) under himself.[50] However, the distinctly lukewarm reaction and the desire to avoid following the same path to confrontation as Russia prompted Kravchuk to rescind the decree five days later, after parliament voted 228:18 to agree to hold twin confidence referenda for both parliament and president on 26 September 1993.[51]

When parliament reassembled in August, however, it soon became clear that the referenda were on hold, and political deadlock resumed.[52] It was only the threat of national strikes organized by all parts of the political spectrum (Rukh, the independent trade unions and the Donbas miners) and the eruption of political crisis in Russia when Boris Yeltsin decreed the dissolution of the Russian parliament on 21 September that forced a resolution of the crisis. Leonid Kuchma finally made good on his repeated threats to resign, and on 24 September parliament agreed by 243 votes to 39 to dispense with the confidence referenda and proceed straight to pre-term elections for parliament on 27 March 1994, and for the presidency on 26 June 1994.[53]

Hiatus

With Kuchma now at least temporarily out of his hair, Kravchuk attempted once again to consolidate his position. He appointed an east Ukrainian ally, Yukhym Zviahil's'kyi, as acting prime minister on 22 September, but on the 28th demoted him to acting first deputy prime minister, and suspended the post of prime minister. On the same day, Kravchuk appointed himself head of a new "coordinating committee for implementing market reforms and overcoming the economic crisis,"[54] and proceeded over the Winter of 1993/94 to take a more active role in more important sessions of the cabinet of ministers, especially those concerned with economic matters, often leading rather than merely presiding.[55]

However, the committee seemed more concerned with "overcoming the economic crisis" rather than with "implementing market reforms." Kravchuk passed up another opportunity to overhaul Ukraine's collapsing economy and instead passed a series of decrees reversing even the limited liberalizing measures passed by Kuchma. The episode confirmed Kravchuk's paradoxical political persona; radical and increasingly nationalist since 1990 in the sphere of politics and foreign policy, but still wedded to the economic dogmas of the late communist period.[56]

Yet another draft of the new constitution published in October 1993 largely reflected the new status quo, neither restoring substantial powers to the presidency nor reducing them still further, although the general trend remained away from a strong presidency.[57] It was proposed to reduce the president's role in the formation of governments. The power to "form the cabinet of ministers" and make individual appointments would now be exercised "on the advice of (*za podanniam*) the prime minister" (Article 133). No mention was made of the seven reserved appointments. The cabinet of ministers was now described as merely "working out the program of the president," and was defined as "accountable to the Supreme Council" (Article 143). The draft proposed that the president could be impeached by a three-quarters vote of all deputies (Article 140), but in return granted him a proper legislative veto which would require a two-thirds majority to overturn (Article 121).

As the June 1993 decision to hold confidence referenda for both parliament and president was probably unconstitutional (according to the July 1991 law on referenda, referenda are called if citizens' initiatives succeed in attracting the necessary 3 million signatures),[58] the new draft included a provision for either the president or parliament to propose the other's pre-term election in a national referendum, subject to the proviso that if the vote was lost, the proposer could be the one facing early elections if the victor so desired (Articles 135 and 140). However, as is often characteristic of mixed presidential/parliamentary systems, there was still no clear-cut mechanism for resolving disputes between the two main branches of state.

The 1994 elections

Kravchuk hoped that the Spring 1994 parliamentary elections would be sabotaged by low turnout, and his own position consequently strengthened, possibly even allowing him to delay the presidential election promised for June. However, his strategy unravelled when 338 out of 450 seats were filled (more than the necessary quorum of 300), with the left block (communists, socialists and agrarians) winning a convincing plurality of seats (145 out of 338).[59] After the new parliament confirmed an early presidential election, Kravchuk was forced to develop an alternative strategy of trying to build a new electoral coalition to win a second term. His main opponent was Kuchma, who had been carefully preparing his bid since September 1993 (or arguably even earlier). The other main candidates were Oleksandr Moroz, leader of the Socialist Party and the new chairman of parliament; Volodymyr Lanovyi, the liberal former minister of economics; Ivan Pliushch, former parliamentary chairman; independent businessman Valerii Babych; and Petro Talanchuk, then minister of education.[60]

Given his awful economic record and the supposedly Russophile views of Kuchma, Kravchuk decided that his best chance of reelection lay in turning the vote into a second referendum on Ukrainian independence. His shift to the right was encouraged by Ukrainian nationalists, who concluded from the parliamentary results that one of their own would have no chance of victory, and therefore backed Kravchuk.[61] Consequently, the main themes of Kravchuk's campaign were statehood, respect for Ukrainian language and culture, an independent foreign policy identity and linkage to Central and Western Europe.[62]

Kuchma, on the other hand, argued that Ukraine was a natural part of a common "Eurasian space" in close alliance with Russia, and that regional differences in Ukraine that reflected this perception (i.e., stronger Russophile sentiment in eastern and southern Ukraine) should be accorded greater respect, in particular the day-to-day use of the Russian language.[63] Kuchma placed more emphasis on economic reform than Kravchuk, but the issue does not seem to have divided the electorate. The election was largely fought on the national issue.[64] All Ukrainians were concerned about economic decline, but, with the problem filtered through different world-views, more nationally conscious Ukrainians tended to conclude that economic salvation would come by building a stronger independent state with links to Europe, while more Russophile Ukrainians diagnosed the necessity of restoring links with Russia. On the other hand, both Kravchuk and Kuchma defended the powers of the presidency against the outspoken attacks of Moroz.[65] Although Kuchma campaigned for a general decentralization of power in Ukraine, he also promised the restoration of a strong hand in government, and demanded that "the state must be prepared to take harsh action to secure conformity with the law."[66]

Juan Linz has argued that presidential systems in general, and second ballot majoritarian voting in particular, produce polarized elections.[67] Certainly the nationalist camp saw the election as a winner-take-all struggle in which Ukraine's very independence was at stake, and the direct confrontation between Kravchuk and Kuchma in the second round tended to squeeze out more moderate voices. The result was ethnolinguistic and regional polarization (Tables 3.2 and 3.3 in the appendix give the breakdown of the vote in the first and second rounds; the minor candidates in the first round – Babych, Pliushch, and Talanchuk – are grouped together as "Other"). The most in-depth survey of the election reported a remarkably high 0.82 correlation between citizens' language and political preferences. More than three-quarters of Ukrainophones supported Kravchuk and a similar proportion of Russophones backed Kuchma.[68] In the second round, Kuchma won every oblast in eastern and southern Ukraine, plus the Left Bank of the river Dnieper (see Figure 3.4).[69] Kravchuk on the other hand led throughout the Right Bank (except in Kirovohrad) and in western Ukraine. Socio-economic issues, on the other hand, although prominent in voters' minds, had much less effect on the *distribution* of votes between Kravchuk and Kuchma. The support groups for both men contained both supporters and opponents of market reform. In fact, of those who opposed the development of private industry, more voted for Kuchma (29 percent) than Kravchuk (14 percent) or even Oleksandr Moroz (27 percent).[70]

However, the resurgence of the national issue was largely a product of changed political circumstances in comparison to 1991, serving to accentuate underlying historical divisions, rather than the presidential system itself. As argued above, the 1991 election had been more of a multipolar contest, in which the simultaneous referendum and the temporary rout of communist conservatives left the national issue submerged. In 1994 three years of economic crisis, political dislocation, and Russophone resentment against Kravchuk's supposed "nationalizing" policies brought it back to the surface. Nevertheless, the 1994 election emphasized two truths first made apparent in the 1990 parliamentary and 1991 presidential elections. Ukraine is a deeply divided society, but it is easier to bridge that divide from the center-left (east) than from the right (west). It is extremely difficult, in current circumstances probably impossible, to win Ukrainian elections on a nationalist ticket. Kuchma won the election by the close but comfortable margin of 52.1 percent to 45.1 percent.

Kuchma in office

Although Kuchma had campaigned on a platform of devolving power to the Ukrainian regions and had frequently condemned his predecessor's behavior as unconstitutional, the new president soon found himself faced with many of the same problems as Kravchuk; parliament continued to contest the president's control over the executive, relations with the prime minister remained difficult and the presidency lacked an adequate mechanism to ensure that its orders were implemented at a local level. In comparison to Kravchuk, however, Kuchma made more decisive steps to

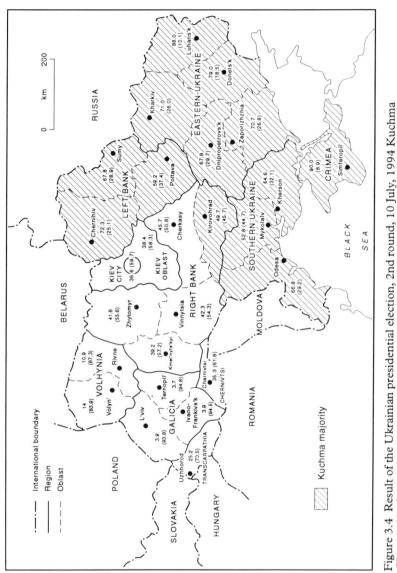

Figure 3.4 Result of the Ukrainian presidential election, 2nd round, 10 July, 1994 Kuchma (Kravchuk). Overall: 52.1 percent–45.1 percent

consolidate his power. Initially at least, Kuchma also won a wider constituency of support for constitutional change. Liberals bought his argument that stronger powers were a necessary precondition of effective economic reform, and his increasingly pragmatic foreign policy won over many Ukrainian nationalists who had originally backed a stronger presidency as a shield against Russian pressure. Only the left continued to rail against the formation of a "presidential republic."[71]

Kuchma's first move was to claim greater control over the executive through an August 1994 decree that declared that the "president of Ukraine in carrying out his functions as leader of the cabinet of ministers determines the main directions of its activity," and that "the most important questions concerning economic transformation, the formation of market relations and the social defence of individuals are decided by the cabinet of ministers with the direct participation of the president," who would also "determine the agenda of the cabinet." Apparently, Kuchma attended most crucial meetings of the cabinet of ministers, where he led discussion much "in the manner of a British prime minister."[72] Furthermore, the president would now "appoint and dismiss the leaders of state committees of Ukraine, other organs subordinate to the cabinet of ministers of Ukraine, directors of ministries and heads of other central organs of state executive power."[73]

Kuchma issued a second decree in August to tighten his control of local authorities, declaring that "the heads of oblast councils, Kiev and Sevastopil' town councils, and their executive committees are accountable to, and under the control of, the president" (direct elections of council heads had been organized in the Summer after the demise of the prefect system).[74] However, Kuchma also offered regional leaders a significant concession through the creation of a Council of the Regions in September 1994, an "executive advisory" body composed of the president, prime minister, and the heads of local councils.[75] Kuchma then granted the Council first look at the draft economic reform program, indicating that if necessary, like Yeltsin in Russia or Kravchuk in 1992, he would bypass parliament and the Cabinet of Ministers to rule. Moreover, the National Security Council, under Kuchma's close ally Volodymyr Horbulin, was revamped in October 1994 and began to trespass on the formulation of domestic policy in a similar fashion to its counterpart in Russia.[76] Kuchma also announced an expansion of the president's staff in order to cope with new responsibilities, and, like Kravchuk before him, was soon being accused of vesting too much power in unelected advisers, especially his young chief of staff, Dmyto Tabachnyk.[77]

Kuchma's next step was to press for an overhaul of the constitution to institutionalize a more powerful presidency. In parallel to the creation of a forty-one-strong Constitutional Commission (fifteen of its members were appointed by the presidency, fifteen by the Supreme Council, the others represented the judiciary and the Republic of Crimea), Kuchma presented a "Law on Power" or mini-constitution to parliament, which proposed to grant the president a proper veto power and the right to form a cabinet of ministers without parliamentary approval (Kuchma dropped his original demand for the power to dissolve parliament). The draft law also envisaged that the powers of local councils would be considerably downgraded.[78] The proposals were too ambitious, with many deputies proposing instead to resurrect the October 1993 draft constitution. Although the right and center factions supported the law, the communists and socialists, who controlled 30 percent of the seats in parliament, were resolutely opposed. Although the law passed two readings, it failed to receive the necessary two-thirds majority.[79]

The 1995 constitutional agreement and the 1996 constitution

In Spring 1995 Kuchma decided to force the issue by copying the tactics used by Yeltsin in March 1993 and threatening to hold a national confidence referendum on both parliament and president. As Kuchma was still riding high in the polls, parliament realized it would lose any direct confrontation. Moreover, the left block was beginning to split, with the socialists and agrarians distancing themselves from the communists and attempting to remodel themselves as national parties of the left. On 7 June 1995 parliament voted by 240 votes to 81 to accept a grand "Constitutional Agreement," with only the communists voting solidly against, in return for Kuchma withdrawing his referendum proposal.

The agreement (*dohovir*) was to function for a year, by which time a new constitution was to have been adopted, and, on paper at least, considerably expanded presidential power. The agreement described the president as "exercising his power as head of the state executive power through heading the government – the cabinet of ministers of Ukraine – and the system of central and local organs of state executive power" (Article 19). After the president appointed the prime minister and "formed" the cabinet of ministers, the latter would present its program to parliament within two months. Once parliament accepted the program it could not then propose a vote of no-confidence for a year (Article 22). The president was finally granted a full veto power, requiring two-thirds of "the actual number" of deputies to overturn (Article 23), and his appointment powers were expanded to include the head of the Constitutional Court (this appointment only would be made "together with the head of the Supreme Council"), half of the court's judges, the head of the

Supreme Arbitration Court, the state prosecutor and the head of the National Bank of Ukraine, all subject to approval by parliament (Article 24). The president now had the power to remove heads of local administration (Article 58). The president could "issue decrees in the area of his competence," including "on questions of economic reform, in areas not covered by the existing laws of Ukraine, which [would remain] effective until the passing of appropriate laws" in that area (Article 25), and could organize (*pryznachyty*) national referenda (Article 26). The president could not dissolve parliament, and parliament could not impeach the president. There would be a moratorium on referenda for a year, unless they were to be held to ratify the new constitution.[80]

However, the agreement did not function in practice as Kuchma's supporters had expected. Parliament continued to harass the government and Kuchma made relatively circumspect use of his decree powers. Most importantly, controversy continued to rage over the new constitution. Kuchma assumed that it would be based on the principles laid down in the agreement, but Moroz and the left argued that everything was still open for debate. Moreover, they were joined by a number of liberals, worried that too much power was being concentrated in the president's hands.[81] Almost half a dozen drafts of the new constitution were therefore circulating by early 1996, including the official October 1993 version. The presidential draft went even further than the Constitutional Agreement by proposing to grant the president an explicit power of legislative initiative (Article 93), broader degree powers (Article 105), and the right to dissolve parliament if it twice rejected the government's program within sixty days of submission (Article 90). Impeachment procedures were made deliberately complex (Article 109).[82]

The draft that emerged from the Constitutional Commission, with the approval of twenty of its forty-one members, was closest to Kuchma's version. It passed its first parliamentary reading on 4 June 1996 by 258 votes to 109, but further progress was prevented by the delaying tactics of the left. Their deadline was not the anniversary of the Constitutional Agreement, but the Russian presidential elections. The communists sought to spin the process out until a hoped-for Zyuganov victory, but liberal doubters and the more nationally minded socialist and agrarian factions were swayed by the contrary fear that both a text and a stronger president needed to be in place in case either Zyuganov or Yeltsin under pressure from Zyuganov were to take a more aggressive line towards Ukraine in the future. Kuchma's threat to hold a referendum on the unamended constitution in September was sufficient to persuade all but the hard left to fall into line, and on 28 June the final version was approved by 315 votes to 36.

In terms of defining presidential power, the constitution broadly followed the principles laid out in the Constitutional Agreement. Changes included clearer impeachment procedures, which required a vote of three-quarters of deputies (Article 111). A Constitutional Court was finally to be elected "within three months of the constitution becoming valid"; president, parliament, and a "congress of judges" were each to pick six of the court's eighteen justices, who would then choose their own head (Article 148). Parliament clawed back the right to approve Kuchma's appointment of the head of the National Bank (and itself chose half the members of the board), but Kuchma was granted the power to issue economic decrees for the rest of his term, now fixed to end in October 1999. Decrees would automatically become law if parliament failed to overturn them after thirty days. No mention was made of referenda powers, except in cases of "changes to the constitution," which either president or parliament could propose (Articles 72 and 156).[83]

By 1996 Kuchma had therefore won a more decisive aggrandizement of his powers than Kravchuk had either achieved or sought, but without breaking the mould of the president/parliamentary system. Kuchma had been unable to win the power of dissolution or to radically reshape the constitution along Russian lines.

A president-parliamentary system

How then to assess the powers of the Ukrainian presidency? One analyst described it in 1993 as "something in the nature of a constitutional addendum to the parliament rather than an attribute of the executive branch."[84] Another has argued that Ukraine has effectively become a "delegative democracy" where weak parties and political institutions effectively allow the president "to govern the country as s/he sees fit for the duration of the term to which s/he has been elected."[85] Ukrainian deputies have repeatedly argued that both presidents have tried to usurp powers properly belonging to parliament.[86] Other studies have described Ukraine as a "semi-presidential" system,[87] and argued that because of the victory of the "unified bureaucratic faction" in the 1990 Ukrainian elections, a presidential autocracy has since been established to protect its interests.[88]

Historical tradition, such as it is, is not much of a guide to assessing the Ukrainian system, as it includes elements of both parliamentarianism and personal rule. The Cossacks of the sixteenth to eighteenth centuries were led by powerful "Hetmans," but the latter were elected by popular assemblies (*viche*). Ukrainian nationalists tend to argue that, without a strong tradition of political organization, it was precisely Ukrainians' supposed tendency towards anarchic individualism that set them aside from "Aristocratic Poland" and "Autocratic Russia." The short-lived Ukrainian People's Republic in 1917–20 elected a president, Mykhailo Hrushevs'kyi, but failed to define his powers, and was in any case temporarily overthrown in 1918 by the dictatorship ("Hetmanate") of Pavlo Skoropads'kyi. In its even briefer existence in 1918–19 the West Ukrainian People's Republic was forced by immediate military crisis to vest all power in a would-be dictator, Yevhen Petrushevych.[89] Opinion polls in Ukraine have shown a marked preference for a presidential form of government (53 percent agreed with the statement that the president should be both head of state and head of the government in Summer 1994),[90] but this may be due simply to the unpopularity of the political class in general.

Without clear historical precedents, the still-evolving Ukrainian constitution has largely been shaped by circumstance. Although it does not fit any ideal-type exactly, Ukraine is probably closest to a "president-parliamentary regime," where "both the president and the parliament have authority over the composition of cabinets."[91] The president is directly elected and can appoint and dismiss ministers, but they are also subject to assembly confidence. The president normally appointed the seven leading ministers directly and discussed other appointments from a list drawn up by his nominee for prime minister (both also consulted with the chairman of parliament).[92] This procedure, however, was dropped in October 1992, when the new prime minister, Kuchma, demanded and obtained collective approval from parliament for his new cabinet of ministers in a single vote. Moreover, both Kravchuk and Kuchma have claimed, and on occasion exercised, the unilateral power of dismissal.

On the other hand, new governments are subject to parliamentary confirmation, and, once in office, to votes of no-confidence. There is therefore a situation of "'confused' control over cabinets" with "both of the electorate's agents [granted] considerable authority in matters of government formation,"[93] although parliament's power of censure was diminished by the 1995 Constitutional Agreement (see above).

Confusion was also generated by the absence of a Constitutional Court. A law creating such a court was actually passed in June 1992, and Leonid Yuzkov, then chairman of the Constitutional Commission's working group, appointed as its head.[94] However, it proved impossible for the deadlocked parliament to agree on further nominations. A particularly bitter controversy erupted in early 1993, when the nationalist opposition interpreted the nomination of leading former communists as an attempt to pack the court in advance of a ruling on the relegalization of the CPU. Eventually the frustration of heading a phantom institution led Yuzkov to resign. Moreover, the possibility of prolonged legal struggle over privatization and the restitution of former Communist Party property made it likely that elections to the court would always be a controversial affair, even after the 1996 constitution attempted to establish a more consensual process (see above).

However, the court was intended to act as a constitutional arbiter and to police the separation of powers. Without it, confusion reigned (although the president's power to cancel acts of ministers and other state institutions "if they conflict with the constitution and laws of Ukraine" arguably amounted to the presidency usurping the functions of a constitutional court). For example, before 1995, parliament had no right to veto the president's decrees, only the power to refer them to the Constitutional Court, but in practice arrogated the power to itself, as in November 1993, when Kravchuk's proposal to introduce dollar-denominated "National Resource Bonds" to encourage foreign capital investment with state property as security was voted down by 239 votes to 33.[95] Moreover, there was no-one to rule on the separation of powers between the president, cabinet of ministers, and the presidium of parliament. The latter's role was now supposed to be confined to managing the legislative program, but its output included over 200 "decisions of an executive character" in 1993 alone. Parliament continued to issue "regulations" (*postanovy*), with supposed executive force – over fifty in 1993.[96]

Lastly, the president's apparent power was severely checked by his inability to dissolve parliament, and, until 1996, by parliament's monopoly on enforcing constitutional change. According to one source, "the Ukrainian president has more formal power than his equivalent in France, but this is balanced by the fact that his position could be abolished overnight."[97] The accumulation of presidential power was therefore not a linear process. Kravchuk lost powers over the Winter of 1992/93 and in the face of the strong left-wing campaign to limit the powers of the presidency in 1993–94.[98] Kuchma was able to use the belated drive for economic reform after 1994 to brow-beat the left and expand his powers, but was never able to win the key power of dissolution.

If Shugart and Carey's index of presidential power is used to assess the powers of the Ukrainian president before 1995, the result is a comparatively low score of seven points, despite relatively stronger non-legislative powers.[99] The president had no real veto power, only the power to return bills for reconsideration (0 points), no partial veto (0 points), limited decree powers (1 point), and no reserved policy areas (0 points). The president introduced the budget, but parliament could amend it at will (half a point), and he had no powers to propose referenda, although the October 1993 draft constitution would have granted him the right to propose the dissolution of parliament (0 points). The president appointed the prime minister and leading members of the cabinet of ministers, subject to parliamentary confirmation (two and a half points), and could dismiss individual cabinet ministers, although he had never tried to dismiss them *en masse* (3 points). The assembly could censure the cabinet of ministers (0 points), and the president had no power to dissolve the assembly (0 points).

The 1995 Constitutional Agreement, however, increased the score to eleven and a half, given that Kuchma now had a proper veto power that required a two-thirds' majority to overturn (plus two points), stronger decree powers (plus one point), and slightly clearer powers over cabinet formation (plus half a point), plus the fact that parliament's censure abilities were reduced (plus one point). Arguably, a further point could have been added between 1995 and 1996 when the president had the theoretical right to initiate referenda.

On the other hand, the Ukrainian president scores relatively highly using James McGregor's system for evaluating presidential power, thanks to a high score on his list of "political" and "ceremonial" powers.[100] After the constitutional revisions of Spring 1992 the Ukrainian president scored between 22 and 26 points, or between 51 percent and 60 percent on McGregor's unweighted scale (the range of possibilities is due to the president's uncertain relations with the cabinet of ministers and the lack of a Constitutional Court), rising to the mid 60s percent after the 1995 Constitutional Agreement. The first score would place the Ukrainian presidency on a par with its equivalents in Poland and Lithuania, the second would have it closing on the Russian president. However, as McGregor himself indicates, an element of subjective assessment of the relative importance of particular powers should be taken into account. As the Ukrainian presidency lacks the crucial power of parliamentary dissolution and many items on McGregor's list are relatively minor, such as the right to grant asylum and amnesties, this would force the Ukrainian presidency lower down the scale (the contrasting results of alternative schema should perhaps make one wary of attempts to quantify presidential power).

Working with parliament

A key aspect of any president's power, particularly in postcommunist systems with weakly developed independent judiciaries, executives, and bureaucracies, but with strong post-Soviet legislatures, is their relations with parliament. Moreover, the weakness of party systems in postcommunist states has often produced fractious and ill-disciplined parliaments, which have tended to fuel arguments for greater presidential power.

Political parties were especially weak in the 1990 Ukrainian parliament, and faction formation was inhibited by the fact that deputies could belong to any two groups. Nevertheless, one comprehensive survey of voting behavior has established that, of the 450 deputies, 129 (29 percent) were regular supporters of nationalist positions, 244 (54 percent) could be classed as conservatives, and 77 (17 percent) were centrists.[101] Kravchuk's group was therefore pivotal, but always in a minority. In the 1994 parliament factions were more clearly defined, although the overall political balance was little different to that of 1990. By July 1994 parliamentary factions had stabilized, with the nationalists controlling 85 seats (25 percent), the left 145 (43 percent), and the center 88 (26 percent). A further 20 (6 percent) belonged to no particular faction.[102]

In neither parliament therefore was there a strong "presidential" party, or even any real national parties as such. At various times in 1990–94, Kravchuk could count on the support of moderate nationalists, centrists, and his own "national communist" faction, but the three groups formed neither a cohesive whole nor a natural majority. Although one author argues that Ukraine possessed a more-or-less "united bureaucratic faction" in 1990, the so-called "party of power" soon fell victim to the same severe factionalism as the political parties of the left and right. Political stalemate and highly disparate party politics has, temporarily at least, made Ukraine more of "a balanced republic" than a consolidated presidential autocracy.[103]

Kuchma's position in parliament was even weaker than Kravchuk's. His own "Interregional Group" and the "Unity" faction (the Russian-speaking half of the political center) could normally be counted on as supporters, but they only controlled 50 deputies out of the 338 elected in Spring 1994 (15 percent). Moreover, neither Kravchuk nor Kuchma was able to shift the balance of power in parliament in their favor through a "coat-tails effect."[104] Both Kravchuk (in December 1991, nineteen months after the March 1990 parliamentary elections) and Kuchma (in July 1994, three months after the Spring 1994 elections) were elected after, rather than before, parliamentary elections. In fact the closeness of the two elections in 1994 makes it possible to speak of a "counter-honeymoon election," with the earlier parliamentary elections exerting more influence on the presidential election than vice versa.[105]

Nevertheless, the two presidents' legislative records were markedly different. Kravchuk initially enjoyed close relations with parliamentary chairman Ivan Pliushch, and they worked closely together to avoid parliamentary defeat.[106] However, Kravchuk never had a positive legislative program as such, despite having the "right of legislative initiative," and consistently avoided pushing controversial issues, economic reform above all. Kravchuk introduced the state budget in 1992–4, but in every year it was amended out of recognition by free-spending deputies. Kravchuk was also repeatedly frustrated by his inability to wrest control of two key economic institutions, the National Bank of Ukraine and the State Property Fund (supposedly responsible for privatization) from parliament. Moreover, by 1993 Pliushch's own presidential ambitions and growing personal faction amongst collective farm leaders and local soviets were making relations with Kravchuk increasingly difficult.[107] Kravchuk's use of his decree powers was also discreet, although parliament still attempted to obstruct them on occasion, despite their lack of constitutional power to do so (see above). Kravchuk used his power to return legislation (never a proper veto) on less than half a dozen occasions in the 1990–94 parliament.[108]

Legislative gridlock was not institutionally determined, however. Kuchma was temperamentally disposed toward confrontation rather than compromise, and after October 1994 fought a long and often successful war of attrition against left-wing deputies to force through Ukraine's first serious program of economic reform (although he suffered serious defeats over privatization and plans to open the Ukrainian economy to Russian capital). After the Constitutional Agreement Kuchma used his newly acquired veto to good effect, for example, twice blocking a land bill designed to enrich collective farm managers. On the other hand, Kuchma was unable to displace the left-wing chairman of parliament Oleksandr Moroz.

"Confused control" over the cabinet of ministers meant that both presidents were similarly constrained in the "appointment game."[109] Both presidents had problems with finding a prime minister they could work with. In October 1992 Kravchuk seems to have misjudged parliament's indifference point by initially pushing the candidature of Valentyn Symonenko.[110] Kuchma's eventual appointment, and the transfer of powers from the presidency to the prime minister represented a substantial political defeat for Kravchuk. In September–October 1993, on the other hand, Kravchuk fared much better. Parliament's indifference point had moved both to the left and to the east. The June 1993 strikes and the revival of left-wing and regional political lobbies based in the Donbas prompted Kravchuk to propose an east Ukrainian, but in Yukhym Zviahil's'kyi he found a close supporter and a more congenial replacement for Kuchma. Moreover, as described above, Zviahil's'kyi was only made "acting prime minister," and Kravchuk seized back important powers in the economic field.

In May 1994 the left's victory in the spring parliamentary elections limited Kravchuk's freedom of maneuver, as did the pattern of electoral sequencing, with Kravchuk hoping that some leftist and east Ukrainian voters in the forthcoming presidential election might be won over by his choice. Nevertheless, Kravchuk maximized his options by circulating a list of six possible candidates, all on the left, and securing the election of Vitalii Masol, a former colleague and representative of the old guard, rather than a member of the revivalist Communist and Socialist parties.[111] Kuchma displayed considerable post-election caution, and respect for the fact that his 50 or so supporters in parliament were considerably outnumbered by the left's 145, in leaving Masol in place until February 1995. However, his replacement, Yevhen Marchuk, the supposedly reform-minded former head of the Ukrainian KGB, was about as radical a candidate as the parliamentary left could reasonably be expected to accept. Marchuk, like Kuchma under Kravchuk, soon developed presidential ambitions of his own and in May 1996 was replaced by Pavlo Lazarenko, a close ally of Kuchma's from his home base of Dnipropetrovs'k.

Both presidents guarded their seven reserved appointments jealously. Turnover was rare and spectacular, as when Kravchuk promptly dismissed defense minister Kostiantyn Morozov after his public criticism of the September 1993 Massandra summit with Russia as a sell-out of Ukrainian national interests.[112] At lower levels, however, both men had less control, especially as the cabinet of ministers remained large and unwieldy. Kravchuk was particularly cautious, leaving most of the conservative old guard in office, despite a sprinkling of appointments to placate the nationalist opposition. Kuchma was also more flexible than might have been expected. His first ministry was a curious mixture of cronies from his home base of Dnipropetrovs'k, Russophiles, and economic reformers.[113] The prominent radical Viktor Pynzenyk, with whom Kuchma had frequently quarreled during his previous stint in office in 1992–3, returned as deputy prime minister in charge of economic reform in November 1994. Although Pynzenyk was demoted in June 1995, IMF pressure has supported minister of economics, Roman Shpek, and the head of the National Bank, Viktor Yushchenko, despite public criticism by Kuchma of both men.

Conclusion: competitive dyarchy, or representation over efficiency?

Neither Ukrainian president has enjoyed a natural majority in parliament. Neither has been able to build a strong presidential party. One possibility therefore is that Ukraine will follow the same route as Russia, and president and parliament will increasingly diverge, creating in effect a system of "dual democratic legitimacy" or "competitive dyarchy,"[114] in which the struggle for political control "will increase the danger that either a president or an opposition assembly will reject the claims to executive authority of the other."[115] Such a confrontation was only narrowly averted in the Summer of 1993 and the Spring of 1995. Ukraine could even be described as a "tryarchy," given the rivalry between president, prime minister, and chairman of parliament. Both Ivan Pliushch, elected parliamentary chairman in December 1991 as Kravchuk's chosen successor, and Oleksandr Moroz, elected in May 1994, have tended to build up their own independent power-base, much as Ruslan Khasbulatov attempted in Russia in 1992–93.

Ukrainian politics would then become a zero-sum game in which conflict would replace compromise. The absence until 1996 of a constitution to spell out a clear separation of powers added to this danger. The rules of the game were not clear; instead of their delimiting politicians' behavior, a battle to define them was itself part of the political contest.[116] As with Poland in 1995, two presidential elections where the contest was for a post with uncertain powers probably added to uncertainty and anxiety and bred unnecessary polarisation. The passing of the 1996 constitution was a step toward *constitutionalism*, the willingness of politicians to allow their behavior to be guided by constitutional norms, but not a sufficient condition for its long-term development.

On the other hand, there are some perfectly good reasons for Ukraine's hybrid system and for the relative weakness of the presidency to date. Ukraine is a deeply divided society, marked by profound ethno-linguistic, regional, and ideological differences. At different times different groups have pressed for a stronger presidency (nationalists in 1991–92, economic reformers in 1994–96), but never with permanent success as rival groups have always feared the consequences of the president's untrammelled power spilling over into other areas. Even Kuchma's attempt to build a stronger presidency was hampered by his supporters' fear that his successor could be an anti-market and/or Russophile leftist.

As pointed out by Juan Linz, the dangers of winner-take-all presidential majoritarianism are therefore acute in states such as Ukraine.[117] Given the possibility of a partisan winning the presidency, it perhaps makes sense that Ukraine has consistently stopped short of building a strong presidential system. The 1994 election would have been even more sharply polarized if greater powers had accrued to the winner. However, any Ukrainian president will therefore find it difficult to construct a national program that is more than the lowest common denominator. The price of avoiding political conflict is likely to be that "decisive government" remains elusive.

APPENDIX

Table 3.1 *Votes in the Ukrainian presidential election, 1 December 1991*

Oblast		Kravchuk	Nationalist Three	Hryn'ov
(i)	**Galicia**			
	L'viv	11.5	85.0	0.8
	Ternopil'	16.8	80.2	0.4
	Ivano-Frankivs'k	13.7	82.2	0.6
(ii)	**Volhynia**			
	Rivne	53.1	42.6	0.8
	Volyn'	51.7	43.5	0.8
(iii)	**Other West**			
	Transcarpathia	58.0	35.4	1.3
	Chernivtsi	43.6	49.1	1.4
(iv)	**Right Bank**			
	Kirovohrad	74.8	20.1	1.7
	Cherkasy	67.1	28.0	1.4
	Vinnytsia	72.3	23.0	1.4
	Zhytomyr	77.6	18.3	1.1
	Khmel'nyts'kyi	75.5	20.3	1.2
(v)	**Kiev city**	56.1	36.6	3.5
	Kiev oblast	66.0	28.4	1.7
(vi)	**Left Bank**			
	Poltava	75.0	19.1	2.5
	Sumy	72.3	20.4	2.5
	Chernihiv	74.1	19.9	1.5
(vii)	**East**			
	Kharkiv	60.8	22.7	10.9
	Donets'k	71.5	13.6	11.0
	Luhans'k	76.2	12.7	6.8
	Zaporizhzhia	74.7	17.4	3.9
	Dnipropetrovs'k	69.7	21.8	3.2
(viii)	**South**			
	Mykolaïv	72.3	18.0	5.6
	Kherson	70.2	21.3	3.3
	Odesa	70.7	16.7	8.4
	Crimea	56.7	10.9	9.4
	Sevastopil'	54.7	13.6	8.4
Total		61.6	29.5	4.2

Source: *Uriadovyi kur"ier*, 38–39 (December 1991). Taburians'kryi won 0.6 percent. The "nationalist three" were Chornovil (23.3 percent), Luk"ianenko (4.5 percent) and Yukhnovs'kyi (1.7 percent).

Table 3.2 *Ukrainian presidential election, 1994 – first round*

Oblast		Kravchuk	Kuchma	Moroz	Lanovyi	Other
(i)	**Galacia**					
	L'viv	89.3	3.5	1.2	1.6	1.1
	Ternopil'	89.7	2.5	1.1	1.9	1.3
	Ivano-Frankivs'k	87.8	3.1	1.4	3.0	1.5
(ii)	**Volhynia**					
	Rivne	75.7	6.0	5.1	7.0	2.3
	Volyn'	68.7	5.4	7.5	10.6	3.7
(iii)	**Other West**					
	Transcarpathia	49.7	16.8	4.2	10.3	9.9
	Chernivtsi	54.0	20.5	6.4	7.3	5.2
(iv)	**Right Bank**					
	Kirovohrad	30.0	21.0	21.2	18.9	4.6
	Cherkasy	39.1	18.0	20.9	12.7	4.7
	Vinnytsia	44.4	19.6	15.2	9.7	5.0
	Zhytomyr	46.4	19.6	14.0	10.7	4.4
	Khmel'nyts'kyi	40.1	15.8	23.6	11.4	5.0
(v)	Kiev city	38.7	18.2	8.3	25.2	6.4
	Kiev oblast	41.1	18.4	13.6	16.5	5.7
(vi)	**Left Bank**					
	Poltava	29.5	28.4	18.3	14.2	5.3
	Sumy	23.1	30.3	25.0	11.5	4.9
	Chernihiv	22.5	45.2	14.5	7.1	6.0
(vii)	**East**					
	Kharkiv	24.4	34.2	22.2	9.5	4.7
	Donets'k	16.1	53.6	16.3	6.2	3.3
	Luhans'k	9.7	53.6	25.4	4.5	2.9
	Zaporizhzhia	23.8	48.5	12.4	7.7	3.6
	Dniproetrovs'k	26.3	43.5	8.7	11.9	5.7
(viii)	**South**					
	Mykolaïv	36.1	33.4	12.5	8.8	4.4
	Kherson	25.9	35.7	19.5	9.8	3.9
	Odesa	23.0	41.8	14.0	11.4	4.5
	Crimea	7.4	82.6	1.3	3.4	2.4
	Sevastopil'	5.6	82.1	2.4	4.0	1.7
Total		37.7	31.2	13.1	9.4	4.1

Source: Arel and Wilson, "Ukraine under Kuchma . . ." "Other" includes Valerii Babych
(2.4 percent), Ivan Pliushch (1.2 percent), and Petro Talanchuk (0.5 percent).

Table 3.3 *Ukrainian presidential election, 1994 – second round*

Oblast		Kravchuk	Kuchma
(i)	**Galicia**		
	L'viv	93.8	3.9
	Ternopil'	94.8	3.7
	Ivano-Frankivs'k	94.5	3.9
(ii)	**Volhynia**		
	Rivne	87.3	10.9
	Volyn'	83.9	14.0
(iii)	**Other West**		
	Transcarpathia	70.5	25.2
	Chernivtsi	61.8	35.3
(iv)	**Right Bank**		
	Kirovohrad	45.7	49.7
	Cherkasy	50.8	45.7
	Vinnytsia	54.3	42.3
	Zhytomyr	55.6	41.6
	Khmel'nyts'kyi	57.2	39.2
(v)	Kiev city	59.7	35.6
	Kiev oblast	58.3	38.4
(vi)	**Left Bank**		
	Poltava	37.4	59.2
	Sumy	28.9	67.8
	Chernihiv	25.1	72.3
(vii)	**East**		
	Kharkiv	26.0	71.0
	Donets'k	18.5	79.0
	Luhans'k	10.1	88.0
	Zaporizhzhia	26.8	70.7
	Dnipropetrovs'k	29.7	67.8
(viii)	**South**		
	Mykolaïv	44.7	52.8
	Kherson	32.1	64.6
	Odesa	29.2	66.8
	Crimea	8.9	90.0
	Sevastopil'	6.5	92.0
Total		45.1	52.1

Source: As Table 1.2

NOTES

1 The author would like to thank Dr. Robert Elgie and an anonymous reviewer for their helpful comments on early drafts of this chapter.

2 Matthew Soberg Shugart and John M. Carey, *Presidents and Assemblies. Constitutional Design and Electoral Dynamics* (Cambridge: Cambridge University Press, 1992), pp. 24–25.

3 The law can be found in *Holos Ukraïny*, 27 July 1991. Wherever possible citations are from *Holos Ukraïny*, as this is the most readily available source in the West.

4 Dominique Arel, "The Parliamentary Blocs in the Ukrainian Supreme Soviet: Who and What Do They Represent?," *Journal of Soviet Nationalities*, 1, 4 (Winter 1990–91), pp. 108–154.

5 Roman Solchanyk, "Ukraine and the Union Treaty," *Report on the USSR*, 3, 30 (26 July 1991).

6 Roman Solchanyk, "Ukraine Considers a New Republican Constitution," ibid., 3, 23 (7 June 1991).

7 See for example Mykola Koziurba, "Yakoiu buty nashii respublitsi – prezydents'koiu chy parlamentarnoiu?," *Holos Ukraïny*, 7 May 1991; Kravchuk's speech in favor of a presidential system, ibid., 15 May 1991; Volodymyr Filenko and Artur Bilous, "Ternystyi shliakh vid deklaratsiï do konstytutsiï," ibid., 16 May 1991, on the pros and cons of a "strong" and "weak" presidency; and Petro Martynenko, "Prezydent – garant stabil'nosti," ibid., 21 May 1991.

8 *Zakarpats'ka pravda*, 30 April 1991.

9 Levko Luk"ianenko, "Ukraïntsi i ïkh konstytutsiia," *Samostiina Ukraïna*, 11 (August 1991).

10 The CPU's rival proposals can be found in *Pravda Ukrainy*, 26 January 1991; and *Radians'ka Ukraïna*, 24 April 1991.

11 Vladyslav Nosov, people's deputy, former secretary to the Constitutional Commission and one of the authors of the October 1993 draft constitution, interviewed by the author and Dominique Arel, 28 June 1994.

12 Author's interview with Al'bert Kornieiev, presidential adviser on parliamentary affairs, 27 October 1994.

13 *Holos Ukraïny*, 6, 9, and 20 July 1991 reported on the passing of the law.

14 Ibid., 27 July 1991.

15 Author's interview with Volodymyr Shapoval, head of department on human rights, Kiev Shevchenko University, 30 June 1994. See also Shugart and Carey, *Presidents and Assemblies*, pp. 136–137.

16 Taras Kuzio and Andrew Wilson, *Ukraine: Perestroika to Independence*, (London: Macmillan, 1994), pp. 171–173; Roman Solchanyk, "Ukraine: Kravchuk's Role," *Report on the USSR*, 3, 36 (6 September 1991); Valentyn Chemerys, "Serpnevi podiï 91-ho. U zv"iazku z tym, shcho zdiisneno antykonstytitsiini zakhody..," *Holos Ukraïny*, 29 April 1994; and L. S. Taniuk and G. P. Krymchuk (eds.), *Khronika oporu* (Kiev: Vik-Dnipro, 1991) – a collection of documents on the coup period in Ukraine, Kravchuk's actions are detailed at pp. 102–123 and p. 170; Valentyn Chemerys, *Prezydent: Roman-ese* (Kiev: Svenas, 1994) concentrates on Kravchuk's actions in 1991.

17 *Holos Ukraïny*, 31 October 1991.
18 See the interview with Tkachenko, "Ya spoviduiu Marksyzm" (I believe in Marxism), *Holos Ukraïny*, 6 November 1991.
19 *Holos Ukraïny*, 4 November 1991; *Rabochaia gazeta*, 11 October 1991 and 6 November 1991.
20 *URP-inform*, 19 (3 September 1991), details the arguments at the meeting of the Grand Council of the main opposition movement Rukh on 1 September.
21 On the 1990 elections, see Arel, "Parliamentary Blocs"; on the December 1991 polls, see Peter J. Potichnyj, "The Referendum and Presidential Elections in Ukraine," *Canadian Slavonic Papers*, 33, 2 (1991), pp. 123–138. Ukraine's historical regional and ethno-linguistic differences are discussed in more detail in my *Ukrainian Nationalism in the 1990s: A Minority Faith* (Cambridge: Cambridge University Press, 1996).
22 Shugart and Carey, *Presidents and Assemblies*, pp. 57–58.
23 See Alexander J. Motyl, "The Conceptual President: Leonid Kravchuk and the Politics of Surrealism," in Timothy J. Colton and Robert C. Tucker (eds.), *Patterns in Post-Soviet Leadership* (Boulder, CO: Westview, 1995), pp. 103–121.
24 Valerii Khmel'ko, "Referendum: khto buv 'za' i khto 'proty'", *Politolohichni chytannia*, 1 (1992), pp. 40–52.
25 *Narodna hazeta*, 7 (February 1992).
26 *Za vil'nu Ukraïnu*, 14 December 1991; Stephen Foye, "The Ukrainian Armed Forces: Prospects and Problems," *RFE/RL Research Report*, 1, 26 (26 June 1992).
27 "Pro vnesennia zmin i dopovnen' do konstytutsiï (osnovnoho zakonu) Ukraïny," *Holos Ukraïny*, 7 April 1992; see also the reports in ibid., 11 and 15 February 1992; and Roman Solchanyk, "Ukraine: Political Reform and Political Change," *RFE/RL Research Report*, 1, 21 (22 May 1992).
28 Alexei Sekarev, "Ukraine's Policy Structure," *RFE/RL Research Report*, 1, 32 (14 August 1992).
29 The Duma's statute was in *Holos Ukraïny*, 12 March 1992; see also *Pravda Ukrainy*, 27 February 1992.
30 The law was published in *Holos Ukraïny*, 20 March 1992.
31 *Demokratychna Ukraïna*, 29 February 1992.
32 Oleksandr Yemets', "Nasha pravova systema shche duzhe nedoskonala," *Uriadovyi kur"ier*, 20 (May 1992).
33 Sekarev, "Ukraine's Policy Structure."
34 A list of the Duma's members can be found in *Holos Ukraïny*, 10 April 1992.
35 *Holos Ukraïny*, 2 June 1992.
36 Sekarev, "Ukraine's Policy Structure."
37 Volodymyr Lytvyn, *Politychna arena Ukraïny: Diiovi osoby ta vykonavtsi* (Kiev: Abrys, 1994), pp. 389–390.
38 Author's interview with Ivan Tymchenko, head of the presidential legal service, 28 June 1994.
39 Author's interviews with Nosov and Shapoval.
40 Author's calculations from the biographies published in *Holos Ukraïny*, March–May 1992, passim.
41 *Holos Ukraïny*, 17 July 1992.

42 Kravchuk called a formal "round-table" of all major political parties and social organizations in February 1992; *Holos Ukraïny*, 25 and 28 February 1992. Although the practice was not regularized or institutionalized, the meeting was the first of several.

43 Author's interview with Nosov.

44 *Holos Ukraïny*, 8 July 1992. A separate motion, passed by 238 votes to 81, asked Kravchuk to "reexamine the composition" of the government by September.

45 Such as measures to limit profit margins to 25–40 percent and to compensate savers from the price rises of January 1992; *Moloda Halychyna*, 10 March 1992.

46 Lanovyi's account of his departure from government can be found in Mykhailo Romanstov, *Volodymyr Lanovyi: "zaliznoï zavisy vzhe ne bude – ne vystachyt' zaliza"* (Kiev: Molod', 1994), p. 84–111.

47 Remarks by Kravchuk at University of Birmingham conference on Ukraine, 13–14 July 1996.

48 *Proekt Konstytutsiia Ukraïny*, dated 28 January 1993, in author's possession. The status of this document is unclear, so I have not quoted from it extensively.

49 Oleksandr Moroz, Ivan Musiienko, and Oleksii Yushchyk, "Pro 'konstytutsiinist' proiekty novii konstytustii Ukraïny," *Holos Ukraïny*, 29 May 1993; Anatolii Tkachuk, "Prezydent bez vlady, a radam – vsevladdia?," ibid., 21 May 1993.

50 *Holos Ukraïny*, 18 June 1993.

51 Leonid Kravchuk, "Koly meni povernuly konstytutsiini povnovazhennia, ya pochav diiaty rishuchishe," *Holos Ukraïny*, 22 June 1993.

52 Ibid., 31 August to 3 September 1993.

53 Ibid., 22–25 September 1993.

54 Ibid., 29 September 1993.

55 Author's interview with Shapoval.

56 A useful guide to the development, or non-development, of Kravchuk's views is Leonid Kravchuk, *Ye taka derzhava – Ukraïna* (Kiev: Globus, 1992), a collection of speeches and interviews.

57 The draft was in *Holos Ukraïny*, 30 October 1993.

58 The text was in *Holos Ukraïny*, 26 July 1991; 3 million signatures, compared to Russia's then requirement of 1 million from a population almost three times the size of Ukraine's, was a formidable barrier indeed. A campaign by Rukh in favor of pre-term elections to parliament in Autumn 1992 received only 1,175,068 signatures; *Samostiina Ukraïna*, 2 (January 1993).

59 Dominique Arel and Andrew Wilson, "The Ukrainian Parliamentary Elections," *RFE/RL Research Report*, 3, 26 (1 July 1994). The large number of empty seats was due to the twin provision in the electoral law requiring majority turnout (50 percent + 1) and a majority vote for election. Three rounds of repeat elections raised the number of seats to 405 by December 1994. After a year's moratorium, 21 more seats were filled in December 1995 and April 1996.

60 Dominique Arel and Andrew Wilson, "Ukraine under Kuchma: Back to 'Eurasia'?" *RFE/RL Research Report*, 3, 32 (19 August 1994).

61 See, for example, the debate in the Ukrainian Republican Party; *Pozacher-hovyi z"izd Ukraïns'koï Respublikans'koï Partiï* (Kiev: URP, 1994), pp. 19–58.

62 See especially the mammoth interview with Kravchuk serialized in *Kievskie vedomosti*, from 23 April 1994 onwards.

63 Oleksii Mustafin, "Lytsar sumnoho imidzhu," *Visti z Ukraïny*, 22 (1994); and Mar"iana Chorna, "Leonid Kuchma. Vchore, s'ohodni, i . . .," *Post-postup*, 13 (29 April–6 May 1994).

64 Valerii Khmel'ko, *Koho oberemo prezydentom? Za dva tyzhni do vyboriv prodov-shuvav lidyruvaty Kravchuk* (Kiev: International Institute of Sociology, 1994), paper kindly supplied to the author by Dr. Khmel'ko.

65 Moroz's program is in *Tovarysh*, 24 June 1994; See also *Kievskie vedomosti*, 14 June 1994; and *Rabochaia gazeta*, 22 June 1994.

66 Leonid Kuchma, "Ukraïna, yakoiu ya ïï bachu," *Holos Ukraïny*, 17 June 1994.

67 See, for example, most recently, Juan L. Linz, "Presidential or Parliamentary Democracy: Does it Make a Difference?," in Linz and Arturo Valenzuela (eds.), *The Failure of Presidential Democracy* (Baltimore: Johns Hopkins University Press, 1994), pp. 3–87.

68 Khmel'ko, *Koho oberemo prezydentom?*

69 The Left Bank became a part of Russia in either 1522 or 1654, whereas the Right Bank remained under Polish rule until 1793–95. Hence Ukrainian national consciousness is stronger on the Right Bank. This was the first Ukrainian election since 1989, however, in which the difference between the Left and Right Bank had been so marked (the polarity between east-ern/southern and western Ukraine has always been acute).

70 Khmel'ko, *Koho oberemo prezydentom?*

71 Heorhii Kriuchkov, "Shche odyn krok do dyktatury? (Pro novyi variant proektu Konstytutsiï Ukraïny," *Komunist*, 49 (December 1995).

72 Author's interview with Kornieiev, 27 October 1994.

73 *Holos Ukraïny*, 11 August 1994; *Post-postup*, 18–24 August 1994.

74 *Holos Ukraïny*, 11 August 1994.

75 Ibid., 23 September 1994.

76 *Narodna armiia*, 26 October 1994.

77 Iryna Pohorielova, "Ferz', abo Dmytro Tabachnyk yak vlastyvist' ukrïns'koï derzhavnosti," *Post-postup*, 8–14 September 1994; and *Uriadovyi kur"ier*, 11 August 1994.

78 *Uriadovyi kur"ier*, 6 December 1994; Lidiia Kryvenko, "Doktrynu pryiniato, doktrynu zruinovano," *Holos Ukraïny*, 2 February 1995. Kravchuk had at-tempted to table a similar law in the Winter of 1993–94, but without success.

79 In December 1994 it passed first reading by 176 votes to 135, and in May 1995 second reading by 223 to 93, on the latter occasion with support from the "Agrarian" faction.

80 "Konstytutsiinyi dohovir mizh Verkhovnoiu Radoiu Ukraïny ta Prezydentom Ukraïny. Pro osnovni zasady orhanizatsiï ta funktsionuvannia derzhavnoï vlady i mitsevoho samovriadyvannia v Ukraïny na period do pryiniattia novoï Konstytutsiï Ukraïny," *Holos Ukraïny*, 10 June 1995, pp. 3–4.

81 Petro Symonenko and Heorhii Kriuchkov, "Ne mozhna nekhtuvaty voliu narodu. Chomu komunisty ne mozhut' pidtrymaty novyi proekt Kon-stytutsiï?," *Holos Ukraïny*, 26 December 1995; see also the centrist critique by

Serhii Kudriashov et al., *Rosiis'ka Konstytutsiia Ukraïny* (Kiev: Ukraïns'ka perspektyva, 1996); and the comment in *Holos Ukraïny*, 16 February 1996.

82 From the draft published by the International Foundation for Electoral Systems, Kiev, February 1996, later in *Uriadovyi kur"ier*, 21 March 1996. It was not clear how, if at all, parliament could veto presidential decrees. If parliament was dissolved, its successor was safe from dissolution for a year. The author would like to thank Kataryna Wolczuk for providing this source.

83 For the text see *Zerkalo nedeli*, 13 July 1996; only changes to Section 1 ("General Provisions") and the amendment rules themselves had to be by referendum.

84 Ihor Markov, "The Role of the President in the Ukrainian Political System," *RFE/RL Research Report*, 2, 48 (3 December 1993), p. 35.

85 Paul Kubicek, "Delegative Democracy in Russia and Ukraine," *Communist and Post-Communist Studies*, 27, 4 (December 1994), pp. 423–441, at p. 424.

86 See the article by Lidiia Kryvenko, "Prezydent Ukraïny: konstytutsiino-pravovyi status," in the parliamentary journal *Viche*, 12 (December 1994).

87 Thomas F. Remington, "Introduction: Parliamentary Elections and the Transition from Communism," in Remington (ed.), *Parliaments in Transition: The New Legislative Politics in the Former USSR and Eastern Europe* (Boulder, CO: Westview, 1994), pp. 1–27, at p. 14.

88 Phillip G. Roeder, "Varieties of Post-Soviet Authoritarian Regimes," *Post-Soviet Affairs*, 10, 1 (January–March 1994), pp. 61–101, at pp. 66, 71–72, 75.

89 A. H. Sliusarenko and M. V. Tomenko, *Istoriia ukraïns'koï konstytutsiï* (Kiev: Znannia, 1993), pp. 71, 123–4; D. Yanevs'kyi, "XI Konstytutsiia Ukraïny v XX storichchi?," *Filosofs'ka i sotsiolohichna dumka*, 8 (1991), pp. 83–91.

90 *Holos Ukraïny*, 14 June 1994; a Democratic Initiative poll with 1,807 respondents. Another Democratic Initiative poll showed support for a presidential republic grow from 32 percent in June 1993 to 37 percent in November 1993. However, support for a mixed "presidential-parliamentary' republic also increased from 19 percent to 28 percent over the same period; Yevhen Holovakha, "Suchasna politychna sytuatsiia i perspektyva derzhavno-politychnoho ta ekonomichnoho rozvytku Ukraïny," *Politychni portret Ukraïny*, 4 (December 1993), p. 7.

91 Shugart and Carey, *Presidents and Assemblies*, p. 24; Volodymyr Shapoval, "Shcho buduiemo?," *Uriadovyi kur"ier*, 28 June 1994.

92 Author's interview with Shapoval.

93 Shugart and Carey, *Presidents and Assemblies*, p. 7.

94 The law was in *Holos Ukraïny*, 2 July 1992.

95 Ibid., 13 November 1993.

96 Author's interview with Tymchenko.

97 Author's interview with Shapoval.

98 Kravchuk hoped to use a renewed mandate from his reelection in July 1994 to see off the left-wing campaign; author's interview with Tymchenko; see also Artur Bilous, "Triumf radians'koï vlady," *Post-postup*, 10–16 February 1994.

99 Shugart and Carey, *Presidents and Assemblies*, pp. 148–158. The scores reflect actual practice rather than whatever was proposed in the various drafts of the new constitution. Two and a half points rather than three were awarded for

cabinet-making powers, as the president appoints the premier and seven leading ministers, not the whole cabinet.

100 James McGregor, "The Presidency in East Central Europe," *RFE/RL Research Report*, 3, 2 (14 January 1994).

101 Dominique Arel, "Voting Behaviour in the Ukrainian Parliament: The Language Factor," in Remington (ed.), *Parliaments in Transition*, pp. 125–158, at p. 138.

102 *Holos Ukraïny*, 12 July 1994.

103 Roeder, "Post-Soviet Authoritarian Regimes," pp. 80–84, 87–89.

104 Shugart and Carey, *Presidents and Assemblies*, chs. 11 and 12.

105 Ibid., pp. 264–265.

106 Author's interview with Nosov.

107 See, for example, former defense minister Kostiantyn Morozov's memoir in *Ukraïns'ka gazeta*, nos. 1–4, 1994.

108 Author's interview with Tymchenko. Examples include the bills on rent and local self-government in spring 1994.

109 Shugart and Carey, *Presidents and Assemblies*, pp. 107–108 and 121–126.

110 In November 1990 the replacement of Vitalii Masol by Vitol'd Fokin was a clear victory for Kravchuk. Conservative communists would have preferred to stick with Masol, or appoint Oleksandr Bulianda, director of the giant Azovstal factory: V. M. Lytvyn and A. H. Sliusarenko, "Na politychnii areni Ukraïny (90-ti rr.). Rozdumy istorykiv," *Ukraïns'kyi istorychnyi zhurnal*, 1 (1994), pp. 9–30, at pp. 28–29; and Ivan Salii, *Ya povertaius* (Kiev: Dovira, 1993), p. 136. However, the example is not discussed here as Kravchuk was only parliamentary chairman at the time.

111 *Holos Ukraïny*, 14 June 1994.

112 Bohdan Nahaylo, "The Massandra Summit and Ukraine," *RFE/RL Research Report*, 2, 37 (17 September 1993). See also note 107 above.

113 *Post-postup*, 18–24 August 1994; and *Kievskie vedomosti*, 20 August 1994.

114 Shugart and Carey, *Presidents and Assemblies*, p. 56.

115 Ibid., p. 75.

116 Lidiia Kryvenko, "Khto zh vidpovidal'nyi za derzhavy. Konstytutsiinyi status Prezydenta potrebuie vdoskonalennia," *Holos Ukraïny*, 21 October 1994.

117 Linz and Valenzuela, *Failure of Presidential Democracy*; and Alfred Stepan and Cindy Skach, "Constitutional Frameworks and Democratic Consolidation: Parliamentarianism Versus Presidentialism," *World Politics*, 46, 1 (October 1993), pp. 1–22.

4   Kazakstan: Nursultan Nazarbaev as strong president

Martha Brill Olcott

A strong president

At the time of independence, and for much of the time since, Kazakstan's first president, Nursultan Nazarbaev, has been a highly popular political figure. This popularity has helped make possible the introduction of two constitutions for Kazakstan since independence, the first of which formally created, and the second of which strengthened even further what both documents call a "presidential democracy," a system of government which gives the president and his office control over almost every aspect of the republic's political and economic life. President Nazarbaev's presidency has been extended, without election, until 2000 and can presumably be further extended again, if necessary. This has had a significant chilling effect on the development of political life in Kazakstan, but has done little to address the problems and pressures of independence which had begun to erode both the popularity and the power of Nazarbaev.

On 1 December 1991, on what proved to be the eve of their unexpected independence, more than 80 percent of Kazakstan's voters chose Nazarbaev to be their president. Strong public support for Nazarbaev was further reflected in the republic's first constitution, ratified in January 1993. While that constitution provided significant guarantees of individual liberties, and accorded a fairly large role to the republic's Supreme Council, or parliament, the greatest part of power in the republic was vested in the presidency. Among the many powers of the presidency were the right to name the government and prime minister (subject to parliamentary agreement), to initiate legislation, and to formulate and conduct foreign policy. The president also was given the right to rule by decree in broadly defined situations, which Nazarbaev expanded in October 1994 to include the right to conduct economic policy in strategically important sectors.

Because Kazakstan is constitutionally defined as a unitary state, Nazarbaev also was given the right to appoint local governments and executives who answer directly to him, rather than to the immediate constituents.

These administrators, or *hakim*s, must work with local legislatures elected by the local populations, but the areas of responsibility for such councils are sharply limited both legally and (what may be more important) financially, since taxes are collected and distributed centrally.

In addition to the powers which he enjoyed legally from that first constitution, Nazarbaev also has a broad spectrum of informal or extralegal powers which accrue from his years in the Communist Party hierarchy, and from the years which his constituents spent as Soviet subjects. The president has a staff of several hundred who can conduct informal interventions or offer necessary persuasion in situations where the more formal powers are inadequate, or might work too slowly.

On two occasions in the short history of independent Kazakstan these informal powers were particularly in evidence: the first was in December 1993, when Nazarbaev successfully pressured the existing legislature, elected in 1990, when Kazakstan was still a Soviet republic, into premature "voluntary" dissolution; the second was in March 1995, when Nazarbaev invoked a technicality of the 1993 constitution to allow him to declare the republic's first post-independence parliament invalid, and so to impose direct presidential rule. Subsequent to that dissolution, Nazarbaev used two extra-constitutional referenda to get public approval for postponing presidential elections (meant to be held by 1996) until at least the year 2000, and to ratify a second national constitution, which further weakened the powers of the legislative and judiciary branches of Kazakstan's government, while expanding those of the executive.

The president's first show of strength

Nazarbaev's first demonstration of strength came shortly after Russian President Yeltsin had used tanks in October 1993 to disband Russia's parliamentary counterpart to Kazakstan's legislative body. Kazakstan's parliament at independence consisted of 350 members who had been elected in 1990, under the Soviet constitution, for a five-year term. Over the opposition of most of the existing political parties, Nazarbaev and his staff were able to convince the deputies, without using force or threats, to relinquish the last eighteen months of their mandates in spite of the fact that forty-five major pieces of legislation then under consideration were left in limbo or abandoned.[1]

Kazakstan's first post-independence constitution had not specified either the size of the new legislature or the means by which candidate slates would be drawn up, giving Nazarbaev and his aides considerable scope in shaping the resultant body.

Elections for what it had been decided would be 177 mandates were held in March 1994. Forty of these were to be chosen directly from candidate lists selected by the president, but considerable attention was also paid to increasing the likelihood that most of the other deputies in the parliament would also be "presidential men." Registration of political parties was made very difficult, and campaigning was sharply restricted, making it difficult for voters to learn the political affiliations, and to some degree even the platforms, of the candidates. The majority of candidates came from slates put together by the government, and many of them had little time to reflect on the nature of the duties that they would be expected to perform if elected, or what their own personal policy prefer- ences were. Even the actual manner of voting, which required that voters cross off the names of candidates whom they did not wish to have represent them, was sufficiently closely "stage-managed" that European observers sent by the Conference on Security & Cooperation in Europe (CSCE) were initially reluctant to endorse the election as free and fair.

The second show of strength

It was the real or supposed inadequacies of that election which provided the occasion for Nazarbaev's second show of strength. On 6 March 1995, the Constitutional Court, one of the republic's three supreme courts (see below), unexpectedly rendered a decision upholding the complaints of one Tatiana Kviatkovskaia, a disappointed candidate for parliament who had sued ten months previously to have the 1994 election in her district annulled for violating the one person one vote and equal representation clauses of Kazakstan's constitution. Although her complaint referred only to one district of Almaty, the capital, the decision was immediately interpreted as an invalidation of the legitimacy of the entire parliament. The constitution gave President Nazarbaev ten days in which to appeal the court's decision, but his response team filed their objection just two days later, in spite of the fact that 8 March was a national holiday.

The appeal had only two elements: an assertion that the question of voting procedures was in the jurisdiction of a general court, not the Constitutional Court, and a reminder that the court's decision would further complicate socio-economic reform in the republic. The Constitu- tional Court reaffirmed its original decision on 11 March, at which point Nazarbaev took advantage of the ruling to go before parliament and inform the deputies that they were an improperly assembled body that now had to be abolished, and that all the decisions and laws it had passed, including those that had confirmed the government of the new prime minister, Akezhan Kazhegeldin (appointed in October 1994) had to be annulled. Using the powers of emergency presidential rule which had been given him by the 1990–94 parliament just before it disbanded, Nazarbaev reappointed Kazhegeldin, named a new temporary government, and asserted his own imposition of direct presidential rule, pending elections to the new parliament, which were ultimately held in December 1995.

About ten days later, on the ancient Central Asian holiday of Nauruz, Nazarbaev assembled an unprecedented "People's Assembly." This presidentially sponsored "advisory committee" is not mentioned in Kazakstan's 1993 constitution but seems to have resembled Turkmenistan's Halk Maslahaty, a presidentially appointed "council of elders" which convenes when necessary to rubber-stamp presidential decisions. Nazarbaev's assembly adopted a resolution calling for Nazarbaev to remain president, without election, until December 2000. Nazarbaev agreed, but also submitted the issue to a national referendum, held on 29 April 1995, which he won overwhelmingly: 91.3 percent of the population turned out to vote, and 95.8 percent of the ballots cast supported extending presidential rule.[2]

Nazarbaev also scheduled a second referendum, conducted on 30 August 1995, which had voter participation of 91 percent, with 89.1 percent of those voting in favor of the hastily drafted second constitution. In addition to creating the bi-cameral legislature which Nazarbaev had been pressing for, the new constitution also formalized further increases in President Nazarbaev's power, beyond what was already granted him under the 1993 constitution. The republic's new basic law continues to define Kazakstan as a unitary state with a presidential form of government. The president is the highest state officer, responsible for determining the basic course of domestic and foreign policy. It is his role to name the government (subject to parliamentary approval) and all other republic officials. He is elected for a term of five years with a maximum of two terms. He has the power to declare states of emergency which put the constitution into abeyance, and is the sponsor of all legislation. He also functions as the guarantor of the constitution and of the workings of government. Importantly, he has the power to override the decisions and actions of local authorities and councils. The only grounds on which a president can be removed from his position are infirmity and treason, either of which must be proven by a majority of the joint upper and lower houses of the new parliament. Decrees which Nazarbaev issued in December 1995 further gave him the power to order new parliamentary elections, annul any laws, and demand the resignation of the government. Clearly, Kazakstan had been transformed into a strong presidential system.

The new parliament, elected in December 1995 and convened 30

January 1996, consists of two houses, a Senate and a Majilis, both operating in continual session. Each of Kazakstan's nineteen oblasts and the city of Almaty, which has oblast status, was to have two senators. Rather than being elected directly by the populace, the senators are chosen by joint sessions of the oblasts' representative bodies, for terms of four years. An additional seven senators are appointed directly by the president. In addition, ex-presidents (should there ever be any) will be senators-for-life.

The Majilis has sixty-five representatives, one each from districts which are drawn to have roughly equal populations. Elections for half the seats were to be held every two years. Members of the government may not serve in either house, or be members of other representative bodies. The first legislature to be elected was disproportionately Kazak; nearly two-thirds of the representatives (sixty-seven) were ethnic Kazaks, while thirty-one were Russian, with five others from other nationalities.

Initiative for most legislative actions was to come from the president. If parliament passes a law which the president vetos, a two-thirds vote of both houses is required to over-ride; a similar margin is required to express no confidence in a prime minister. Presidential authority was similarly strengthened at the local level, where it was already quite strong. Almaty and Leninsk, the support city for the Baikonur launch facility, both had oblast status. The oblasts are divided into rayons (regions), consisting of a number of settlement points. Each oblast, rayon, and, usually, even settlement has its own elective council, called a *maslikhat*, which is charged with drawing up a budget and supervising local taxation. Cities have their own local councils as well, and large cities are divided into rayons, each with its own council. None of these local legislatures has the authority to choose the local executive, who has the job of ensuring that republic governmental decisions are enforced and that the republic constitution is observed. Instead, oblast and rayon heads of administration, known as Glavs or hakims, are presidential appointees. The head in turn appoints the members of his staff, who are the department heads of the oblast.

Erosion of presidential power

There has been considerable speculation that Nazarbaev may have orchestrated the circumstances leading up to the parliament's dismissal in 1995, because, up until it rendered its March 1995 decision putting into question the legal status of the parliament, the Constitutional Court had been a notably unproductive organ of power, reaching only eight decisions in over two years. There are other aspects of the annulment which also struck observers as strange: Marash Nurtazin, an ex-deputy who had brought a similar complaint to that of Kviatkovskaia, supported the decree in principle but declared it invalid in fact, since Article 14 of the republic's basic law imposed a six-month statute of limitations on such decisions. Others were puzzled by the president's rapid but strangely insubstantial objection to the court ruling, followed by his swift and apparently well-prepared implementation of the consequences of the decision. And a number of observers found it strange that the court should make a decision so convenient for the president when it did, after having held the case for more than ten months.

Perhaps more important for fuelling speculation that either the president or his staff had maneuvered the annulment of parliament, the closure spared Nazarbaev a number of political inconveniences, not the least of which was an increasingly assertive legislative body. The extraordinary lengths to which Nazarbaev and his men had gone to attempt to insure a compliant legislature makes it all the more remarkable how quickly the 1994–95 parliament had begun, not only to assert its independence, but also to strengthen and consolidate itself as an institution. At that time it was conceivable that a more mixed presidential-parliamentary system might evolve.

In part, the deputies, 70 percent of whom were first-time office holders, were reflecting a confidence bred by a growing culture of political pluralism which had begun to develop in the republic following independence. By early 1994, Kazakstan had developed an increasingly more independent press, and the growing prominence of the non-governmental press in particular made it increasingly difficult for the Nazarbaev government to stifle public debate on alternatives to government policy.

This in turn gave the new national legislature a greater sense of institutional empowerment than the drafters of the republic's constitution had intended. As a result the legislature was quick to flex its muscles, testing its powers.

Despite some fairly broad threats from the presidential office to the effect that the new deputies should not be in a hurry to give up their old jobs or apartments,[3] almost immediately upon taking their seats a group of deputies in the new parliament organized themselves into a left-center opposition bloc, called Respublika, which brought together such disparate political groups as the socialists (the legal successor to the banned Communist Party), the social-democrats, the new Communist Party, the Russian nationalist party Lad (Harmony), the Kazak nationalist party Azat (Freedom), and even the tiny Tabigat group, Kazakstan's Greens.[4] Soon afterward, a sub-group of Respublika, called Legal Development of Kazakstan, went so far as to organize a formal "shadow cabinet," with the stated intention of providing alternative viewpoints and programs in competition with those of the government.

In May 1994 the parliament passed a vote of no confidence in the government of Sergei Tereshchenko, whom Nazarbaev had appointed as prime minister even before independence. In addition to being a long-time close associate of Nazarbaev, Tereshchenko was also an important symbolic figure, because he was an ethnic Ukrainian, born in Russia; importantly, and highly unusual for a Slav, Tereshchenko spoke fluent Kazak, which made him especially well suited to be the highest ranking non-Kazak in the government. The motion of no confidence was brought with 139 deputies present, 111 of whom voted against Tereshchenko.

Although Nazarbaev immediately stated unequivocal support for Tereshchenko, saying that the prime minister would stay in office at least another two years, or until the completion of the round of privatization and economic reform then underway, parliamentary pressure continued to mount, leading in July to parliamentary overrides of presidential vetoes on two consumer-oriented economic bills.[5] Potentially more disruptive was the fissioning of Respublika, which now spawned a new "non-constructive" opposition that began to call for the replacement of both Tereshchenko and Nazarbaev. Calling itself Otan-Otechestvo ("Fatherland" in Kazak and Russian respectively), this coalition brought together representatives from: the (largely Russian) Workers' Movement; the Kazak nationalist party Alash; the new Communist Party, the All-Union Communist Bolshevik League, and the All-Union Communist Leninist Youth League (all mostly old nomenklatura of both ethnic groups); the Russian nationalist groups Lad and Russian Community; and the Democratic Human Rights Community (Russian and Kazak intellectuals). Even more embarrassing for Nazarbaev were the accusations of malfeasance made against the Tereschenko government's minister of economics and minister of the interior, widely publicized in the republic's media in September 1994. Both men were quickly dismissed, and criminal charges were brought against M. Urkumbaev, the economics minister,[6] but this was not sufficient to save the Tereshchenko government. In mid-October parliamentary and public pressure forced Nazarbaev to reverse his position. The Tereshchenko government resigned *en masse*.

Nazarbaev attempted to regain a modicum of his eroded power by imperiously appointing the successor government of Akezhan Kazhegeldin – the nomination was put forward in a hastily called special session at which no discussion of the candidate was permitted. It was clear, nevertheless, that for all its imperfections and problems, Kazakhstan's legislature was by mid-1994 beginning to demonstrate that it could become a body which might provide a real check and balance on the powers of the presidency.

This demonstration of their power emboldened the legislators, who increasingly saw the parliament as a "bully pulpit" from which to air a wide variety of concerns, both public and those that were more self-interested. One of the unforeseen consequences of creating a "professional" parliament which met in nearly continuous session was that most of the deputies came to understand that their responsibilities were to the particular group of constituents which had elected them and so, presumably would reelect them, if they felt themselves to have been well served. This "change of allegiance" is particularly surprising, given that nearly 90 percent of the legislators had been senior state administrators.[7]

Regional and ethnic constraints on executive power

This growing responsiveness to voters' concerns (perceived or real) inevitably meant tht the 1994–95 parliament began to develop regional and economic blocs, as well as ethnic ones, as a consequence of the wide differentiation in the social and ethnic makeup of the republic. Comprising a surface area as large as all of Europe, Kazakstan's comparatively small population of about 17 million was scattered in regional clusters regardless of whether the populace were ethnically uniform. However, as has been frequently pointed out, the republic at independence was almost evenly split between ethnic Kazaks and Russians, each of whom represented about 40 percent of the population.

It has been widely noted that each of these groups regarded independence in very different, even antithetical ways, and that each is affected by the further course of Kazakstan's development in different ways. What is less often remarked upon, however, is that neither the Russian nor the Kazak community within the republic is uniform. Some of this diversity is the legacy of Soviet developmental patterns, which sited factories, cities, and transportation networks in ways which benefited the all-union economy, rather than the individual republics. Thus, for example, there are virtually no roads or railroads which cross the republic east to west or north to south; transportation links in the north were built to run through Russia, while in the south they pass through Uzbekistan. It was not until many months after independence that it even became possible to *fly* directly between cities in the republic's extreme east and extreme west, since air traffic had been routed with Moscow as the hub.

These patterns of development have left marked regional differences and orientations within the republic. Communities in the northeast, for example, are inextricably linked with Russia, mining coal for electrical generating plants which are located in Siberia, and from which they get their electricity. The population here is heavily Russian, and is closely integrated with the Siberian cities over the border; those Russian cities have already once declared the existence of a "Siberian republic," and could do so again, drawing in the Kazakstani cities.

By contrast, further west along the 3,000 mile border with Russia, the communities are more agricultural. Here the dependency is of a different sort. Kazakstan has no silos in the north, and no flour mills; all of these were built in Russia.

The far west, near the Volga, is also Russian, but it is more oriented toward Moscow and central Russia. This is also the first territory which the Russians took from the Kazaks, at the end of the seventeenth century, so there is here the strongest claim to Russian "ownership." This is also a region where the Cossacks are influential, asserting their right to establish a "homeland." Further south, in Mangyshlak, there is abundant oil, but no means to refine or ship it since both refineries and pipeline are in Russia. To complicate matters further, the existing pipeline runs west, out of the republic, rather than east, to Kazakstan's industrial centers.

In the south, which is ethnically much more Kazak, development follows the same sort of pattern of dependence upon another republic. Tashkent was the major hub city along the southern flank of the USSR, so that most road and rail traffic for the southern oblasts lies within Uzbekistan. Since the independence of the five Central Asian republics, the imposition of customs and currency laws has made it all but impossible to maintain the Soviet spaceport of Baikonur; although physically on Kazakstan's territory, the complex was supplied out of Tashkent, which came to mean that even typewriters and air-conditioners could not be sent out for repair, to say nothing of more complex equipment. The same integration obtains in the southeast, where the economy of Kyrgyzstan has become heavily dependent upon that of its larger neighbor. Here too, as is true all along the eastern boundary, the proximity to China has created a very different economic and political "microclimate" than in the rest of Kazakstan. Such regional differentiation, taken together with the ethnic division in the republic, seemingly stood in the way of creating strong central authority.

The growth of Kazak identity

It is not only the Soviet legacy which makes Kazakstan's political landscape so diverse; also at work, and making itself increasingly felt, is the growing national self-assertion among the Kazaks themselves, who are in a process of national revival. Although Kazakstan had no indigenous "liberation" movement before independence, there was from the mid-1980s a growing sense among prominent intellectuals that the Kazaks were in danger of disappearing as a people, a language, and a culture.

Their long association with and close proximity to the Russians made the Kazaks among the most Russified of the Soviet peoples. Estimates from the late Soviet era were that as many as 40 percent of the Kazaks could no longer speak their "native" language.

Thus, even before independence there was a gathering movement to resurrect and preserve a Kazak identity. Before independence this advanced primarily along two fronts: a movement, begun in the late 1980s, to make Kazak the official language of the republic; and another movement, spurred by Mikhail Gorbachev's campaign of glasnost, which undertook to expand and rewrite the history of the Kazak people.

Since independence the language issue has become a point of serious contention between the republic's Russians and Kazaks. As a number of deputies to the short-lived parliament – both Russian and Kazak – pointed out, independent Kazakstan's first constitution, adopted in January 1993, was ambiguous on the question of whether or not the state is an ethnically defined entity. Although Article 1 of the first constitution guaranteed citizens of Kazakstan equality of rights and freedoms regardless of race, nationality, sex, language, and a number of other conditions of status, the preamble to the same document claims that the right to adopt a constitution springs from the "unshakeability of Kazak statehood," and declares as its first basis that the republic is a form of statehood "self-determined by the Kazak nation." The republic's second constitution, adopted by a popular referendum in August 1995, is similarly ambiguous about whether or not Kazakstan is ethnically defined, although it too specifically prohibits discrimination based upon ethnicity, native language, place of origin, and a number of other factors which might be considered ethnic.

Both the first and the second constitution stipulate, however, that the official state language is Kazak. The 1993 constitution relegated Russian to the nebulous status of "language of inter-ethnic communication"; the 1995 constitution was more specific but no clearer, saying that, "In government offices and in offices of local administration Russian is officially used equally with Kazak."

In 1990, in the context of the Russian-dominated USSR, the adoption of a law protecting Kazak as a state language did not seem a serious threat to most Russians. By 1995, however, linguistic requirements began to make themselves increasingly felt for entry into universities, for job security, and even for public entertainment, as Russian-language media became more inaccesible.

Although less immediately contentious than the language issue, history too is a potentially explosive issue. The Russians see northern Kazakstan as Russian frontierland, where the embattled native Kazaks sought the protection of the tsars in the eighteenth century. The Kazaks view the same events as tactical alliances which their khans had intended to be short-lived, save that the Russians abrogated the agreements and stole the Kazaks' land. Thus, to the Kazaks, independence is a restoration of a national right they had long been denied, while to the Russians it is a disaster, leaving them stranded on the wrong side of an arbitrary border.

Although the Kazaks were converted to Islam quite late in their history, and never assimilated the religion as deeply into their culture as did their more southern neighbors, the general religious revival in Central Asia is also adding a dimension to this growing Kazak self-assertion. The cultural antagonism between Russians and Muslims has always been strong, but has grown even stronger among the so-called "stranded Russians" in the new republics since the civil war in Tajikistan and the Russian attack on Chechnia. Moscow has portrayed both conflicts as the product, at least in part, of "fundamentalist Islam," making Russians elsewhere even more apprehensive about the growing number of mosques.

Paradoxically, this growth of Kazak national self-awareness has also had the effect of promoting a fissioning of the Kazaks themselves, as they return to earlier terms of self-identification. To build support therefore, Nazarbaev must do more than proclaim himself a Kazak nationalist. Historically the Kazaks had been organized into three groups of clans and tribes; called *zhus*, or Hordes, each had traditional territories. The Small Horde controlled western Kazakstan, the Middle Horde migrated in what today is northern and eastern Kazakstan, and the Large or Great Horde was dominant in the south. The Small and Middle Hordes came under Russian control first, in such a way that the hordes' nobility managed to retain many of their privileges, and even to educate their sons in Russian schools. These sons became the first Kazak nationalists, and so it was *their* sons who were destroyed when Stalin's purges decimated the Kazak intelligentsia.

The Great Horde came under Russian control later, when colonial rule was much harsher. The few Great Horde Kazaks who were political became socialists, not nationalists, so that it was they who came to dominate in the Soviet era, particularly after Kazakstan's capital was moved from the Small Horde town of Orenburg (now in Russia) to a Great Horde wintering spot, Almaty. Dinmukhamad Kunaev, who led the republic for twenty-five years during the Brezhnev era, and Nursultan Nazarbaev are both from the Great Horde, although they come from unrelated clans.

Clan and *zhus* always had some importance in the Soviet period, but strict Soviet punishment for nepotism reduced its impact upon patronage. Since the collapse of the Communist Party and its patronage networks, and in the absence of any other functional equivalent, clan and *zhus* membership has come to play an increasingly important role in the economic and political life of the republic, both at the national and oblast level. Naturally this further alienates the republic's Russians, who see clan and *zhus* patronage as yet another way in which they are excluded from economic and political advantages.

At the same time, however, the rising importance of clan puts Great Horders at odds with Small and Middle Horders, since in the event of a Russian secession, the latter would lose most of their land, while the Great Horde lands would remain intact, even if the people themselves would be very much impoverished. *Zhus* politics is also said to be behind the generally leisurely pace of implementation of plans to move the republic's capital from the Great Horde territory of Almaty to the Middle Horde territory of Akmola.

Gathering challengers

For all the tensions arising from ethnic, geographical, and cultural differences, it is probably the state of Kazakstan's economy which has offered the greatest challenge to Nazarbaev's power. As is true elsewhere in the former Soviet Union, Kazakstan has since independence seen an enormous transfer of power and wealth, while also suffering a catastrophic decline in productivity (by some accounts, the republic's GNP dropped by one-half between 1990 and 1994).

For approximately the first year of independence, the Soviet-era administrators and political authorities enjoyed enormous economic advantages because of their opportunities for "spontaneous privatization" (or theft). This advantage was not universal, but most administrators who had access to stocks of metals or minerals were able to use contacts in Russia and elsewhere to make substantial private fortunes selling these on the world market. This first phase of "spontaneous privatization" predominantly benefited Russians, or the Kazaks who worked closely with them, because it was they whom the Soviet system had put in power.

The introduction and execution of the government's privatization scheme, however, systematically shifted economic advantage toward the Kazaks. Kazaks control virtually the entire apparatus of republic government, meaning that they have a monopoly on the granting of export licenses and tax concessions, and other important bureaucratic functions. Even more important, though, certain Kazak families have been able to use the voucher system of privatization to secure control of huge portions of the state economy.

The voucher system which the Kazaks adopted was similar to the model used in the Czech republic; citizens were issued vouchers that they could deposit in holding companies, which would then be able to buy up to 20 percent of large companies being privatized. In theory, Kazakstan's citizens had a wide choice of funds; about 170 were eventually registered. In fact, however, just 20 companies were able to accumulate nearly 60 percent of the coupons, and another 19 companies accumulated more than 20 percent. Thus, one-quarter of the companies control more than three-quarters of the privatization vouchers, while half the companies have less than 4 percent among them. One company, Butia-Kapital, received nearly 10 percent of the vouchers, the largest single holding.

While it may not be true, as is widely rumored, that this company is controlled by one of Nazarbaev's relatives, there is no doubt that the system of privatization has put most of the nation's new wealth into a small group of privileged Kazak hands. There are also a number of complaints that the process of privatization itself is fixed, with the prices for choice properties set artificially low and the number of bidders strictly controlled. The perception that the privatization process is rigged was further cemented in the public mind by the scandals of autumn 1994, which eventually brought down the Tereshchenko government.

Although some Russians have been able to enter the new Kazak commercial structures, they have done so only as junior partners; the majority of the republic's Russians have felt themselves to be entirely excluded from the new wealth that is being created. The same may also be said of many of the republic's Kazaks, of course, but with the important difference that Russians find an ethnic explanation for their economic disenfranchisement, while the Kazaks have explanations only of clan, horde, and other "insider" connections.

Many of the former nomenklatura – a large percent of whom are Russian – who have now fallen on harder times had extensive training in the various Soviet hierarchies, which they were able to use with considerable effect in Kazakstan's complex political environment, particularly when the economy was in precipitous decline. Nazarbaev's insistence on continuing his economic and social policies regardless of public support for them, at a time when the republic's GDP was declining by 25 percent and its industrial production by 28 percent, permitted the politically skilled but otherwise disempowered deputies to use the 1994–95 parliament to forge anti-presidential coalitions of disparate, even antagonistic, groups. As noted, the Respublika bloc was elastic enough to contain both the Russian nationalists and the Kazak nationalists, while Otan-Otechestvo was able to use the widespread desire to return to the political and social structures of a decade earlier as a way to forge a coalition of Russians, Kazaks, and even Cossacks.

Even more disturbing, from a presidential point of view, was the growing professionalism of the parliament. This is perhaps best exemplified by the changing political role of Speaker A. Kekilbaev. Formerly a minor member of the presidential staff, Kekilbaev was a compromise candidate for speaker who seemed to have been chosen largely for his loyalty to Nazarbaev. While that loyalty was never disavowed, the new speaker became increasingly insistent about the institutional functions belonging to parliament, demanding that government actions and decrees must have a basis in law. Kekilbaev also began to insist that normal democratic practice was to have the parliament, not the president, propose new legislation, and he expressed concern about the lack of a legal framework for the economic and political transformations which Nazarbaev was attempting to impose. Kekilbaev was particularly active in resisting Nazarbaev's attempt to create a bi-cameral legislature without amending the constitution.

Kekilbaev also used parliamentary resources to educate his deputies, sending legislators to study how other parliaments and legislatures functioned. Under Kekilbaev's leadership, work in the parliament moved into standing committees and away from the long-winded, unfocused floor debates of past parliaments. Indeed, citing the practice of the nomadic Kazaks in the fifteenth through eighteenth centuries, who reached major decisions in councils of elders, or *bii*s, Kekilbaev began to assert that the Kazaks have a native parliamentary tradition which they must resurrect and defend. As Kekilbaev put it, the parliament, not the presidency, embodies the democratization of the people, and leaders must not be permitted to forget to render account for their actions to the people whom they lead.[8]

Inevitably, this proliferation of parliamentary opposition blocs and parties also began to push forward candidates with presidential aspirations of their own. As we recall, Nazarbaev was originally elected president for a five-year term, meaning that he would have had to stand for reelection by the end of 1996 at the latest. Continued economic decline and the general disenchantment which followed independence reduced Nazarbaev's popularity, until by early 1995 speculation began to surface that presidential elections might be held early, or even that Nazarbaev might not stand again.

A number of parliamentarians spoke openly of their plans to run against Nazarbaev. These included Serik Abdrakhmanov, a former Komsomol leader turned ecologist and the first head of SNEK (the presidential political party); Olzhas Suleimenov, a poet and folk hero who was head of the Congress Party (and who was also trying to take over the Respublika opposition); S. Abildin, who had been speaker of the 1990–93 parliament and who became head of the Socialist Party; and Gazziz Aldamzhanov, also of the socialists, who had made a bid to become speaker of the new parliament (the bid failed but was sufficiently strong to keep the post from K. Sultanov, head of SNEK, who was Nazarbaev's original choice). Although a presidential election, had it been held, would almost certainly have been closely controlled by the incumbent, even manipulated, this abundance of skilled opponents would have meant at the very least that Nazarbaev would have had to campaign hard for a second term.

The Constitutional Court and the presidency

In fairness to Nazarbaev and his advisers, it must be pointed out that there is ample evidence that the Constitutional Court may have acted entirely on its own initiative in 1995 when it chose, in effect, to close parliament. There is little question that the original case had merit; not only were there wide discrepancies in the size of the legislative districts, and so in the number of voters that each deputy would represent, but voters were asked to cross out the names of candidates whom they did not want, which allowed vote counters to interpret a single ballot as having been cast for many people at once if a voter had not followed instructions. The result, in many districts, was that more votes were cast than there were voters.

Perhaps more important, the Constitutional Court was at the time involved in a bureaucratic fight for its own existence. Until the adoption of the 1995 constitution, Kazakstan had three "supreme courts" – the Constitutional Court, the State Arbitrage Court, and the Supreme Court – which employed a total of sixty-six judges. Of the three, the Constitutional Court was widely regarded as the most expensive and least effective, as well as the most poorly administered. Arrears for services had become so large that in late November 1994 the court had its telephone service cut off and its automobiles revoked for two weeks. In spite of these financial problems, the eleven justices of the court had taken thirty-five trips abroad at state expense since 1993, including two trips to France made by Chief Justice Baimakhanov, and another trip to the United States on which Baimakhanov and his deputy, Amanzhol Nurmagam-betov, substituted themselves for lesser deputies at the last moment. Nurmagambetov later went to Moscow for a year's legal study, while remaining on the state payroll.[9] Furthermore, two of the judges, Udartsev and Malinovskii, were the subjects of recall attempts for actions they had taken against student demonstrators in the aftermath of the December 1986 Alma-Ata riots, when they were, respectively, dean of the Kazak

University Law Faculty and assistant head of that faculty's party committee.[10] In addition, the court moved extraordinarily slowly, rendering no decisions at all in the first ten months of 1994.[11]

The powers of the Constitutional Court were accordingly under steady attack. In mid-1993, Kazakstan's earlier parliament had taken from the court the right to institute legal proceedings on its own or to question presidential, parliamentary, or presidium decrees, and had attempted unsuccessfully to cut the court's support staff. That effort was finally successful in November 1994, when staffing and funding were both reduced.

There was also growing demand in parliament and in some parts of the government to do away with the court entirely, creating instead a single supreme court on the model of that in the United States. The most vocal advocate of this approach was Minister of Justice Shaikenov, who was simultaneously pushing for a fundamental revision of the republic's constitution. As long as the president enjoyed full power of judicial appointment, with no public airing of the way in which candidates for top judicial positions were selected, Shaikenov argued, it would be impossible to create a genuinely independent judiciary in the republic.[12] In fact, the 1995 constitution did abolish the Constitutional Court, replacing it with a Constitutional Council of six members; two are appointed by each chamber of parliament, and two by the president.

The Constitutional Court itself was also deeply divided, with the judges split into various warring factions, over which Chief Justice Baimakhanov had little control. Indeed, Baimakhanov was described as an intellectual but ineffectual man who long ago had ceded effective administration of the court to his secretary, Igor Rogov.

Cui bono?

Whether the inception of direct presidential rule in Kazakstan was planned or contingent (on this question see chapter 8), public opinion in the republic accepted its imposition with little objection. This was in part because the issues to which parliament had paid the greatest attention while in session, and immediately after its dissolution, were questions of the members' own emoluments and benefits. International public opinion voiced a few token objections, such as US Secretary of Defense William Perry's warning to Nazarbaev that failure to hold timely elections would be regarded with disfavor (apparently contradicting the approval which the US ambassador had earlier expressed for parliament's annulment). The world financial community, however, seemed to welcome the annulment of parliament. The International Monetary Fund, which had long complained of the republic's failure to institute and promulgate foreign investment laws, applauded Nazarbaev's actions, and promised to release a pending tranche of loans, presumably because laws favorable to foreign investment became easier to establish with both parliament and presidential elections out of the way.

Indeed, given that Turkmenistan's President Niiazov and Uzbekistan's President Karimov also "submitted to the will of their people" by agreeing to remain head of their respective nations until the next millennium, long-term presidential rule appears to be the future norm for Central Asia. After Nazarbaev's extension of his term of office, President Akaev of Kyrgyzstan also flirted with the idea of postponing presidential elections, until dissuaded by a loud chorus of foreign disapproval from his donor nations.

In Kazakstan the imposition of direct presidential rule seemed to bring several immediate advantages. As suggested above, politics in the republic had become fragmented, with a number of blocs and coalitions beginning to attract considerable public followings, and their leaders to emerge as credible political rivals to Nazarbaev.

Significantly, perhaps, Nazarbaev has been unsuccessful in gaining widespread support for a "presidential party" which might serve as the functional successor to the Communist Party, imposing discipline on junior members as it trained them for senior positions. Nazarbaev lost control of his first two attempts at aligning with parties, the Socialists and the People's Congress Party (NKK). Under the leadership of one-time Nazarbaev ally Olzhas Suleimenov, the latter particularly became a backbone of the parliamentary Respublika opposition. A third party, SNEK, has proven marginally more successful in that it remains identified as Nazarbaev's party. But even with considerable government help, SNEK failed to produce enough deputies to allow Nazarbaev to control the parliament. Closing parliament and postponing presidential elections not only reduced the viability of Nazarbaev's rivals and their parties but also may have given SNEK and its new allies, such as the entrepreneurial party For Kazakstan's Future, the opportunity to develop into stronger entities.

Closing parliament also obviated that body's growing encroachments on what Nazarbaev views as executive prerogative. While being notably unproductive itself – the body passed only seven laws in its year of existence – parliament had managed to impede the progress of privatization, including stopping further distribution of vouchers. What may have seemed worse, at least from the presidential point of view, was that parliament was supported in its opposition to privatization by the republic's procurator and the State Arbitration Court. Further, in January

1995, parliament had put forward its own proposed New Economic Policy, which would have slowed the pace of privatization, overhauled the tax structure, and given pronounced preference to local producers, rather than to foreign investors or trading companies. At the end of 1994 parliament even attempted to censure the Cabinet of Ministers for its faulty execution of the state budget (including steep arrears on wages and pensions), and to assume oversight for future dispensation of funds. Parliamentary commissions were also preparing to publish and turn over to the procurator the findings of investigations into the activities of the Economic Transformation Fund that Tereshchenko and his fellow discredited ministers had established after their resignation. This fund, it was alleged, had taken over funds that had been appropriated for other uses (including considerable funds that were diverted to help build Nazarbaev's vast new presidential palace).

Presidential rule and the Russians

In the short run, imposition of direct presidential rule in Kazakstan in 1995, and of all but direct presidential rule which has emerged since an extremely weak bi-cameral parliament began operation, is likely to reduce some of the various ethnic and economic tensions within the republic. The ethnic constituency most affected by the strengthening of the presidency is that of the Russians, both within the republic and in Russia proper. Stability in Kazakstan is overwhelmingly shaped by developments in the Russian Federation, even more so if Russia returns to a more reintegrationist policy. Kazakstan's vulnerability to Russian political and economic intervention (to say nothing of military) is so great that it must be assumed that Russian interests, national and ethnic, played a considerable part in Nazarbaev's calculations. The fact that Russia voiced no objection to Nazarbaev's retreat from democracy suggests, at the least, that authorities in Moscow did not find it either a surprise or a negative development.

Although Kazakstan has always been mindful of the wishes of its northern neighbor, under Prime Minister Kazhegeldin the two republics have grown even more interdependent economically. Kozykorpesh Esenberlin, president of the State Property Commission under Prime Minister Tereshchenko, had conducted privatization in a way that favored the large voucher holding companies that are, as noted, Kazak dominated. By contrast, his replacement under Kazhegeldin, Sarybai Kalmurzaev, not only began to permit privatization auctions to be held for cash (including rubles), as well as for vouchers, but also began the practice of giving Russia rights of first refusal for large industrial plants, especially those which had been of military significance in the Soviet era. Kalmurzaev also favored raising the stake that investment funds might take in enterprises from one-fifth to one-third.

The Kazhegeldin government, unlike the virtually all-Kazak Tereshchenko government, returned the key Finance Ministry to a Russian, Aleksandr Pavlov, and gave the Economics Ministry to Altai Tleuberdin, a Middle Horde Kazak from the Russified north. Two first deputy prime ministers were appointed, one Kazak and the other Russian; the Russian, Vitali Mette, was however removed from office in March 1996.

Nazarbaev used his period of direct presidential rule to increase the linguistic and cultural rights of the republic's Russians. Nazarbaev is likely to remain firm in rejecting the formal dual citizenship that Russian leaders demand, and a treaty he and President Yeltsin signed in late January 1995 all but obviated the question. The treaty allows citizens of the two countries to own property in either republic, to move freely between them, to sign contracts (including for military service), and, if requested, to exchange one citizenship for the other.

Nazarbaev also has had to backpedal on the language issue. His Navruz speech to the People's Assembly concluded with the observation that there was no need for adult Russians to have to learn Kazak, but that all Kazaks must learn Russian. Still, a draft law in 1997 set 2006 as the year Russians in government had to know Kazak.

The impact of Nazarbaev's presidency on the Russians can also be gauged by examining local government. The Constitutional Court and President Nazarbaev both made it immediately clear that the 6 March 1995 decision applied only to the national parliamentary elections, not to the elections to various local representative councils which began in 1994. Despite strenuous efforts by the central government to control the results, the new councils began inevitably to represent the interests and demands of the populations that elected them.

The issues that confront local councils vary by region, but the overall effect is, in the opinion of one journalist, that the oblast structures were already moving out from under the authority of the presidentially appointed hakims.[13] These presidential representatives were temporarily strengthened by the imposition of presidential rule, but there was no letup in the demands of certain oblasts, particularly those in the Russian north, to make the post of hakim elective rather than appointive. If this were to occur (and Nazarbaev announced before the dissolution that he would consider it), the result would be to increase the power of regional political authorities and to lessen central authority, including that of the president. However, the new constitution provides only that the local maslikhats can express no confidence (by a two-thirds vote) in the hakims. As noted, the president also has the power to override or revoke decisions taken by the maslikhats, while the hakims will have the power to control budgetary decisions taken by the local councils, suggesting that the power of the local bodies over their immediate administrators is at best only slightly enhanced under the new constitution. However, election results for the new parliament suggested that the Russian-dominated regions of northern and eastern Kazakstan remained unhappy with Almaty's policies. Non-government candidates each won one seat for Semipalatinsk and Kokchetau oblasts, while the other two seats for each remained unfilled. In East Kazakstan, where Nazarbaev attempted to impose a Kazak administration on a district which is more than 80 percent Russian, two of the four representatives elected were independents, rather than government candidates.[14]

Should the northern and eastern oblasts continue their demands for greater autonomy, it may be that the local councils could be dissolved as was the national parliament. Although the voting districts for those council seats were different from those for parliamentary elections, the method of voting (crossing out unwanted candidates) was the same. However, the many concessions that Nazarbaev made to Russian interests in his handling of parliament and his appointment of an interim government suggest that he would be unlikely to attempt to rein in the councils of the northern regions, or to be successful if he were to try.

If the northern councils were permitted greater powers, it seems inevitable that the southern, Kazak-dominated councils would also claim them. That would present Nazarbaev with the dilemma of whether to permit the further dilution of his power, or to crack down on the Kazaks for claiming freedoms given to the Russians.

Even without that dilemma, however, Nazarbaev seems certain to face opposition from his own people if concessions to the republic's Russians continue. If the constitution is amended to permit two official languages or to permit dual citizenship, the Kazaks will feel they have lost their hard-won privileged status. It is difficult to predict what form opposition would then take, since, as noted, the Kazaks are seriously divided by clan and family differences, as a result of which some of them share more interests with the Russians than they do with their ethnic fellows. The Kazaks also have no alternative institutions which could transmit their political will; despite a wave of mosque building since independence, Islam is not well established in much of the republic and certainly has no republic-wide network through which it might mobilize disaffected Kazaks.

The gamble that Nazarbaev has undertaken in imposing presidential rule is that it may permit him to transform the republic's economy and buy off the opposition, producing widespread improvement of living standards. Certainly the republic has the natural resources and industrial potential to make that a credible wager.

At the same time, however, Kazakstan faces enormous obstacles before it realizes its potential, or even returns to the relatively threadbare beginnings from which most citizens have tumbled since independence. Deconstructing the old Soviet economy is a challenge everywhere in the former USSR, but defining an economic existence independent of Russia is proving a special challenge in resource-rich Kazakstan, where the republic's vast natural wealth particularly fosters Russia's claims to rights of special privilege.

Russia is capable of taking advantage of Kazakstan's geographic isolation to use control of transit routes as an effective tool of both political and economic control. The Russian government is able to starve the Kazak government into submission, because if Kazakstan cannot realize a profit from its fossil fuel over the next five years, it will have no choice but to become a *de facto* dependency of Russia.

Over the next several years Russia is certain to continue to elaborate its distinction between "inner" and "outer" former Soviet republics, with the Kazaks clearly falling within the "inner" group. Foreign economic relations of the "inner" group of states will probably become more closely integrated, along the lines of the Russia-Belarus-Kyrgyzstan-Kazakstan customs union under discussion. Of course, should Russia prosper economically and make firm, irreversible steps toward becoming a democratic state, then the chances of Kazakstan not only surviving but becoming more democratic will be substantially enhanced.

A democratic Russia, were it to come about, would create an incentive for the Kazaks to promote democracy on their side of the border, particularly if Kazakstan also succeeds in gaining full control of its own resources and economy. However, in the absence of external pressure, Kazakstan's current elites are unlikely to become strong advocates of democracy.

Presidential power and Kazakstan's future

No president of Kazakstan will ever enjoy the advantages of ethnic homogeneity, economic prosperity, and distance from Russia that could contribute significantly to democratization in the country. In addition, it is clear that Nazarbaev was not an instinctive democrat. His long years of service in the Soviet hierarchies of the Communist Party and Kazakstan's Council of Ministers predisposed him to adopt a managerial approach to governing. Under this model, it was the responsibility of the authorities to provide a large array of services to the population in return for its submissiveness to central authority. Such a mindset was not surprising for a political leader who had spent his entire life in a one-party system. Nazarbaev understood the vacuum created by the collapse of the Communist Party of the Soviet Union in 1991 in Soviet terms. He remained convinced at that time that society could be changed through a model of social engineering that was designed by the government and that filtered through society from the top down.

On the other hand, Nazarbaev took the rhetoric of the late Gorbachev period about creating the rule of law seriously. In the aftermath of the unsuccessful August 1991 coup in Moscow, he joined the Union-wide rush to ban the Communist Party. But almost immediately he undertook to create a structural successor for it. As discussed earlier, the search for a presidential party took Nazarbaev from the Socialist Party to the People's Congress Party (built on the highly successful Nevada–Semipalatinsk anti-nuclear movement), to the SNEK. This fact is itself salient to an understanding of Nazarbaev's conception of the presidency. Unlike the presidents of his Central Asian neighbors, Uzbekistan and Turkmenistan, Nazarbaev did not exhibit a marked tendency to enlarge his power for its own sake nor to establish a personalistic system. Although Kazakstan in the mid-1990s came to display many features of one-man rule, Nazarbaev attempted to institutionalize his bases of power. His presidential style was, where necessary, to use veiled threats rather than direct force or intimidation – a rare quality in the post-Soviet environment.

If Kazakstan was not situated in such a vulnerable geopolitical position, there would be good grounds for supposing that the first shoots of genuine political pluralism (such as the nascent multiparty system and the assertive 1994–95 parliament) might well flourish in the republic. Although he was frustrated by what he viewed as the messy processes of democracy, Nazarbaev resisted the temptation to squash these structures (though, as noted at the outset, there are some who see Nazarbaev's hand behind the March 1995 Constitutional Court decision dissolving parliament).

As an economic reformer, Nazarbaev was equally cautious. In the first year after independence he showed a fundamental distrust of the private sector. His own training as a Soviet-era manager inclined him to regard management of the most important industrial and agricultural enterprises as a government responsibility. But by degrees Nazarbaev expanded his understanding of the advantages of a market economy, and he announced an ambitious privatization program in 1993. As criticism of economic reforms increased, the president insisted on staying the course until the end of 1995, regardless of public support for them or not.

Indeed Nazarbaev's economic record may ultimately determine

whether the institution of the presidency is viewed in positive or negative terms. In addition, a strong presidency may be less necessary or desirable in conditions where economic growth has been spurred and sustained.

If economic reform in Kazakstan can stimulate the development of a middle class, then Kazakstan will develop into a more democratic state than it is today. The next president might then be chosen in a competitive, or at least quasi-competitive election, the legislature might evolve to serve as a partial check on the executive branch (as would the judiciary), and local governments might come to share executive and legislative authority with the national government.

Barring unusual changes in national direction, however, the more likely course for Kazakstan seems to be the continued ossification of the existing political order, in which constitutional democracy will come increasingly to resemble the legal fiction that it is now in Uzbekistan or Turkmenistan. Closing of the 1994–95 parliament and the use of referenda rather than elections to fashion an ever-weaker parliament are symptomatic of a growing tendency not only in Kazakstan, but across the entire region, to regard the present elites as the only ones which can be trusted to govern. Faced with the realities of how difficult the transition to independence can be, Nazarbaev and his advisors appear to be falling back increasingly on the political instincts formed during their careers in the Brezhnev, Andropov, and Chernenko eras. The ideal of reform has taken on a life separate from that of the society which Nazarbaev and his men are nominally trying to reform, and the people of Kazakstan, who are supposed to benefit from the reform process, have instead become identified as its enemy.

Ethnic Kazaks are likely to enjoy, and even increase, their present disproportionate share of political power, while ethnic Russians may hope for limited local autonomy (in the Russian-dominated oblasts of the north), with only minimal political representation at the national level. This balance of political power is likely to be hastened by a slow but continuous emigration of Russians out of Kazakstan, which will probably leave the Kazaks an absolute majority in the republic within a generation or less.

Until that occurs, however, Kazakstan remains two ethnic entities bound within a single border, each of which tends to see the gain of the other as its own loss. For all its balkiness and imperfections, Kazakstan's 1994–95 parliament emerged as a genuine partner in the process of economic and political transformation in Kazakstan. Whatever frustrations that partnership may have caused President Nazarbaev, it had offered him an institution and other political leaders with whom he could share responsibility for painful radical policies. By taking upon his office the entire burden of government after March 1995, Nazarbaev gave both of Kazakstan's ethnic groups, and all the republic's dissatisfied citizens, a target upon which they could focus their opposition – the failings of the president himself. As many political scientists have concluded, this is the most serious disadvantage of a strong presidential system.

NOTES

1 *Literaturnaia gazeta*, 16 March 1994, pp. 1–2, as reported in *Daily Reports. Central Eurasia*, FBIS-USR-94-031, 30 March 1994, p. 104.
2 *OMRI Report*, 2 May 1995.
3 *Nezavisimaia gazeta*, 2 April 1994, p. 3.
4 Ibid.
5 The bills defined a minimum consumer budget and a minimum wage. In both instances the parliament objected that the president's figures were far too low. *Panorama*, 30 July 1994, p. 11, as reported in *Daily Reports. Central Eurasia*, FBIS-USR-94-086, 9 August 1994, p. 102.
6 *Interfax* 16 September 1994, as reported in *Daily Reports. Central Eurasia*, FBIS-SOV-94-181, 19 September 1994, p. 59.
7 *Izvestiia*, 12 May 1994, p. 4.
8 *Sovety Kazakhstana*, 2 November 1994, pp. 1–2, as reported in *Daily Reports. Central Eurasia*, FBIS-USR-94-124, 15 November 1994, p. 87.
9 *Ekspress*, 1 November 1994, p. 1.
10 *ABV*, 21 January 1994, p. 2.
11 *Ekspress*, 1 November 1994, pp. 1, 3.
12 *Nezavisimaia Gazeta*, 24 November 1994, p. 3, as reported in *Daily Reports. Central Asia*, FBIS-USR-94-137, 20 December 1994, pp. 89–90.
13 *Ekspress K*, 4 November 1994, p. 5, as reported in *Daily Reports, Central Eurasia*, FBIS-USR-94-125, 15 November 1994, pp. 92.
14 *OMRI Report*, 22 December 1995.

5 Poland: Wałęsa's legacy to the presidency

Krzysztof Jasiewicz

Jestem niezależny, samorządny, i nazywam się prezydent.
(I am independent, self-governed, and my name is President)
Lech Wałęsa to reporters on 27 September 1994

From Piłsudski to Wałęsa

Since Poland regained its independence in 1918, each Polish constitution was tailored for the man who would be president: sometimes to suit him well, sometimes to create a corset limiting his freedom of movement and the scope of his powers.[1] The so-called March Constitution of 1921 was drafted by a fragmented parliament to prevent Marshal Józef Piłsudski (from 1918 to 1921 the head of state, or *Naczelnik Państwa*, and an obvious choice for president) from assuming too much power. In turn, Piłsudski refused to declare his candidacy for president, not satisfied with the scope of presidential powers. In 1926 he organized a military coup against what he mockingly called "sejmocracy," and became a *de facto* dictator of Poland. But not a president: formally elected by the National Assembly in 1926, he declined to accept this honor, maintaining a low profile – and assuming almost unchecked executive power, as minister of military affairs, and, occasionally, prime minister. His lieutenants drafted a new constitution, but the opposition in parliament was strong enough to block its passage until 1935. When the so-called April Constitution was finally accepted, Piłsudski was already on his deathbed. Ignacy Mościcki, president since 1926, was reelected; he received the powers designed for Piłsudski, but lacking Piłsudski's leadership and charisma was never able to use them effectively to the benefit of the country.

Lech Wałęsa, the former chairman of the independent, self-governing trade union, Solidarity, and Polish president from 1990 to 1995, didn't mind being compared to Piłsudski. One of the posters used in his 1990 electoral campaign carried a picture of Wałęsa styled after a well-known photograph of Piłsudski. Not surprisingly, Wałęsa's supporters saw him as the leader of a successful quest to regain the nation's independence – just as Piłsudski's supporters once saw him as a father of the country. Wałęsa's critics, on the other hand, believed that the comparison should end where it began: with the similarity of their moustaches. But Wałęsa did become president, a position that eluded Piłsudski, either by fate or design. In spite of this success, however, Wałęsa faced many challenges remarkably similar to those confronted by Piłsudski.

The communist-led government after World War II pronounced the April Constitution of 1935 invalid on the basis of a technicality. The 1921 March Constitution was in effect until 1947, when the Sejm adopted a constitutional provisorium, known as the "small constitution," and chose the leader of the communists, Bolesław Bierut, as president. But these were the times of *Il Principe Nuovo*, when the official ideology promoted the collective over the individual. The new 1952 constitution abolished the presidency and replaced it with the State Council. This collective presidency, along with the parliament (the Sejm) and the cabinet (the Council of Ministers), was a mere window-dressing extension of the real center of executive, legislative, and judicial powers – the Communist Party, with its Politburo and first secretary.

In 1989 party rule came to an end. The so-called Roundtable Accords, negotiated by the communist regime and the Solidarity-led opposition, outlined in great detail a power-sharing scheme for the years to come. Several constitutional amendments, necessary for the accords to work, were accepted by the Sejm on 7 April 1989. Designed to establish a system of checks and balances, these amendments protected each of the signatories from being outmaneuvered during the transitional power-sharing period. The two most important amendments led to the reestablishment of the presidency and of the Senate – the upper chamber of parliament. The reasons for these changes were both symbolic and political. On the symbolic level they represented a break with the insufficiently legitimized institutional framework of a communist party-state, while establishing continuity with the institutions of the precommunist political order. The political reasons were, however, more important. In the context of electoral arrangements for the Sejm (which guaranteed the communists and their allies a 65 percent share of the seats), the freely elected Senate would give the entire arrangement more legitimacy and enhance the balancing power of the democratic opposition (should it, as expected, win the election). In contrast, the president – to be elected by the National Assembly for a six-year term, exceeding by two years the tenure of the parliament – would come from the ranks of the communists, thereby preserving their balancing power and providing the whole arrangement with a specific legitimacy aimed at Poland's Warsaw Pact allies (at a time when the Brezhnev doctrine was not yet pronounced dead). The obvious choice for president was General Wojciech Jaruzelski, since 1981 the undisputed leader of the communist government. The specific powers of the presidency were designed to fit both Jaruzelski's role as a guarantor of continuity in Poland's foreign and military policies, and his personal preference for being an arbiter rather than the chief of the executive branch.² After some turbulence caused by the magnitude of Solidarity's victory in the June 1989 parliamentary elections (it swept all but one of the seats it contested in both chambers), Jaruzelski eventually became president. He wore this custom-tailored suit for a year and a half, admittedly with some style. But then the presidency passed to a man of quite a different posture and background; a man with different ambitions and a different vision of the presidency.

In mid-1990, Lech Wałęsa, the man who had led Solidarity through the best and the worst of its times, a statesman of international stature and Nobel Peace Prize laureate, was still just the chairman of a trade union. In 1989 he neither ran for parliament nor contested Jaruzelski for the presidency, assuming that for the period 1989–93 Poland would be at best a "35 percent democracy," and that he would be most comfortable and influential as the leader of a powerful trade union, having no constitutional powers or responsibilities (and no accountability). But only a year after the historic 1989 elections this position was increasingly marginalized. Power had shifted not only from the communists to Solidarity, but also, within Solidarity, from the leadership of the trade union to its representation in government and parliament. Knowing that he had played a crucial role in the downfall of communism and the rise of democracy, and clearly not content to fall into obscurity, Wałęsa decided to step in and force Jaruzelski out of office. Most of his former associates and advisors, Prime Minister Tadeusz Mazowiecki among them, opposed this decision. They felt that a vicious political campaign would destroy the fragile balance of power in Poland and erase the first achievements of the economic reforms that had been enacted. They also believed that things should be done in reverse order: first a new constitution drafted by the "contractual" parliament and subjected to a referendum, then parliamentary elections, and finally presidential elections. Wałęsa had no wish to wait that long. He and his camp decided to channel the growing popular discontent with austerity measures against the residua of the old system and against the Mazowiecki government, which was allegedly too slow in implementing reforms. Mazowiecki, reluctantly, decided to run against Wałęsa.

The idea of electing the president by a popular vote rather than by a vote of the National Assembly originated in Mazowiecki's camp. Although Mazowiecki's public opinion ratings were still quite high, Wałęsa and his supporters realized that the prime minister's popularity was fading and consequently accepted the challenge. A potential constitutional crisis was avoided when Jaruzelski – too proud merely to step down – submitted to the parliament a constitutional amendment, which in essence ended his term prematurely on the grounds that a change in the mode of presidential election had been proposed. The amendment was accepted by the Sejm on 7 September 1990, and the first presidential election by direct universal suffrage in Poland's history took place on 25 November (first round) and 9 December (runoff) 1990.

The 1990 election and its consequences

The vote was subsequently burdened with the dysfunctional consequences pointed out by Juan Linz[3] as typical for a two-round majority election by universal suffrage. The most conspicuous was, of course, the strong showing of a virtually unknown outsider, Stanisław Tymiński. With 23.1 percent of the popular vote, he managed to finish second to Wałęsa, and to eliminate Mazowiecki from the run-off. But the institutional design can only partially be blamed for the "Tymiński surprise." Since 1990 similar – *toutes proportions gardées* – candidates have entered electoral contests in the East and West: from Zhirinovsky to Lukashenka, from Perot to Berlusconi, from North (in Virginia) to Huffington (in California). The Berlusconi case seemed to indicate, for example, that parliamentary systems, contrary to Linz's assumption, are not immune to the "outsider[s] to the party system with no congressional base" syndrome.[4] Proliferation of Tymiński-like candidates in democracies with different institutional designs and political traditions may indicate more complex and more universal conditions characterized by an anti-establishment popular backlash.

Of the other dysfunctions outlined by Linz, one: "In a highly fragmented system the two leading candidates might enjoy only small pluralities with respect to the other candidates and might represent positions on the same segment of the political spectrum,"[5] clearly did not occur: the margins separating the leading candidates were substantial (Wałęsa 40 percent, Tymiński 23 percent, Mazowiecki 18 percent), and the two front runners represented polar opposites on the political playing field. But the following expectations presented by Linz were fully confirmed:[6]

(1) The majority that voted for Wałęsa did not represent a real coalition of parties or even a politically homogeneous electorate. Wałęsa's electorate, apart from an overrepresentation of less-educated and older voters, in general reflected the demographic and social heterogeneity of Polish society, along with the political diversification of the Solidarity movement. Shortly after the election, the camp of Wałęsa's supporters disintegrated politically, and gradually became alienated from the president himself.

(2) The winner, even if supported by only a plurality of the eligible

voters (in the first round 24 percent: 40 percent votes of the 60.6 percent turnout; in the run-off 39 percent: 73.4 percent votes of the 53.4 percent turnout), has apparently felt "that he represents 'a true and plebiscitary' majority."[7] This has led to numerous quarrels with parliament and other democratic institutions, as discussed below.

However, the last negative consequence pointed out by Linz,[8] a proliferation of candidates in the first round reinforcing the existing political fragmentation, did not occur in the 1990 election (though it did in the 1995 one). Only six candidates registered, and a partial explanation of this rather low number may be found in the relatively high threshold of citizens' support needed for registration (a requirement to collect 100,000 signatures on the petition to register a candidate). But, more importantly, those candidates did represent the major options viable in Polish politics. Thus, the 1990 presidential vote set in motion a process of crystallization and consolidation of the Polish political scene and party system. This process, with its ups and downs, and sharp turns to the left and to the right, continued through the 1991 and 1993 parliamentary elections, the 1994 municipal elections, and the 1995 presidential contest. While Wałęsa's constituency reflected, as already indicated, general demographic and social characteristics of Polish society, with a somewhat Christian-democratic ideological flavor, the constituencies of his defeated rivals had a better defined social and/or political profile: Mazowiecki's supporters represented a liberal-democratic orientation among the educated urban population; Bartoszcze's (the candidate of the PSL, Polish Peasant Party) – agrarian populism; Cimoszewicz's (the candidate endorsed by the former communists) – socialist egalitarianism; and Tymiński's and Moczulski's – political populism[9] and an anti-system protest vote. The two major, crosscutting political cleavages were between those identifying with Solidarity and those unsympathetic to this movement, and between urban and rural populations.

In 1990, these differences were painted in broad brush strokes. They became much more evident in the 1991 (and, subsequently, 1993) parliamentary elections. In 1991, more than 100 parties and quasi-parties participated in the election, and more than 30 won at least one seat in one of the two houses. This plurality of parties must not be confused, as Dahl[10] and Sartori[11] warn, with genuine political pluralism. But the seeds of such pluralism were already in place. As several analysts[12] had anticipated, voting behavior was guided by four or five major political cleavages: political and economic liberalism versus populism, secularism versus religiosity, political authoritarianism versus democracy, Westernization versus nationalism, and (mostly for the constituencies of fringe parties) a stance for or against decommunization. The layout of these cleavages corresponds to the four-dimensional framework introduced by Sartori[13] for the analysis of party systems in advanced pluralist democracies, as well as to the classical Lipset and Rokkan hypothesis on political cleavages and nation-building in Western Europe.[14] Moreover, an examination of the first two of these cleavages, and the relative positions on them occupied by the constituencies of relevant (in a Sartorian sense)[15] parties in the 1991 and 1993 elections, allows one to identify four major political options viable in Polish politics: liberal-democratic, conservative-Christian democratic, socialist, and populist.[16] Surprising as it may seem, these options resemble the three major political orientations and traditions of political thought which have evolved in Western Europe since the early nineteenth century: liberalism, socialism, and conservatism, and subsequently the twentieth-century addition – populism. In addition, one can point out the existence of at least two other options: radical anti-system opposition (fragmented and highly diversified ideologically: from the Beer Lovers to the libertarian Union of Real Politics to the proto-fascist Self-Defense and Tymiński's party X), and the "silent majority" – those who voluntarily disfranchised themselves and refused to participate in the elections (in 1991, 57 percent, in 1993, 48 percent, in the 1994 municipal elections 66 percent, and in 1995 35 percent of eligible voters).

On the other hand, the process of consolidating the four major options since 1991 has advanced not only on the mass (electorate) level but on the elite level as well. In the 1993 election, the socialist and populist options were represented by one party each (Democratic Left Alliance, SLD, and Polish Peasant Party, PSL, respectively). Since the election, the two parties representing the liberal-democratic option (Democratic Union and Liberal Democratic Congress) have merged, assuming the name of Freedom Union. Even the notoriously fragmented Christian-conservative right managed to form several successful local coalitions in the 1994 municipal elections, and three nation-wide alliances. As a result, in many Polish localities the classical left–center–right political continuum reemerged.

Thus, the 1990 presidential vote established a basis for the development of relatively stable and well-defined political alignments, with the major political options traceable to the candidates participating in the first round. This development occurred despite the repolarization of the political scene in the second round in 1990 (with the old Solidarity camp rallying behind Wałęsa, and the anti-Solidarity forces supporting Tymiński), and despite the subsequent fragmentation of the party system.

Round one: Wałęsa versus a postcommunist parliament

Once elected, Wałęsa, regardless of his actual support which was limited to no more than 40 percent of the eligible electorate, acquired a position of superiority *vis-à-vis* parliament. His legitimacy stemmed from an unquestionably democratic election, while the lower and, according to the constitution, politically more important chamber, the Sejm, was elected in an only "35 percent democratic" vote, with 34 percent of the seats reserved in advance for the communists, and an additional 31 percent for their allies. The Sejm, without hesitation, accepted Wałęsa's choice for the new prime minister, a relatively unknown man from Gdańsk and a leader of the minuscule Liberal-Democratic Congress, Jan Krzysztof Bielecki. Wałęsa seemed to understand that the limited democratic legitimacy of the Sejm would allow him to make liberal use of the constitutional powers he had inherited from Jaruzelski. The position of president was defined in Article 32 of the constitution (as amended in April 1989, December 1989, and September 1990) as follows: "The President of the Polish Republic is the supreme representative of the Polish State in internal and external relations." The president "safeguards the observance of the Constitution of the Polish Republic and defends the sovereignty and security of the State, the inviolability and integrity of its territory, as well as the observance of international political and military alliances." The constitution also made him the commander-in-chief of the armed forces and the chairman of the National Defense Committee. The president's specific powers included: the right to initiate legislation; to veto legislation passed by parliament (but no line item veto); to remit laws for a review of their constitutionality by the Constitutional Tribunal (should his veto be overridden by a 2/3 majority in the Sejm); to designate the prime minister, the president of the National Bank, and the chief justice of the Supreme Court, for a final nomination by the Sejm; to appoint judges; to convene the Council of Ministers and preside over its sessions; to impose – under specified conditions – martial law or a state of emergency; to dissolve the parliament, if: (1) the Sejm was unable to nominate the prime minister and his cabinet in three months; (2) the Sejm was not able to approve the budget within three months of its submission; (3) the Sejm accepted an act preventing the president from performing his functions as the guarantor of Poland's international obligations.[17]

The last of these prerogatives, once again emphasizing the above-mentioned president's responsibility for control over the observance of international political and military alliances, was a specific legal safeguard designed for Jaruzelski, should the parliament fall under the domination of anti-communists and begin to jeopardize Poland's relations with the

Soviet Union. Its intentionally vague wording gave the president substantial discretionary power. But this regulation, within a few months of its introduction, became obsolete. The East European revolutions, initiated by the Roundtable Accords and the June 1989 Polish elections, brought an end to the alliances and obligations this clause was designed to protect. Jaruzelski didn't have an opportunity to use it; Wałęsa didn't need it at all.

But Wałęsa wanted to expand his powers in other areas. The constitutional framework in force at the time of Wałęsa's election fitted the category of semi-presidentialism, as defined by Duverger,[18] or premier-presidentialism, as defined by Shugart and Carey almost perfectly.[19] The president was elected by popular vote and had considerable powers, but the executive functions were performed by the premier and his cabinet, nominated by the parliament and subject to its confidence. Wałęsa, a man of action, never felt comfortable in ceremonial roles. He always wanted the ability to intervene directly in government affairs, whenever necessary. In particular, he sought the right to nominate and dismiss state officials,[20] and wanted to have such rights guaranteed in the new constitution. As proven by the swift nomination of Bielecki to the premiership, Wałęsa, with his "legitimacy advantage" over the Sejm, did not need to feel directly threatened by parliament's actions. But parliament was in charge of drafting the new constitution. Wałęsa couldn't be sure that the former communists and their allies would give the president the powers he sought.

From the outset of his presidency, Wałęsa also faced another challenge. His electoral campaign was based on promises of "acceleration" – a rapid improvement in the standard of living for all Poles. In particular, the public expected a relaxation of the austerity measures imposed by the Mazowiecki government in accordance with the IMF and World Bank policy requirements. Bielecki, however, reappointed Leszek Balcerowicz, the architect of Poland's economic recovery plan, as minister of finance and deputy prime minister in charge of economic affairs. Both Bielecki and Balcerowicz opted in favor of continuing tight, anti-inflationary monetary policies. These policies were also endorsed – to the astonishment of many – by Wałęsa himself. Wałęsa's shift of position alienated many of his supporters, among voters as well as among political elites. Critical opinions were voiced even by the members of the president's Chancellery staff, including the chief of chancellery, Jarosław Kaczyński (the leader of the Center Alliance, and a major architect of Wałęsa's electoral victory). The apparent lack of consensus on economic policy fueled rivalry between the cabinet and the staff of the president's Chancellery. This rivalry came to an end in October 1991, when Wałęsa fired Kaczyński and several other staff members.

The growing frustration of the electorate was channeled by Wałęsa and his associates against the Sejm. Despite profound changes in its composition (as the Communist Party and, to a lesser extent, the Solidarity camp disintegrated) and in the attitudes of the incumbents, this Sejm, given its origin, had become an obvious anachronism by 1991. Nonetheless, those who portrayed the Sejm as the major force obstructing reforms seemed to exaggerate the argument. Pro-reform bills were generated by the house at a steady pace, which in the opinion of some was too slow considering the range of areas requiring new legislation, but which in the opinion of others was too fast considering the desired quality of legislative acts.

While there was a consensus that new parliamentary elections were necessary, there was nevertheless no agreement on when to hold them. The president, his staff, the Bielecki cabinet, and numerous political groupings not represented in parliament pressed for a May 1991 date; most of the parliamentary factions preferred a later, October 1991, date. The Sejm prevailed and the elections were set for October. Wałęsa could now put the full blame for stalling reform on the Sejm. He sought an open confrontation with the postcommunist parliament, and as the arena of this showdown he chose the debate over electoral legislation. A long and sometimes very emotional conflict ensued which included a presidential veto, subsequently overridden by the Sejm. Participants of this debate had their overt and covert agendas and often changed their positions. In general, the postcommunist majority in the Sejm, joined by some post-Solidarity groupings, was in favor of proportional representation (PR) while the president and major post-Solidarity parties advocated various mixed electoral systems. Eventually the postcommunist parliament prevailed once again and a PR system was adopted.

Round two: Wałęsa versus an anticommunist parliament

This was perhaps the outcome Wałęsa was really hoping for. Almost thirty political entities were represented in the Sejm, with the strongest party, the Democratic Union, led by Mazowiecki, controlling a mere 13.5 percent of the seats, and with no majority coalition of fewer than five parties being possible. A weak parliament, unable to generate and support a stable coalition government, and vulnerable to the criticism of public opinion, would have to yield to the president. If this was indeed the outcome Wałęsa desired and tried to stimulate by his tug-of-war with the old Sejm over the electoral law, he apparently overdid it. The deputies, very well aware of their vulnerability, were determined to prevent the president from assuming a dominating position at their expense. And the president did not have many allies in the Sejm either. While the postcommunist Democratic Left Alliance had been his traditional foe, new opponents emerged from the ranks of his former followers. In addition to Mazowiecki and his Democratic Union, some staunch supporters of Wałęsa's bid for president turned also into his critics. Most of them joined the Center Alliance. The coalition-building process was, under these circumstances, both slow and painful. At some point Wałęsa indicated that he himself might assume the duties of prime minister (Polish legal experts differed as to the constitutionality of such a decision) but clearly preferred Bielecki to remain at the post. This solution, however, was unacceptable to the leaders of several parties that opposed Bielecki's policies. In a surprise move, Wałęsa nominated Bronisław Geremek, the leader of the Democratic Union parliamentary faction, as prime minister, but after consultations with all major parties Geremek gave up his efforts to form a government. In the following weeks a minority coalition of five parties emerged, with Jan Olszewski of the Center Alliance as their choice for the premiership. This coalition could obtain the required absolute majority of votes in the Sejm. After prolonged hesitation, Wałęsa nominated Olszewski to the post of prime minister on 5 December, and the decision was accepted by the Sejm. Despite a defection of two of the five parties from the coalition, Olszewski's cabinet was eventually approved by the Sejm on 20 December, 1991.

The Olszewski cabinet, the self-proclaimed "first truly non-communist government in Poland since World War II," lasted only twenty-four weeks. Three facts are essential for understanding this brief tenure: (1) it was formed by parties that harshly criticized the austerity policies of the Mazowiecki and Bielecki governments during the electoral campaign; (2) it was formed by people who often had distinguished themselves in the anti-communist opposition, but were not elevated to prominent positions after Solidarity's rise to power; (3) while most of these people had associated themselves closely with Wałęsa and actively supported his bid for the presidency, in 1991 President Wałęsa rejected their services. Consequently, they initiated a series of conflicts with the president which proved to be fatal to them.

Shortly after assuming their offices, Olszewski and his ministers realized that the condition of the state treasury would not allow them to fulfill the economic promises they had made before the elections. In fact, the Olszewski government continued the economic policies of the two previous administrations and presented a state budget proposal closely resembling the one developed by Bielecki. In attempting to distinguish itself from its predecessors and to gain or maintain popular support, the Olszewski government launched a campaign of "decommunization." This campaign was aimed not only at the remnants of the communist *nomenklatura*, but also at the core parties and individuals of the two previous Solidarity-based governments who, between 1989 and 1992, allegedly tolerated or even supported former communists. The campaign took the form of a personnel purge, among others.

Particularly controversial were new personnel policies in the Ministry of Defense and in the armed forces, designed to initiate decommunization. The new minister of defense, Jan Parys, the first civilian minister of defense since World War II, forced two civilian vice-ministers out of the ministry, and sent several military commanders, including his ministerial predecessor, Admiral Piotr Kołodziejczyk, into early retirement. Parys did all of this without consulting the president, the nominal commander-in-chief. When these decisions were criticized by the president's aides, Parys responded with the accusation that the president's staff was obstructing decommunization of the armed forces. President Wałęsa himself expressed the opinion that all Polish top officers were recruited and trained under communism, and replacing one postcommunist general with another did not equal decommunization. Accusations were traded back and forth. Eventually, in April, Parys implied that the president was conspiring with some officers to prepare a military *coup d'état*. Prime Minister Olszewski had no choice but to first send Parys on leave, and then to dismiss him.

The ill-conceived decommunization scheme and the antagonistic relationship with the president did not strengthen the position of Olszewski's government (a minority one after all) in the parliament where the opposition began to regroup. Pro-Olszewski media accused several leaders of the opposition, as well as some people close to the president, of being "collaborators" and beneficiaries of various privileges under communism, or, worse still, informers for the communist secret police. In an atmosphere of growing hysteria, the Sejm in May obliged (in a form that arguably violated constitutional provisions) the minister of internal affairs to disclose the content of the SB (former secret police) files, thereby exposing the true informers and exonerating the falsely accused.

The decommunization strategy backfired. As Robespierre antagonized the Convention (and sealed his fate) by proclaiming that he knew who was corrupt while not giving any names, the internal affairs minister, Antoni Macierewicz, antagonized the Sejm by delivering lists with the names of individuals about whom the communist secret police kept records (and sometimes approached with an offer of collaboration), but not of individuals whose services for the SB were proven beyond reasonable doubt, or, at least, seemed reasonably likely. The lists, as state secrets, were never officially published, but, according to numerous leaks, several prominent leaders of the former anti-communist opposition, including veteran political prisoners, were among those implicated. One deputy, Kazimierz Świtoń, himself a veteran dissident, implied in a speech in the Sejm that even Wałęsa was on the list.

The Sejm reacted to all these accusations with anger and shame (after all, Macierewicz had acted to fulfill the Sejm's own resolution). Wałęsa moved for immediate dismissal of the government. Olszewski responded with a dramatic speech on live TV, equating the fall of his government with the return of communism. It was to no avail as, on 5 June 1992, the Sejm voted him out of office.

Enter Wałęsa. The president, who during Olszewski's tenure had remained isolated due both to his own antagonistic policies and Olszewski's efforts, now moved in to fill the leadership vacuum. In a surprise move, he proposed Waldemar Pawlak, the young leader of the Polish Peasant Party, as the new prime minister. On 6 June, the Sejm, still stunned by the "Macierewicz files" revelations, approved this candidature.

There are several possible explanations for Wałęsa's choice of Pawlak as "his" prime minister. The president could have hoped that the elevation of a young, inexperienced leader of a party still bearing the stigma of its pro-communist past would buy him Pawlak's unconditional loyalty and give him direct control over the day-to-day management of state affairs. Or perhaps Wałęsa hoped that the nomination of an outsider would serve as a sobering warning to the divided post-Solidarity elites. He could have seen also a need to involve the non-Solidarity forces in the governing process; to make them more responsible – and accountable – for the reforms.

No matter what the president's intentions were, his *protégé* failed to form a cabinet. On 2 July, Pawlak offered his resignation, but Wałęsa refused to accept it and threatened to use his "constitutional powers" (possibly calling new elections) if a compromise was not reached. This threat generated another round of negotiations among a broad group of post-Solidarity parties. In early July they overcame numerous ideological and political differences, and decided to form a coalition which would command a slight majority in the Sejm. Wałęsa, apparently surprised by the formation of a workable coalition and at its choice of premier, without much hesitation withdrew his endorsement of Pawlak and nominated Hanna Suchocka of the Democratic Union as prime minister.

The interim constitution

The Sejm, thus far busy with cabinet formations and dismissals, now could finally move on to other vital state affairs. There was a consensus that some constitutional matters, specifically the relationship between the executive and the legislative branches of government, had to be regulated in a new way. Deputies were pressed by two conflicting considerations. On the one hand, the misfortunes of the Olszewski administration and the pains of the coalition-building processes convinced the deputies that there was a need to create an institutional framework that would allow for the formation of a strong, stable executive (cabinet), even within the context of a fragmented parliament. On the other hand, having experienced Wałęsa's formidable efficiency during crisis situations, and being aware of his ambitions, the deputies wanted to specify (and limit) the conditions under which the president could exercise his authority over the cabinet and directly or indirectly influence the processes of legislation and cabinet formation. Since work on the drafting of a new constitution was not yet far enough advanced, the parliament chose to adopt an interim constitutional regulation.

On 17 October 1992 the Sejm adopted the Constitutional Act on the Mutual Relations Between the Legislative and Executive Institutions of the Republic of Poland and on Local Self-government. In principle, this Act abrogated the previous constitution, which had – despite many amendments, especially during the 1989–92 period – originated in the Stalinist era. In actuality, the abrogation of the old constitution had only symbolic significance because in content the amended constitution diverged substantially from the text of the original 1952 document.

The Constitutional Act of 1992 was intended as only a temporary act that regulated specific limited areas of the system of government. Accordingly the Act is known as "the small constitution" in Poland. This is a typical colloquial phrase with historical connotations. Twice before, in 1919 and 1947, temporary constitutional acts were proclaimed, each known as "the small constitution." The provisions of the current Act regulate the legislative branch (i.e., the bi-cameral parliament), the positions of the president of the republic and the Council of Ministers (i.e., the executive branch of the government), as well as relations between them. Furthermore, the Act regulates the system of local government. But it does not cover the judicial branch, nor does it regulate the area of civil rights.

Article 1 of this interim constitution outlines the separation of powers in the Republic:[21]

The state organs of legislative power shall be the Sejm and the Senate of the Republic of Poland, executive power shall be the president of the Republic of Poland and the Council of Ministers, and judicial power shall be independent courts.

The powers of the president are discussed in the third chapter. According to Article 28:

1. The president of the Republic of Poland shall be the supreme representative of the Polish state in internal and international relations.
2. The president shall ensure observance of the constitution, safeguard the sovereignty of the state, the inviolability and integrity of its territory, as well as upholding international treaties.

Article 29 stipulates election of the president by secret ballot in general, equal, and direct elections for a five year term. If none of the candidates gains an absolute majority in the first round, a run-off between two front-runners will take place in fourteen days. Article 31 states: "The president shall hold no other office and shall be neither deputy nor a senator" – an apparent response to Wałęsa's threat in November 1991 that he would assume the duties of prime minister.

Presidential powers include:

general supervision in the field of international relations with the power to appoint and recall ambassadors. This supervision is to be exercised "through the appropriate minister dealing with foreign affairs" (Article 32);

the power to ratify and denounce international treaties (Article 33);

general supervision in the area of external and internal state security (Article 34);

as the supreme commander of the armed forces of the Republic of Poland the president, in agreement with the minister of national defense, appoints and dismisses the chief of general staff of the Polish army, and, on the motion of the minister of national defense, other military commanders (Article 35);

the power to introduce martial law (Article 36) and a state of emergency (Article 37);

the right to summon meetings of the Council of Ministers and preside over them (Article 38);

the right to deliver an address to the Sejm or the Senate (Article 39);

the power to propose to the Sejm the appointment and the recall of the president of the National Bank of Poland (Article 40);

the power to grant and revoke Polish citizenship (Article 41);

the power to appoint judges, upon the motion of the National Council of the Judiciary (Article 42);

the power of pardon (Article 43);

the power to confer orders and decorations (Article 44);

the power to issue regulations and executive orders (Article 45). These acts, to be valid, must be countersigned by the prime minister or appropriate minister (Article 46), with thirteen exceptions from this requirement, such as dissolution of the Sejm, nomination of the prime minister and ministers, etc. (Article 47).

The president may "appoint ministers of state to represent him in the matters related to the exercise of his powers" (Article 48). He formulates the rules and regulations of his executive office, the Chancellory, and appoints and dismisses its chief officer. Some additional powers (for instance, the right to nominate three members of the National Broadcasting Council, and to choose its chairman) are granted to the president in the other constitutional provisions in force (the remnants of the 1952 constitution, as amended). Article 50 stipulates the conditions of impeachment:

1. The president may be held accountable for an infringement of the Constitution and the laws, as well as for committing an offence, only by indictment before the Tribunal of State.
2. An indictment may be brought against the president upon the resolution of the National Assembly [i.e., the Sejm and the Senate in a joint session – K.J.] carried by at least two-thirds majority vote of the total number of its members, on the motion of at least one-quarter of its total members.

The relations between the president and the legislature are outlined in the second chapter:

the president, under specified conditions, orders elections to the Sejm and Senate (Article 4), and summons the first sitting of the newly elected parliament (Articles 9 and 26);

the president has, along with the deputies (of the Sejm), the Senate, and the Council of Ministers, the right to introduce legislation (Article 15);

a statute adopted by the Sejm and the Senate is submitted to the president, who within 30 days signs it and orders its promulgation in the Journal of Laws of the Republic of Poland. He may "refuse to sign a statute and refer it to the Sejm for its reconsideration, giving reasons therefore." The president's veto may be overridden in the Sejm by a two-thirds majority vote. The president may, before signing a statute, refer it to the Constitutional Tribunal for an adjudication upon its conformity to the Constitution (Article 18);

the president has the right to order, with the consent of the Senate, a referendum. This right belongs also to the Sejm (Article 19);

he may dissolve the Sejm, if it fails to pass a budget within three months from submission by the Council of Ministers of a draft fulfilling the requirements of the budgetary law (Article 21);

should the Sejm give the Council of Ministers the right to issue regulations with the force of a statute, the president may refuse to sign such regulations (Article 23);

in the cases when the Sejm is not in session, the president may declare a state of war upon appropriate conditions (a military attack against the state, or an international obligation of joint defense) (Article 24).

The most subtle and complex are the regulations regarding the relationship between the two sub-branches of the executive, the president and the Council of Ministers (chapter 4). The procedure for the nomination of the prime minister and his cabinet is outlined in Articles 57 through 62:

1. The president shall nominate the prime minister, and on his motion the President shall appoint the Council of Ministers according to the composition proposed by the prime minister, within a period of 14 days following the first sitting of the Sejm or the acceptance of the resignation of the Council of Ministers. The appointment of the prime minister by the president shall be in conjunction with the appointment of the Council of Ministers.

2. The prime minister shall, within a period not longer than 14 days following appointment by the president, submit to the Sejm a program of activity of the Council of Ministers together with a motion requiring a vote of confidence. The Sejm shall pass a vote of confidence by an absolute majority vote[22] (Article 57).

In the event that the Council of Ministers has not been appointed pursuant to the provisions of Article 57, the Sejm shall choose the prime minister and a Council of Ministers composed as indicated by him, by an absolute majority vote within a period of 21 days. The president shall appoint a government chosen by such means and accept its oath of office (Article 58).

In the event that the Council of Ministers has not been appointed pursuant to the provisions of Article 58, the president shall appoint the prime minister, and on the motion of the prime minister, shall appoint the Council of Ministers pursuant to the provisions of Article 57, provided that the Sejm has passed the vote of confidence by majority vote (Article 59).

In the event that the Council of Ministers has not been appointed pursuant to the provisions of Article 59, the Sejm shall choose a prime minister and a Council of Ministers composed as indicated by him, by majority vote within a period of 21 days. The president shall appoint a government chosen by such means and accept its oath of office (Article 60).

In the event that a Council of Ministers has not been appointed pursuant to the provisions of Article 60, the president shall dissolve the Sejm or, within a period of

14 days, shall appoint the prime minister and the Council of Ministers for a period no longer than 6 months. In the event that the Sejm has not passed the vote of confidence in this government before the expiry of this period or has not passed a vote of nonconfidence pursuant to the provisions of Article 66, para. 4, the president shall dissolve the Sejm (Article 62).

This lengthy regulation reflects the major concern of the deputies who adopted it, namely: how to prevent a stalemate during the coalition building process – a stalemate within the parliament or between the parliament and the president. The Constitutional Act achieves this objective by oscillating the selection of the prime minister from the president to the Sejm and back to the president, by gradually decreasing the threshold of votes in the Sejm necessary to pass the vote of confidence, and finally by giving the president the ultimate "tie-breaking" power. Altogether, the Act assigns to the president a substantial, and possibly critical role in the process of cabinet formation. The electoral law reform passed in May 1993, in particular its threshold clause for representation in the Sejm (5 percent for parties, 8 percent for coalitions), was designed to serve the same purposes.

The other major consideration of the law-makers was how to assure the stability of a government, once the prime minister and his cabinet were nominated and approved. The 1992 Act provides several safeguards against instability. Article 66 introduces the practice of a constructive vote of non-confidence. The article establishes an interval of time between the motion and the actual vote (seven days), and, should the motion be defeated, another three month interval between this vote and a subsequent motion of no confidence. It also establishes the minimum number of deputies needed to present such a motion: 46 for the first motion; 115 for a subsequent motion (there are 460 deputies in the Sejm). The Sejm, having passed a vote of no confidence, may choose a new prime minister (and proceed further pursuant to the provisions of Article 58). If it fails to do so, the president has a choice of either accepting the resignation of the government (and proceeding further pursuant to the provisions of Article 57), or dissolving the Sejm and calling for new elections within three to four months. At first glance, these regulations seem to grant the president substantial powers and a dominant position over the Council of Ministers. In fact, however, the small constitution guards the cabinet against such domination. Once the prime minister and his cabinet are accepted by the Sejm, the president cannot move for a vote of no confidence, or remove the prime minister in any other way. The same is true about the individual ministers: the president appoints the ministers upon the prime minister's motion, and can dismiss them only upon such a motion (Article 68), or if the Sejm passed a vote of no confidence in an individual minister (Article 67). Only in the case of the three portfolios relevant to the president's role as guarantor of national security, and only regarding the appointment process, is the president given some special, even if vague, influence (Article 61: "The prime minister shall lay a motion to appoint the ministers of foreign affairs, national defense, and internal affairs after consultation with the president").

Nevertheless, the presidential powers, as delineated in the Constitutional Act, while not necessarily satisfying Wałęsa's expectations,[23] can still be viewed as substantial. James McGregor, in his innovative comparative analysis of presidential power in fourteen new East European democracies[24] classified Poland, along with Hungary, at the top of his ranking of the relative constitutional power scores of East European presidents. But the Hungarian presidency, McGregor acknowledged, is usually viewed as a weak one, in contrast to the Polish, Croatian, or Romanian presidency. This seems to prove the old truth that constitutional powers notwithstanding, the actual role of the president is very much defined by the personality and actions of the incumbent. So while Hungarian president, Arpad Göncz, tended to maintain a low profile, Wałęsa felt uncomfortable if left far from the madding political crowd.

The system established by the small constitution locates Poland, in the terms outlined by Shugart and Carey, in the premier-presidentialism category, despite certain strengthening of the president's powers in comparison to the 1989 arrangements. Of the three constitutive features of such a system,[25] all apply to the Polish case:

the president is elected by popular vote;

there also exist a premier and cabinet, subject to assembly confidence, who perform executive functions;

the president possesses considerable powers (he can issue regulations and executive orders, can initiate legislation, and has a veto power over the statutes passed by the legislature), including the power to dissolve the parliament (although only under very specific circumstances).

"Very specific" doesn't necessarily mean "rare." Even if Wałęsa had preferred to stay away from the center of Polish politics, he could hardly have afforded to do so. Only a few months after the small constitution was promulgated and went into force, the Sejm passed a vote of no confidence in Suchocka's government without naming her successor. The president, in accordance with Article 66, paragraph 5 of the interim constitution, had a choice of either accepting Suchocka's resignation and nominating a new prime minister, or dissolving the Sejm. He chose the latter.

The president's decision was an unintended, unexpected, and generally undesired outcome of a particular political game. In the first half of 1993, the Suchocka government continued implementing economic reforms that aimed at further privatization of the state sector and expanding the role of the market. The government achieved considerable success by negotiating with the trade unions and the state enterprise managers a package of legislation known as the "Pact on the Enterprise." Before the final version of this pact could be approved by the Sejm, however, a motion for a vote of no confidence in the government was submitted by the trade union Solidarity, one of the partners in these negotiations. The issue in question, one of the major features of the reform policies, was the tight control over the monetary supply introduced in 1989 by Mazowiecki, and continued by Suchocka's cabinet. These monetary policies were particularly harmful for public sector employees and workers in state-owned enterprises. Solidarity's small parliamentary representation, which had been instrumental in setting up the coalition supporting Suchocka in 1992, did not intend to oust her cabinet. Its aim instead was to enhance Solidarity's own bargaining power *vis-à-vis* the government, and improve its eroding popularity among workers. Unfortunately, it overplayed its hand: on 28 May the motion carried by a single vote. Ironically, among the deputies voting against the government were members of two political camps, joined at the moment by their hostility to both Suchocka and Wałęsa but ultimately more hostile to each other – members of Solidarity, and several post-Solidarity parties on the one hand, and deputies of the postcommunist Democratic Left Alliance on the other.

Round three: Wałęsa versus a neo-communist parliament

In dissolving parliament, Wałęsa undermined the political well-being of many of his foes, and did it with their assistance. The outgoing Sejm, during its last session on 29 May, managed to adopt significant changes in the electoral law, designed to limit fragmentation by eliminating weaker parties from the Sejm. Specifically, the following devices were put in place: (1) a threshold of 5 percent for parties and 8 percent for coalitions, nationwide; (2) increase of the threshold for the national list from 5 percent to 7 percent; (3) increase in the number of districts, from 37 to 52, expanding district magnitude to 3 to 17 seats (in 1991: 7 to 17); (4) implementation of the D'Hondt PR system, advantageous to stronger parties, for allocation of all seats (in 1991 seats in districts were allocated according to the Hare-Niemeyer formula, and seats on the national list according to the modified Saint Lague system). Suchocka's cabinet stayed in office until after the 19 September 1993 elections. The major participants of the 1993 electoral campaign were, by and large, the same as in 1991, with one important addition, however. Wałęsa sponsored a new organization, the Non-Party Bloc for Support of Reforms. The Polish acronym of this organization, BBWR, was identical with the acronym of the Non-Party Bloc for Cooperation with the Government, an organization established by the followers of Marshal Piłsudski in the 1920s to counterbalance a fragmented party system. Wałęsa's intentions were apparently similar, and, as always, he certainly didn't mind having his name associated with Piłsudski. The new BBWR, unlike the old one, did not attract substantial popular support, yet still managed to reach the 5 percent threshold.

The elections resulted in a major victory for two postcommunist parties, the Democratic Left Alliance (SLD) and the Polish Peasant Party (PSL). Together they won almost two-thirds of the seats in the Sejm, and almost three-quarters of the seats in the Senate. Many factors contributed to this victory, but analysis of their impact falls beyond the scope of this chapter.[26] One factor ought nevertheless to be mentioned here. The parties of the so-called center-right, led by former Solidarity leaders who had parted company with Wałęsa in 1991, had no ideological reason to run in this election separately. They were competing for the same constituencies, and it was only the ambitions of their leaders that led them to run on separate tickets. As a result, none of them cleared the 5 percent threshold, and they were not represented in the Sejm despite a substantial following (at least 20 percent of the popular vote). They were the major loser in these elections.

From the day of the election it became clear that any future ruling coalition would have to include both the SLD and the PSL. But answers had to be found to some other important questions. Should the ruling coalition be limited to these two parties, or expanded to include other parties? What would the balance of power be between the two major partners? How would this coalition establish a relationship with an ideologically and politically hostile president? The SLD, somewhat overwhelmed by the magnitude of its success, pursued the following goals in the coalition-building and cabinet-formation process: (1) inclusion of some post-Solidarity partners into the coalition to enhance its internal and international legitimacy; (2) a central role reserved to the SLD's coalition partner, the PSL, in order to avoid an impression of a return to the old communist regime; (3) maintaining good relations with the president to avoid an early confrontation that could eventually lead to a constitutional crisis, and perhaps new elections. The SLD failed to accomplish the first goal, but the other two goals were achieved. The coalition's choice for prime minister was Pawlak, the young leader of the PSL and the head of the short-lived caretaker government in 1992. In his cabinet the PSL was also awarded one of the three deputy prime minister positions (with the other two going to the SLD), plus an additional six portfolios (against another four for the SLD). The SLD, in exchange for the more prominent role given to the PSL, secured for itself the key cabinet positions related to the economy: that of the deputy prime minister/minister of finance, and the portfolios of Property Rights Restructuring, and Labor and Social Policy, among others.

With regard to relations with the president, the coalition bowed to his interpretation of Article 61 of the interim constitution, and accepted candidates picked by Wałęsa for the positions of the ministers of foreign affairs, national defense, and internal affairs. None of these nominees was connected to the parties of the coalition. On the other hand, the coalition won a showdown with the president over the political mechanism leading to the nomination of the prime minister. Since the provisions of the interim constitution give the president the first choice of a candidate, Wałęsa was not legally bound to choose a candidate from the SLD or PSL, but would not be able to force any candidacy against the will of these two parties. In a pretended gesture of good will, Wałęsa asked the PSL and SLD to submit a list of three candidates for him to select from. The coalition refused to bow to this request insisting that Pawlak was its only candidate. Wałęsa, who only a year before had nominated Pawlak to form a cabinet, was not happy this time about his candidacy, apparently because Pawlak had managed to establish his own power base and, if nominated, wouldn't owe any favors to the president. After a few weeks' long tug-of-war, Wałęsa yielded and nominated Pawlak.

During the last two months of 1993, Pawlak's government pursued policies not of radical change, but rather of continuity with those of its predecessors. This was true for the monetarist approach to the economy, as well as for Poland's foreign policy of seeking closer ties to the Western economic, political, and military alliances (including a bid for Poland's membership in NATO). Expectations that the "neo-communists" in power would reverse the course of Polish reforms were not, at that time, confirmed. In the first months of Pawlak's tenure, the president and the prime minister avoided open conflicts. Conflicts eventually emerged in 1994. Some conflicts, noted below, had the potential for developing into a constitutional crisis.

One potentially dangerous conflict took place in August 1994 when the president vetoed amendments to the penal code. The amendments were designed to liberalize Poland's restrictive abortion regulations by depenalizing abortions performed for reasons relating to a woman's social and economic situation (thus in fact allowing abortions on demand). Wałęsa made it clear that even if his veto were over-ridden, he would not sign the bill into law. Since the small constitution explicitly requires the president's signature on any statute, Wałęsa's refusal to sign the bill would have left the parliament no other choice but to initiate impeachment procedures. This extreme development was avoided when the Sejm failed, by a substantial margin, to override the veto.

Another bizarre conflict involving constitutional matters developed over the actions and composition of the National Broadcasting Council (NBC). In March 1994, the president issued an executive order firing the Council's chairman, Marek Markiewicz. The parliament, as well as many observers, questioned the constitutionality of this act. The Statute of the National Broadcasting Council gives the president the right to appoint the chairman, but doesn't mention the right to dismiss. The interpretation given by the chief legal adviser to the president, Professor Lech Falandysz, was "he who appoints has the right to dismiss." Other experts disagreed, pointing out that the very philosophy underlying the establishment of the NBC was to secure its independence and to prevent direct political control and misuse of the media. Once appointed, the members of the Council could be recalled before the end of their term only in the case of a serious violation of the law. To this argument the president's staff responded that Markiewicz wasn't dismissed as a member of the NBC, but only as its chairman. The case was eventually heard by the Constitutional Tribunal which ruled in May against the president without, however, indicating if this ruling was retroactive or only an interpretation of the law to be applied in the future.

It is very difficult to judge Wałęsa's intentions here. Even with the power to appoint and dismiss three members of the NBC, he could not control the whole Council. And even if such control were possible, it would by no means assure anyone of control over the electronic media, or any significant portion thereof. Some analysts saw in his actions purely personal motives. But a broader interpretation seems more convincing. By October 1994, Wałęsa essentially began his 1995 reelection campaign. His behavior here would be consistent with past events in 1981 and in 1990. Wałęsa liked to create the impression that he was omnipresent and almost omnipotent. He remarked "People are trying hard (sometimes not hard enough), they commit various errors and mistakes, and I, Wałęsa, have to fix them." Hence the conflicts in which he became engaged simultaneously with several different institutions: the NBC, the prime minister (see below), the parliament. In the past this strategy worked – would it work this time? In the Fall of 1994 the other actors on the political scene seemed more concerned than impressed with the constitutional implications of the president's actions. On 13 October 1994 the Sejm passed an unprecedented resolution, under the heading of "Address to the President," asking him, for the sake of democracy in Poland, to avoid actions that might violate the law. This was only a step short of a threat of impeachment – but, in fact, nobody, perhaps besides Wałęsa himself, wanted to see the president impeached. The post-Solidarity parties, save for some extreme groupings, would see it as an enormous embarrassment. For the postcommunist groups this was too risky a game. Wałęsa would surely attempt to mobilize popular support against such a move as an alleged resurgence of communism and an attempt to reverse the course of history.

The president responded to the Sejm's resolution by questioning the legality of its action (indeed, the Constitutional Act doesn't recognize the procedure of an "Address to the President"). Wałęsa also proclaimed, in an address to the judges of the Constitutional Court, that, in order to get things done, one must sometimes stretch the law a little bit.[27]

But the major area of Wałęsa's confrontations with parliament and government was personnel policy. Such conflicts involved nomination of a new deputy prime minister – minister of finance (after the resignation of Marek Borowski in February 1994, Wałęsa refused to nominate as his replacement the coalition's first choice, Dariusz Rosati, but settled for the second choice, Grzegorz Kołodko, in April 1994); nomination of the commander-in-chief of the state police (Pawlak refused to accept several candidates endorsed by Wałęsa and the minister of internal affairs, Milczanowski); departure of minister of defense, Kołodziejczyk, and the subsequent search for his replacement (in November 1994, Pawlak, without consultation with the SLD, dismissed Kołodziejczyk on Wałęsa's demand, but would not accept Wałęsa's choice for replacement, Zbigniew Okoński); finally, resignation of the minister of foreign affairs, Andrzej Olechowski (Olechowski resigned in January 1995 over disagreements with Pawlak, and to protest against the minister of justice, Włodzimierz Cimoszewicz's, mishandling of an investigation regarding financial indiscretions of state officials, Olechowski among others).

The major issue underlying these conflicts was the question of control over the so-called presidential portfolios: Internal Affairs, National Defense, and Foreign Affairs. Wałęsa maintained that to exercise his constitutional responsibility for the internal and external security of the state he needed more direct control of the three relevant ministries, and specifically full discretion in personnel policies. Most factions in parliament opposed presidential control on political and/or constitutional grounds, as an arrangement that would transform the dual executive into two parallel governments and effectively eliminate parliamentary control over the most vital parts of the executive branch.

With two critical ministerial nominations on hold (possibly even three – Milczanowski would resign as minister of internal affairs had the president so requested), Wałęsa launched in December 1994 a major offensive against the Pawlak government. As the area of confrontation he chose the government's fiscal policies and the state budget. A series of complex legal maneuvers included a presidential veto of the 1995 tax bill (the bill was designed to effectively raise personal income tax), overridden by the Sejm, and subsequently submitted by the president to the Constitutional Tribunal for review of its constitutionality. When the Tribunal ruled against the president on a technical issue, the president signed the bill but resubmitted it for judicial review, broadening the scope of questions (to include, among others, the issue of retroactivity of some regulations). Eventually, in March 1995, the Constitutional Tribunal upheld presidential objections. In the meantime, however, since the 1995 state budget was predicated on the tax law being passed, Wałęsa refused to sign it, too, and submitted it to the Constitutional Tribunal for review (2 February 1995). This decision meant that there would be no state budget within three months of its submission by the Council of Ministers in draft form, thereby not fulfilling the requirements of the budgetary law. According to the provisions of the Constitutional Act (Article 21) this would give the president the right to dissolve the parliament. Wałęsa explicitly threatened such an action, to the almost unanimous outrage of the ruling coalition and the parliamentary opposition. In the deputies' view, the delay in the legislative process caused directly by the president's actions could not serve as grounds for the dissolution of parliament. At this point Wałęsa hinted that he might withdraw his objections to the budget, if the coalition agreed to remove Pawlak from the premiership. Negotiations between Pawlak and Wałęsa regarding the two ministerial nominations were conducted concurrently with the tug-of-war over taxes and budget. In these negotiations, Pawlak appeared ineffective and oftentimes disloyal to his coalition partner, the SLD. The SLD, increasingly critical of Pawlak's personnel policies and apparent lack of leadership, accepted Wałęsa's suggestion, and, after additional rounds of bargaining with the president over personnel issues, submitted to the Sejm a motion of a constructive vote of no confidence in Pawlak's government. As the new prime minister, the SLD chose Józef Oleksy, the speaker of the Sejm, a member of the SLD (and its core party, the SdRP), and a former communist *apparatchik*. The motion was accepted by the Sejm on 1 March 1995, and on 6 March the new government took the oath of office. In this government, the three so-called presidential portfolios were assigned to people hand-picked by Wałęsa: Okoński was, at long last, accepted by the coalition as minister of national defense, Władysław Bartoszewski, a veteran opposition intellectual and ambassador to Austria, became minister of foreign affairs, while Milczanowski remained at the internal affairs post.

With the conflict resolved Wałęsa had again accomplished something seemingly impossible. Facing a formidable foe in a ruling coalition that commanded almost two-thirds of the seats in the Sejm, he nevertheless was able to cause the fall of a government supported by this coalition, and to secure himself control over the three critical portfolios. Perhaps the SLD/PSL coalition bowed to Wałęsa only because it hoped for his forthcoming departure, with the new presidential election due before the end of the year.

The 1995 election

As early as Fall 1994, Wałęsa had begun his reelection campaign. He was regarded as a serious contender, not just because he was an incumbent, but above all because he had proven to be an able politician. His ability to act during a crisis remained unmatched in Polish politics, but so too did his ability to cause crises where and when there was no need for them. Many of his ideas that at the time seemed farfetched were later turned into very practical solutions. A good example was the famous "Your President, our Prime Minister" slogan of the summer of 1989 that opened the way to Mazowiecki's premiership. Publicly, the slogan first appeared in Adam Michnik's article in *Gazeta Wyborcza*, but recently published documents suggest that the article was inspired by Wałęsa.[28] In the Polish model of cohabitation, Wałęsa as president survived three by and large hostile parliaments, and six governments, of which only two may be described as moderately friendly to him. On the unstable Polish political scene, his constitutional position – if not always his actions – provided desired elements of stability and continuity. But his fixed term was to end in November 1995. What were his assets and liabilities on the eve of the new elections?

One could expect that, after four years in office, a president would have at his disposal a group of able and loyal advisers, a political machine, and a considerable stable following among the electorate. Lech Wałęsa failed to secure any of the above.

His lack of ability to work effectively with people close to him became proverbial. Over the course of the last fifteen years, Wałęsa alienated almost all of his close aids and advisors:: from Andrzej Gwiazda and Anna Walentynowicz of the Free Trade Unions and early Solidarity times, to Mazowiecki, Geremek, and Michnik, to Bielecki and Jacek Merkel (the manager of Wałęsa's first presidential campaign), to the Kaczyński brothers and Olszewski. In his much-loved motorist metaphors, he liked to compare himself to a driver, with prime ministers serving as bumpers that provided protection against collisions (with popular discontent, for instance), and, therefore, the bumpers had to be replaced once in a while.

Those in the president's Chancellery in 1995 were able (at least some of them) and loyal, but they lacked respect among Polish political elites and the public. Falandysz (privately a renowed expert in victimology), who until his departure in March 1995, was the chief legal advisor to the president, compared himself to a sergeant in the army, who always followed the orders of his commander-in-chief. In other words, his philosophy was "every decision of the president may be justified legally," which the Polish press[29] labeled as the "falandisation of law." Falandysz resigned his position in March 1995, citing disagreements with Wałęsa's closest aide, Mieczysław Wachowski. Wachowski, formerly Wałęsa's chauffeur and bodyguard and since the 1990 election his chief of staff (*dyrektor gabinetu*), in 1993 elevated to the position of minister of state, was the most controversial of all the president's men. Rumors about his murky connections and about the sources of his influence on Wałęsa were countless. In 1992 he was accused by Jarosław Kaczyński of being a former officer of the communist secret police, but the charge lacked any credible evidence.

The president's Chancellery often seemed more like a monarch's court than the staff of a democratically elected office-holder. It is the president's constitutional privilege (Article 48) to appoint and dismiss the Chancellery staff at his discretion without any confirmation process. The Constitutional Act does not regulate the duties and responsibilities of the ministers of state and other officers in the Chancellery, nor does it provide any mechanism for their accountability aside from falling out of the president's favor. This was the case of Jarosław Kaczyński, who attempted to use the Chancellery as his own power base. Wałęsa dismissed him, but there are no institutional checks to prevent a similar development in the future. Moreover, the relationships of the Chancellery with the other state institutions and the delineation of their respective responsibilities are not regulated either. For a time in 1994, Jerzy Milewski served simultaneously as a minister of state in the Chancellory and a deputy minister of national defense. Whether a presidential or a parliamentary system is adopted in the new constitution, it must clearly outline not only the president's own powers and responsibilities, but also those of his staff.

Regarding the lack of a political machine, Wałęsa once had a machine as formidable as one could imagine: Solidarity. It challenged the communist system in 1980–81, it survived persecution in the 1980s, and its political extension, the Civic Committees, swept the 1989 election. Wałęsa balked, in 1989, at turning the Civic Committees into a political party, or any other more permanent organization. He was too comfortable as the leader of a powerful trade union to seek any other institutional base of support. Solidarity and the remnants of the Civic Committees secured his election in 1990. But soon after he and Solidarity parted company. Wałęsa became "the President of all Poles," and Solidarity, losing its best people to political institutions and the state administration, evolved into a radical, populist trade union.

After the 1990 election, several Solidarity politicians, Kaczyński and Olszewski among others, attempted to transform their political organization, the Center Alliance, into "the president's party." But Wałęsa did not like to owe a debt to people around him (Kaczyński was most instrumental in promoting Wałęsa's bid for presidency), and he refused to endorse this enterprise. He also genuinely wanted to be president of all Poles, and rise – like Piłsudski – above partisan politics.

In 1993, after many disappointments, came his attempt to build a new political base, the Non-Party Bloc for Support of Reforms. After its relatively good showing in the 1993 parliamentary election, the BBWR lost momentum and failed to record any meaningful success in the 1994 municipal elections. The movement lacked able leadership, ideological focus, and a well-defined political agenda. Not surprisingly, Wałęsa distanced himself from it quickly. In early 1995, there was practically nobody to run Wałęsa's reelection campaign besides the president himself.

The outlook of his popular following wasn't any more encouraging. Wałęsa, who cast himself as the president of all Poles, and believed that he represented a "true and plebiscitary majority"[30] never, in fact, accomplished this. He won the election by rallying behind him no more than 40 percent of adult Poles, and soon after election his popularity began to wane. To a great extent this decline in popularity was his own fault, since his campaign was filled with promises that neither he nor anybody else could deliver. Those who had taken his slogan of "acceleration" literally were obviously disappointed and turned their political sympathies to other prophets of an easier future, from the right or the left. But there were some other factors as well, factors beyond Wałęsa's control. Many Poles seemed to expect that, once elected, Wałęsa would miraculously turn from a rough-edged electrician and union leader to a dignified statesman, with noble manners, speaking flawless Polish. This transformation could not take place, of course, and the symbolic function of the presidency seemed undermined by Wałęsa's slips of tongue and conduct.

But what hurt Wałęsa's popularity most were his actions and bellicose attitude toward other political actors. Conflict avoidance remains one of the fundamental features of Polish political culture, and public opinion polls indicate strong support for national accord and unity. The Poles

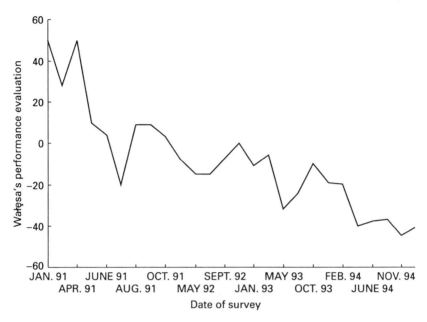

Figure 5.1   Wałęsa's net approval rate, January 1991–January 1995
Source: Compiled by the author from CBOS data

expected that their president would act according to the principles of democracy (75 percent), the rule of law (74 percent), and the will of the majority (72 percent, data from a CBOS poll of June 1994). They believed that Wałęsa, as president, did not conform to these standards. For instance, 55 percent expressed the opinion that he violated the law in his conflict with the National Broadcasting Council (CBOS, October 1994). The polls showed also a steady decline in the president's general approval rating (see Figure 5.1).

Simulated presidential elections also placed Wałęsa well behind his major rivals. Several CBOS polls conducted between January and October 1994 consistently listed Wałęsa, with 5 percent to 10 percent of the vote, behind Aleksander Kwaśniewski (the leader of the SLD, who had 16 percent to 20 percent support), and Pawlak (9 percent to 12 percent). In a simulated pair-wise contest (2–5 September 1994; reported in *Gazeta Wyborcza* on 10–11 September), Wałęsa turned out to be a "Condorcet loser": if he made it to the run-off with any of the four other candidates – Kwaśniewski, Pawlak, Andrzej Olechowski, or Jacek Kuroń (a veteran of the anti-communist opposition, former minister in the Mazowiecki and Suchocka governments) – Wałęsa would lose to each of them.

With no capable advisors, no political machine, and only a handful of

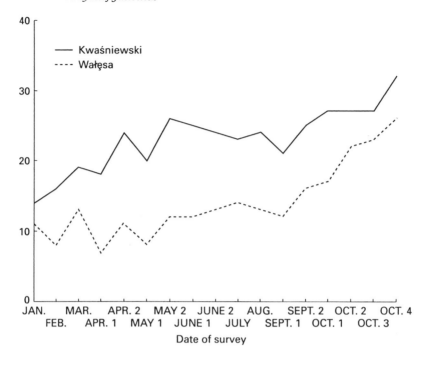

Figure 5.2   Public opinion ratings for Kwaśniewski and Wałęsa, 1995

devoted followers, in the spring of 1995 Wałęsa's chances for reelection looked grim. But Wałęsa did it again – almost. In the CBOS preelection polls his ratings (see Figure 5.2) early in the year were low and unstable (between 7 percent and 13 percent of those declaring that they would vote in the election), placing him behind not only Kwaśniewski, the consistent leader, but also Kuroń and Tadeusz Zieliński (the Ombudsman, candidate of the Labor Union), although ahead of Pawlak (whose popularity began to wane after his departure from the prime minister's post). During the summer, Wałęsa's ratings stabilized at the 12–14 percent level, now ahead of Kuroń and Zieliński. The summer months also saw the rapid rise of yet another candidate, Hanna Gronkiewicz-Waltz, the president of Poland's National Bank. Her campaign posed a serious threat to Wałęsa since she was seeking the support of the center-to-right political forces and was appealing to the socially conservative Catholic constituency, where Wałęsa's popularity was always higher than elsewhere. But Gronkiewicz-Waltz's rapid rise in the polls was followed by an even more rapid decline: from 15–16 percent and second position in early September, to a mere 3 percent in late October, a week before the first round. We cannot examine here the causes and consequences of this "shooting star" candidacy, but obviously there was a strong link between her and Wałęsa's performance in the polls. His popularity began to rise in mid-September, and by mid-October it became obvious that there were only two candidates with chances to make it to the run-off, Kwaśniewski and Wałęsa. Interestingly, the band-wagon effect of the latter's campaign engendered an "underdog" effect on the former's ratings: stable at the 27 percent level for almost a month, on the eve of the election it rose to 32 percent. It should also be noted that the cited data refer to unweighted distribution of preferences among those who declared that they intended to vote. When weighted to reflect the likelihood of actual participation in the vote, the data revealed only a minimal lead by Kwaśniewski: 34–31 percent.[31] Also, in a simulated runoff round, Wałęsa, from a "Condorcet loser" of a year before, became a Condorcet winner, registering for the first time a slight lead over Kwaśniewski (42.4–40.8 percent, with others uncommitted), and beating all other potential rivals comfortably.

The election, conducted according to the same rules as in 1990, took place on 5 November (first round), and 19 November (run-off), 1995. The slim margin of Kwaśniewski's victory in the first round (see official results in Table 5.1) left the run-off contest wide open. The momentum, however, was apparently with Wałęsa: a CBOS poll conducted between both rounds (9–11 November) had Wałęsa one point ahead.[32]

On Sunday, 12 November, the first of two live TV debates took place between the candidates. The campaign had already entered its ugly phase: both sides were trading all sorts of accusations, not all of them unfounded. There was no clear favorite in the debate. Both candidates, regardless of enormous differences in individual styles, had in fact established good records as speakers and debaters. A pivotal role in Wałęsa's (and Solidarity's) reemergence from the political underground in the late 1980s was played by his TV debate with Alfred Miodowicz, the leader of the communist sponsored trade unions (the OPZZ), and a Politiburo member, in October 1988. The witty and relaxed Wałęsa, who had been coached for this confrontation by top Solidarity advisors, crushed and ridiculed his opponent then. But on the night of 12 November 1995 the roles were reversed: the tense, incoherent, and rude Wałęsa wasn't even a shadow of himself of yesteryear, in contrast to the relaxed, focused, and seemingly conciliatory Kwaśniewski. Wałęsa recovered somewhat during the second debate, on Wednesday 15 November, but not to the point of repairing the damage done on Sunday.

For Kwaśniewski, the debates had been planned as the logical climax of his nearly year-long campaign. His image for the whole campaign was designed by a renowned French public relations firm. Wałęsa, on the contrary, came to the TV studio without a consistent plan and well-defined objectives. The recurring theme of his monologues was, as it had been throughout the campaign, "Only I, Wałęsa, can save Poland from a return to communism." In 1995 such a slogan was nothing but an anachronism: nobody, neither Kwaśniewski's supporters nor his foes, believed seriously that his election would mean a restitution of the communist regime. Wałęsa's campaign, as amateurish as his opponent's was professional, failed to respond adequately to the changing mood of the public.

The above-mentioned CBOS poll conducted between both rounds was designed as a panel study. The same people were interviewed twice: before the first debate, and after the second (but before the day of the run-off). A clear majority of respondents (68 percent) saw the winner of the debates in Kwaśniewski. Still, the debates did not influence voting preferences of those who already before the debates were committed to vote for one of the candidates. But among those uncommitted, after the debates 60 percent decided to vote for Kwaśniewski, and only 20 percent for Wałęsa (with the rest remaining undecided). While before the debates Wałęsa led by one percentage point (43–42 percent), after the debates he trailed Kwaśniewski by five points (44–49 percent). On run-off day, he lost by a 3 percent margin (see table 5.1).

Wałęsa lost in 1995 due to his own arrogance. Since 1988, he had gradually severed ties with all those advisers and staffers who could effectively stage his campaign and coach him for the final confrontation. After winning his first term, he never seriously attempted to build his own political machine. Without far-sighted advisors or a political machine, he still recorded a remarkable comeback and rallied behind himself almost half of the voters. But on the apparently decisive nights of the debates, his self-inflicted political isolation turned against him. The clash of personalities and political biographies of the two major candidates overshadowed any substantive issues in this election. Both candidates presented themselves as true proponents of democracy and economic reforms, and neither called for any substantially new policies. Their respective constituencies did not differ much in terms of their demographic and social features: they both reflected, by and large, the demographic and occupational composition of the Polish population. They differed, however, in their political and cultural profile, with religiosity being the best predictor of voting preferences (the more often individuals participated in religious services, the more likely they were to vote for Wałęsa). Also, regional differences were statistically significant.

The 1995 election, as the previous one, can serve as a test for Linz's analysis of the dysfunctional consequences of the two-round ballot. The first ("In a highly fragmented system the two leading candidates might

Table 5.1 *Results of the presidential election, 5 November and 19 November, 1995*[a]

Candidate	Party	First round 5 November, 1995 Turnout: 64.70% (%)	Second round 19 November, 1995 Turnout: 68.23% (%)
Leszek Bubel	Independent	0.04	
Hanna Gronkiewicz-Waltz	Independent	2.76	
Janusz Korwin-Mikke	UPR	2.40	
Tadeusz Koźluk	Independent	0.15	
Jacek Kuroń	UW	9.22	
Aleksander Kwaśniewski	SLD	35.11	51.72
Andrzej Lepper	Samoobrona	1.32	
Jan Olszewski	Independent	6.86	
Waldemar Pawlak	PSL	4.31	
Jan Pietrzak	Independent	1.12	
Kazimierz Piotrowicz	Independent	0.07	
Lech Wałęsa	Independent[b]	33.11	48.28
Tadeusz Zieliński	Independent[c]	3.53	

[a] Compiled by the author from official results published in *Rzeczpospolita*, 259 (4212), 8 November 1995, and no. 570 (4223), 22 November 1995.
[b] Endorsed by the ZChN and Solidarity.   [c] Endorsed by the UP.

enjoy only small pluralities with respect to other candidates and might represent positions on the same segment of the political spectrum"[33]) clearly could not be found here. Kwaśniewski and Wałęsa finished in the first round well ahead of the other candidates (see Table 5.1), and represented polar ends of the political spectrum. The second ("One of the candidates might be an outsider to the party system with no congressional party base"[34]), if applied to all the candidates in the first round, finds solid confirmation: there were several such candidates, not only frivolous ones, but also serious politicians (Zieliński, Gronkiewicz-Waltz). However, if Linz's statement were applied only to the two top candidates (and that apparently was his intention), his expectations may be confirmed only in a most perverse way. Wałęsa, the incumbent running for reelection was in fact "an outsider to the party system with no congressional party base," but by no means an outsider to the political system of the Tymiński or Ross Perot sort.

Whether the third of Linz's points ("The 'majority' generated might not represent a politically more or less homogeneous electorate or a coalition of parties"[35]) is substantiated remains to be seen. Among those who voted for Kwaśniewski, there has been a core group of voters who consistently supported the candidates of the postcommunist SLD in presidential and parliamentary races. According to the author's own post-election survey, if the parliamentary elections were held in 1995 concurrent with the presidential ones, exactly half of Kwaśniewski's supporters would have voted for the SLD. Among the other half, though, there would have been many who, having no pro-SLD or any pro-left sympathies, would have cast their ballots for Kwaśniewski in order to prevent Wałęsa's reelection (according to the cited CBOS panel study, 15 percent of all who voted for him). The proportion of those who supported Wałęsa exclusively to stop Kwaśniewski was even higher (39 percent). Regardless of whether voters' motivations were positive or negative, their emotions were strong, and the level of mobilization high: the turnout in the run-off (68 percent) was higher than in the first round (65 percent, see Table 5.1).

Thus, the very mode of presidential election contributed to repolarization of the Polish political arena, reviving the old Solidarity versus (post)communists cleavage. Given this development, it is unlikely that the fourth of Linz's expectations ("The winner, although initially the choice of a small proportion of the electorate, is likely to feel that he represents a 'true and plebiscitary' majority"[36]) will be confirmed in the foreseeable future. Kwaśniewski faces too much open hostility among citizens and political elites to be able to forget the slim margin of his victory and its scandalous features.[37]

For the question of the institutionalization of Polish democracy, the most important point seems the final one in Linz's analysis,[38] exposing the relationship between the incentives for candidates to enter the first round, and the fragmentation of the party system. Indeed, with the exception of the SLD, during this campaign all other major parties underwent a political crisis of some sort. For some (PSL, UW, UP), the process of candidate selection led to internal feuds among factions and/or personalities. Others (the Christian nationalist ZChN), posting no own candidate, feuded about whom they should endorse, shifting their alliances in the middle of the campaign, which led to a growing confusion among their own membership, candidates, and voters. The most disastrous were the conflicts among the parties of the anti-communist right. Badly defeated in the parliamentary election of 1993, due to lack of unity and cooperation, in 1995, despite this somber experience, they still did not get their act together, and advanced several candidates (at least seven, of which three withdrew during the last week of the campaign). The consolidation process which, as has been argued above, began with the 1990 presidential election, stalled in 1995 if it did not succumb to an outright reverse. This fragmentation, along with the above-mentioned reemergence of the Solidarity-communism cleavage, brought the Polish polity dangerously close to the state of polarized pluralism,[39] where conflict resolution is not possible and no consensus can be achieved.

Lech Wałęsa and the future of presidentialism in Poland

As has been pointed out, Wałęsa possessed a unique ability to act in a decisive and intelligent way during political crises, providing an argument for those who believe that crisis-solving potential may be a major advantage of presidential systems compared to parliamentary ones.[40] But Wałęsa's ability and eagerness to cause unnecessary crises outweighed, most observers agree,[41] any advantages of his crisis-solving skills. A major crisis, whose long-term ramifications cannot yet be assessed, erupted in Polish politics immediately after Wałęsa's electoral defeat, still before the end of his term. On 19 December 1995, Wałęsa summoned to his office the speakers of both Houses and the chiefs of the three high courts (the Supreme Court, the Constitutional Tribunal, and the High Court of Administration). During the meeting, Minister of Internal Affairs Milczanowski presented information about an investigation of spying charges against "a high-ranked state official." The absence of the prime minister, Oleksy, at this meeting was conspicuous. Two days later, responding to a formal demand from the Sejm, Milczanowski delivered a speech to the Sejm (televised live), in which he disclosed that the official in question was indeed Oleksy. Oleksy allegedly maintained continuous contacts between 1982 and 1995 with two consecutive residents of first Soviet and then Russian intelligence in Warsaw, and passed on to them state secrets. In his rebuttal, Oleksy repudiated the charges, and in turn accused the officers of counterintelligence who investigated the case, Milczanowski, and Wałęsa of a provocation aimed at destabilization of the state on the eve of Kwaśniewski's inauguration. He acknowledged a "friendship" with Colonel Alganov, one of the two Russians in question, but refused to admit to any wrongdoing. An extraordinary parliamentary committee was chosen to investigate whether the rule of law was observed by individuals and institutions involved in the Oleksy case investigation. Its preliminary report ruled out the possibility of a provocation, but its final report was delayed until summer 1996. Oleksy for more than a month refused to step down or even to take leave, but eventually succumbed to the pressure of public opinion and resigned his office on 24 January 1996. Simultaneously, the military prosecutor's office, to which the Office for Protection of the State (civil intelligence and counterintelligence service) presented the case, examined the evidence against Oleksy, and reported on 22 April 1996 that it was insufficient to charge him formally with espionage.

Wałęsa's role in this affair is unclear. He, and Milczanowski, maintained that Wałęsa learned about the investigation of Oleksy as late as 5 December 1995. They tried to solve the problem in a discreet manner, without harm to the interests of the state, by contacting President-elect Kwaśniewski on 12 December 1995, and asking him to use his influence to force Oleksy out. Kwaśniewski purportedly promised to look into the case but took no significant action. On the other hand, Oleksy (who on 27 January replaced Kwaśniewski as the leader of the SdRP, the core party of the SLD) and his party colleagues claim that Wałęsa orchestrated the whole affair to take revenge for his electoral defeat.

Regardless of who was telling the truth (and public opinion in Poland doubts if the full truth about the whole affair will ever be revealed), this case illustrates well the dynamics between the constitutional framework of the presidency and the incumbent's personality. Wałęsa used presidential powers as prescribed by the Constitutional Act (oftentimes trying to stretch the limits of these powers) to play the role of an active, "strong" president. His actions were decisive in facilitating the fall of two prime ministers (Olszewski in 1992 and Pawlak in 1995) at times when the prime minister's departure was desirable for the sake of political stability and/or well-being of economic reforms. Kwaśniewski, on the other hand, acting within the same institutional framework, chose the role of a passive, "weak" president. Not only did he ignore the invitation to participate in solving the Oleksy affair as president-elect, but also after his inauguration, when the affair was in full swing, he maintained a very low profile, limiting himself to general statements about the trust he had in his friend "Józek" (Oleksy). The role of the active and authoritative arbiter was played by Józef Zych, the speaker of the Sejm, who oversaw the creation and work of the Sejm extraordinary committee to investigate the actions of the Office for Protection of the State in the Oleksy affair, and who was instrumental in expediting the process of cabinet change. Whether Kwaśniewski would opt for a passive presidency in the future, remained to be seen.

Also the role of presidentialism in the future Polish constitution was not finalized with the 1995 election. Until his election, Kwaśniewski had been chairman of the Extraordinary Parliamentary Committee drafting the constitution. But, paradoxically, his impact on the future shape of the Polish presidency will not, in all likelihood, match that of his predecessor. Surveys and polls indicate that the public preferred a parliamentary rather than presidential model of democracy for Poland, by a two to one margin.[42] So did the authors of six of the seven drafts of the constitution submitted in 1995 for consideration by the Constitutional Committee of the National Assembly. The only project making a case for a presidential democracy was the one submitted by President Wałęsa. In his address to the nation (27 October 1994), Wałęsa spoke in dramatic terms about the need for presidential democracy in Poland. This call, however, was doomed to fall on deaf ears. Political elites and the public witnessed Wałęsa's version of presidentialism, and they saw enough.

Wałęsa's vision of the presidency was best described by Andrzej Wajda, the film director, shortly after the 1990 election. In Wajda's words, Wałęsa saw the role of the president as similar to that of the party's first secretary in the communist regime. The president, with all his omnipotence, travels from town to town, from village to village, from factory to factory, greets those who are happy and helps those who suffer injustice, awards those who contribute and punishes those who don't. If things go wrong, he moves the pawns on the personnel check board. He is a Godfather, loved and respected. This was a vision of the presidency that Wałęsa tried to realize during his tenure in office, with – as it turned out – rather limited success.

Nevertheless, one could derive from Wałęsa's presidency a case for presidentialism. As a president elected for a fixed term, with relatively strong democratic legitimacy, he indeed provided the necessary elements of continuity and stability. If he were a prime minister, sooner rather than later, he would have lost a no confidence vote. He represented Poland in the international arena very well, enjoying considerable popularity among his fellow international statesmen and the public. But if the new Polish constitution adopts a strong parliamentary system and a weak presidency, Wałęsa will be responsible for it more than anyone else.

As noted at the outset, Lech Wałęsa does not mind being compared to Piłsudski. Unlike Piłsudski, he served as president. But will he also, as Piłsudski, be remembered as a controversial, but undeniably exceptional contributor to the development of the Polish nation and state? After Piłsudski, there were the *piłsudczycy* and *piłsudczyzna*. After de Gaulle, there were the Gaullists and Gaullism. There will be no *wałęsowcy* or Wałęsism after Wałęsa. To put it in Weberian terms, Wałęsa failed to institutionalize his charisma. But those familiar with him as a man and a politician know: Wałęsa himself will be around in Polish politics for years to come.

NOTES

1 Research for this chapter has been supported by a Glenn Grant from Washington and Lee University. The author wishes to thank Arista Maria Cirtautas and Ray Taras for their criticism of a draft version of this chapter.
2 See W. Osiatyński, "Jaruzelski," in *East European Constitutional Review*, 2, 4/ 3, 1 (1993).
3 J. Linz, "Presidential or Parliamentary Democracy: Does it Make a Difference?" in J. Linz, and A. Valenzuela (eds.), *The Failure of Presidential Democ-*

racy (Baltimore and London: Johns Hopkins University Press, 1994).

4 Ibid., p. 21.

5 Ibid.

6 Ibid.

7 Ibid.

8 Ibid., p. 22.

9 For discussion of agrarian and political populism, see H. Canovan, *Populism* (London and New York: Harcourt Brace Jovanovich, 1981).

10 R. Dahl, *Dilemmas of Pluralist Democracy. Autonomy vs. Control* (New Haven and London: Yale University Press, 1982).

11 G. Sartori, *Parties and Party Systems. A Framework for Analysis*, vol. I (Cambridge: Cambridge University Press, 1976).

12 See for instance M. Grabowska, "System partyjny – w budowie," *Krytyka*, 37 (1991); K. Jasiewicz, "Polish Politics on the Eve of the 1993 Elections: Toward Fragmentation or Pluralism?" *Communist and Post-Communist Studies*, 26, 4 (December 1993); J. Wiatr, "Fragmented Parties in a New Democracy: Poland," in J. Wiatr (ed.), *Politics of Democratic Transformation: Poland After 1989* (Warsaw: Scholar Agency, 1993).

13 Sartori, *Parties and Party Systems*, p. 336.

14 S. M. Lipset and S. Rokkan (eds.), *Party Systems and Voters Alignments* (New York: Free Press, 1967); S. Rokkan et al., *Citizens, Elections, Parties* (Oslo: Universitetsvorlaget, 1970).

15 Sartori, *Parties and Party Systems*, pp. 121–125.

16 See Jasiewicz, "Polish Politics on the Eve of the 1993 Elections," and K. Jasiewicz, "Poland," *European Journal of Political Research*, 26, 4 (1994).

17 For analyses of the constitutional framework, see S. Gebethner, "Political Institutions in the Process of Transition to a Post-socialist Formation: Polish and Comparative Perspectives," in W. Connor and P. Płoszajski (eds.), *The Polish Road From Socialism* (Armonk, NY and London: M. E. Sharpe, 1992) and W. Sokolewicz, "The Legal and Constitutional Bases of Democratisation in Poland: Systemic and Constitutional Change," in G. Sanford, *Democratization in Poland, 1988–90* (London: Macmillan), 1992).

18 M. Duverger, "A New Political System Model: Semi-presidential Government," *European Journal of Political Research*, 8 (1980).

19 M. S. Shugart and J. M. Carey, *Presidents and Assemblies: Constitutional Design and Electoral Dynamics* (Cambridge: Cambridge University Press, 1992).

20 See Osiatyński, "Wałęsa," pp. 43–44.

21 All quotations are from the official translation of the Constitutional Act: *The Constitutional Act of 17th October, 1992* (Warsaw: The Sejm Publishing Office, 1992).

22 The term "absolute majority" corresponds to the American concept of majority, and means "more than 50 percent of all valid votes." The term "majority," as used in the Constitutional Act, corresponds to the American concept of plurality, and means "more votes in favor than against."

23 Osiatyński, "Wałęsa," pp. 43–44.

24 J. McGregor: "The Presidency in East Central Europe," *RFE/RL Research Report*, 3, 2 (1994).

25 Shugart and Carey, *Presidents and Assemblies*, p. 23.

26 For an analysis of the 1993 election see Jasiewicz, "Poland."

27 Reported in *Gazeta Wyborcza*, 10–11 November 1994.
28 S. Perzkowski, (ed.), *Tajne Dokumenty Biura Politycznego I Sekretariatu KC. Ostatni rok władzy, 1988–89* (London: Aneks, 1991) p. 400.
29 *Polityka*, no. 42/1994.
30 Linz, "Presidential or Parliamentary Democracy," p. 21.
31 CBOS, *Komunikat z badań BS/192/167/95*.
32 CBOS, *Komunikat z badań BS/218/193/95*, unweighted data.
33 Linz, "Presidential or parliamentary democracy," p. 21.
34 Ibid., p. 21.
35 Ibid.
36 Ibid.
37 During the campaign, Kwaśniewski presented himself as a graduate of Gdańsk University with an M.A. degree in economics. Authenticity of these credentials was questioned, and the issue led to official protests challenging the legality of his election. The Supreme Court ruled that Kwaśniewski indeed misrepresented himself, but upheld the legality of the election.
38 Linz, "Presidential or Parliamentary Democracy," p. 22.
39 Sartori, *Parties and Party Systems*, pp. 131–144.
40 T. A. Baylis, "Presidents versus Prime Ministers: Shaping Executive Authority in Eastern Europe," in *World Politics*, 48, 2 (1996).
41 Baylis, p. 320; J. F. Brown, *Hopes and Shadows: Eastern Europe After Communism* (Durham: Duke University Press, 1994), p. 71.
42 Jasiewicz, "Polish Politics on the Eve of the 1993 Elections."

6   The Czech Republic: Havel and the evolution of the presidency since 1989

Sharon L. Wolchik

Introduction

Formally, the Czech Republic is what Alfred Stepan and Cindy Skach have termed a "pure parliamentary" system. The president is elected by the legislature and has a largely symbolic function. The president of the Czechoslovak Federation had somewhat greater powers than the Czech president does. However, the Czechoslovak Federation was also a parliamentary system. According to much of the voluminous literature on the subject of the benefits of the presidential versus parliamentary regimes, these polities ought, thereby, to have avoided the political problems of presidentialism.[1] The stability of the Czech political system, particularly after the dissolution of the Czechoslovak Federation and prior to the 1996 elections, and the Czech economic miracle, seem to be evidence of the political and economic benefits of a parliamentary system in a society that has a number of substantial cleavages and has undergone a radical transformation from an economy that was almost totally under state control to a market economy. Yet the parliamentary system of the postcommunist Czechoslovak Federation failed to satisfy the most basic requirement of effectiveness, the preservation of the state. The president of that Federation, and later of the Czech Republic, Václav Havel, is one of the postcommunist world's most renowned figures whose actual influence exceeds the limited formal powers of his office.

This chapter examines the office of the president in, first, the Czechoslovak Federation and, second, the Czech Republic in light of these facts. It examines the formal powers of the president in both periods; the impact of the first incumbent, Václav Havel, on the office of the presidency; and his relations with the legislative branch and the prime minister. After examining several "case studies" that illustrate the nature of the president's powers and relations with other political actors, it explores the implications of the Czechoslovak and Czech experiences with regard to the political stability and effectiveness of democratic institutions, and for our understanding of the impact of choices about institutional forms for the development and maintenance of democracy.

The institution of the presidency in Czechoslovakia and later the Czech Republic has been shaped by the constitutional definition of the office. As is the case with other institutions, the office has also been influenced by the nature of political life during the transition and the magnitude of the issues with which political leaders and institutions have been confronted.[2] Similarly, the evolution of the office and the way in which it functions have also reflected the personality, values, and political style of its first incumbent, Václav Havel. The office of the presidency has also been shaped by the process that led to the demise of the Czechoslovak Federation in 1992; the institutionalization of political life; and the growing influence of other institutions and individuals.

The powers of the president

The powers of the president of the Czechoslovak Federation were formally determined by the constitution in place when the communist system fell. This was the 1960 constitution, as amended by the 1968 Federation Amendment. Although many of its provisions were subsequently modified in the first year and a half after the end of communist rule, the provisions that dealt with the president's powers were not changed. According to this constitution, and in keeping with the tradition of the interwar Czechoslovak Republic, the formal powers of the president were limited. The president had the power to appoint and recall the prime minister and other members of the government. The president was also entitled to grant amnesties and to dissolve the Federal Assembly if it could not agree on a budget. The president served as the head of state and was charged with representing the country abroad. He or she possessed the right to call for new elections and was to serve as head of the armed forces. In addition, the president had the right to initiate legislation, although not to veto it or return it to the legislature for reconsideration. The president was elected indirectly by the parliament for a five-year term and was not the head of the executive branch.[3] The conditions under which the president could exercise many of these powers were not clearly specified in the constitution. During the communist period, this situation was not problematic, because the presidency, as well as the government and legislature, was subordinated to the direction of the Communist party leadership. However, once the formal institutions of government came to direct the country's affairs with the end of communist rule, the lack of clarity in the constitution concerning these issues, as well as the relatively limited powers of the president, had an important effect on political life. As Mathernova notes, the president's inability to dissolve parliament, except under very limited circumstances, to initiate a referendum, or to rule by decree were all factors that limited

President Havel's ability to intervene in political life to prevent the breakup of the federation.[4]

The Czech Constitution adopted in December 1993 as the basis for the government of the Czech Republic established in January 1993 further reduced the powers of the president. The president continues to fulfill a number of functions. As the head of state, he is charged with receiving foreign visitors and represents the country abroad; he also serves as commander-in-chief of the armed forces. As was the case in the federation, the president is responsible for naming the prime minister and the cabinet (following the suggestion of the prime minister) and appointing judges to the Constitutional Court as well as the chair and deputy chair of the Supreme Court. The president also appoints the president and vice-president of the Supreme Control Office and members of the Banking Council of the Czech National Bank. As with many of the other powers of the office, many of these are circumscribed and several require the consent of other political actors such as the prime minister or the Senate.

The president is empowered to convene the lower house of parliament, the Chamber of Deputies, and can dissolve it if it does not pass a vote of confidence in a new government whose chair has been appointed by the president at the proposal of the chair of the Chamber of Deputies, or if it does not decide within three months on a government-sponsored bill which the government has made a question of confidence. He is also able to dissolve the lower house if the session of the Chamber has been interrupted for a period longer than is admissible or if it has not had a quorum for over three months.

In contrast to the situation under the federal constitution, the Czech president cannot initiate legislation. However, the president has the right to return laws, apart from constitutional laws, passed by parliament for reconsideration. In such cases, a majority of the Chamber of Deputies, the lower, and to date only, house of parliament, is sufficient to pass the law, despite the president's veto. The president also signs laws, together with the prime minister.

The president has the right to participate in meetings of parliament and its committees and commissions; he or she also has the right to speak to parliament at any time he or she requests. In addition, the president has the right to take part in government meetings, request reports from the government and discuss matters within their jurisdiction with the members of the government.[5]

There are several anomalies in the president's relations with parliament under the 1992 Czech constitution. These stem from the fact that the second house of parliament envisioned by the constitution, the Senate, was yet to be constituted. Thus, according to the constitution, the president is to be elected at a joint meeting of both houses of parliament. Since the Senate did not exist, it was the Chamber of Deputies, which was empowered by the constitution to act alone until the Senate was constituted, that elected Havel president of the Czech Republic in February 1993. But from now on the president must be elected by a joint session of the Chamber of Deputies and Senate. A candidate must be nominated by twenty deputies or ten senators and is elected by a simple majority of all deputies and all senators. In the event that no candidate receives such a majority, a second election is to occur within fourteen days; the candidates who have received the highest number of votes in each chamber advance to the second round. In the event of a tie in either or both houses, those who receive the highest votes when the total number of votes received in both chambers are combined participate in the second round. If no candidate receives a simple majority of those deputies present and of those senators present, a third round is held in fourteen days. If no candidate obtains a majority in the third round, new elections must be held.[6] Similarly, although the president is empowered to dissolve the Chamber of Deputies under the conditions noted above, he could not do so in the absence of the Senate.

As this enumeration of the powers of the president illustrates, the formal powers of the office are limited. The prime minister, as head of the government, is responsible for introducing legislation. The government also has the right to issue governmental regulations. As in other parliamentary systems, the prime minister is responsible for exercising the executive function and overseeing the administration of legislation. This pattern has limited the influence the president can exert through his role in the legislative process.[7]

In a comparative study of the powers of the presidency in East Central Europe, James McGregor ranked the Czech presidency near the top among the fourteen postcommunist countries compared in terms of the number of its symbolic and ceremonial powers, as well as appointive powers. However, as he noted, most of these powers, as well as the far more limited political powers of the office, were qualified, i.e., required the agreement of another institution or individual. Overall, the Czech president ranked ninth of fourteen in terms of the constitutional powers of the office.[8]

The power of the president also depends on factors other than the constitutional powers of the office. One of the most critical of these in the case of the Czechoslovak Federation after the end of communism and the Czech Republic established in 1993 was the impact of the transition from communist rule on the composition and working of other institutions, including parliament, the government, and political parties. The influence the president exerted also depended on the holder of the office and the informal resources that the president could bring to bear to influence public debate and the work of the parliament and government.

The role of the first incumbent: Havel as president of Czechoslovakia

As in other new states, or states undergoing transitions from authoritarian rule, the first incumbent, in this case Václav Havel, had a major impact in shaping the office. Elected president of the Czechoslovak Federation in December 1989 by a parliament still dominated by members of the Communist Party, Havel brought to the office of president an authority and prestige unmatched by other political leaders in the country as a result of his literary renown and his lengthy opposition to the communist regime. Although well known in intellectual circles and abroad, he became a public figure in Czechoslovakia largely as a result of his role in founding Civic Forum and leading the Velvet Revolution that ousted the communist system in Czechoslovakia in November 1989. The most visible of the leaders of the Civic Forum, Havel quickly emerged as both the spiritual and *de facto* leader of the country in the immediate post-November days. His election as president sealed the victory of the Velvet Revolution.

Often depicted as a modern philosopher king, Havel played an extremely important role in both symbolic and practical terms in the first two years after the end of communism. As the most visible and popular politician,[9] he brought a good deal of political capital in addition to his unrivaled claim to moral leadership to the office. These resources gave him far greater influence than the powers of his office alone warranted in determining the composition of the federal government, setting the political agenda, and influencing political debate. Prime Minister Marián Čalfa, in his speech nominating Havel as president on 29 December 1989, emphasized the importance of Havel's moral qualifications for president, demonstrated by his activity as a dissident, and claimed that these principles would be a "guarantee that democratic dialogue will remain the basis of our newly born political regime." "It is precisely in the new president's political morality," Čalfa continued, "that the certainty lies that the public's attention and that of their representatives will concentrate on our country's future, on strengthening democracy."[10] Yet, despite his stature and the unusual political resources which Havel brought to the presidency, he was unable to prevent the federation from breaking up. He was also subjected to the ignominy of not being reelected as president by the Federal Assembly in July 1992.

Table 6.1 *Public representatives whom the public trusted, 1989–1990*

	11 Nov.– 1 Dec. 1989		9 Dec.– 12 Dec. 1989		31 Jan. 1989– 5 Feb. 1990		27 Mar.– 4 Apr. 1990	
	Most	Least	Most	Least	Most	Least	Most	Least
V. Havel	10	13	18	11	60	4	51	5
M. Čalfa			4	1	8	7	10	3
V. Klaus					3	1	10	4
A. Dubček	2	2	2	1	7	3	4	3
Čarnogurský	0	0	1	1	0	0	2	2
M. Kňažko	3	2	2	1	0	0	0	0

Source: Institut pro výzkum veřejného mínění, 1990, p. 3.

Havel remained a very popular politician in the Czech Republic throughout his tenure in office. However, as Table 6.1 illustrates, the integrating role he played in the early months after the November 1989 fall of communism declined as the postcommunist period progressed. As tensions between Czech and Slovak leaders escalated, popular trust in Havel declined significantly in Slovakia. Havel also came to be much less popular here than many Slovak politicians.

In July 1992, 60 percent of those polled in the Czech Republic thought Havel should be Czech president. In September, 51 percent thought so, in October, 57 percent, in November, 51 percent, and in December, 45 percent. However, although support for Havel declined, no other figure came close to receiving this level of support. Only 2–4 percent of respondents favored Václav Klaus as president, and only 3–4 percent Miroslav Sládek, leader of the far-right Republican Party.[11] Trust in Havel remained high during his first year as Czech president and increased in 1994 and 1995. In April 1995, 78 percent of those surveyed trusted Havel. Public trust in Václav Klaus, on the other hand, decreased from 71 percent in February 1995 to 54 percent in April 1995. Those surveyed praised Havel's honesty, openness, and support for democracy, but felt that he lacked "political foresight." Positive views of Klaus, on the other hand, focused on his specialized knowledge of economics and his ability to achieve his goals; respondents criticized him for his "lack of sensitivity to the democratic process."[12]

As was the case with others thrust unexpectedly into the role of political leaders, Havel was inexperienced in practical politics when he became president of Czechoslovakia. In a telling response to an interviewer's query concerning his habit of wearing sweaters rather than suits and ties, Havel replied, "First of all, I do wear suits sometimes. However, if people

Table 6.2 *Overall trust in president, government, and parliament, 1993*

	September		October		November		December	
	yes	no	yes	no	yes	no	yes	no
president	69	28	73	25	70	29	69	28
government	57	39	60	37	59	37	56	40
parliament	26	66	23	69	25	68	20	73

Source: Prague CTK: "Poll Shows Most Czechs Still Trust Havel," as reported in FBIS-EEU-93-244, 22 December 1993, p. 13.

trust me they will accept me the way I am."[13] Used to the life of a dissident intellectual, he had to learn the rules of the game of practical politics as head of state. He also had to learn the art of managing a large staff, dealing with foreign and domestic political leaders, and speaking to the press. His early acts as president were also affected by the general confusion in the political system as a whole during the transition period.

As a writer, Havel reflected and elaborated on his conception of the office of president. From these writings, as well as from his actions, it is clear that he held a dual conception of the function of president. The first function was that of symbolic or moral leader of the country. Often described by others as the conscience of his country in the early days after communism, Havel's lengthy opposition to the communist regime and insistence on "living in truth" despite the personal cost made this a natural role for him. On the eve of his election as president, Havel argued that he would not remain in office very long. He also articulated his perception of his role: "If my fellow citizens want to install me there (in the presidency) as a guarantor of a fair and decent election campaign, I will gladly do my duty for the people as a symbolic figure during this time of national understanding."[14]

One of the features of Havel's presidency that was evident in the early months of his tenure in office was his tendency to use symbolic politics and the office of the presidency as a forum for raising controversial public issues. His willingness to discuss topics most other politicians would not touch publicly was clearly evident in his speech on the occasion of the visit of the president of Germany, Richard von Weizsacker, to Prague on 15 March 1990. In his welcoming speech, Havel used the occasion, which coincided with the anniversary of the German occupation of Bohemia and Moravia in 1939, to air sensitive issues in Czech–German relations and call for efforts at reconciliation on both sides.[15] Havel continued to use the symbolic power of the presidency to raise issues he perceived to be important to the strengthening of democracy, throughout his tenure in office.

Havel also insisted from the outset of his term as president that politics and morality were compatible. In a speech to the Federal Assembly in June 1992 after the parliamentary elections, Havel noted:

My lifelong civic and public activities . . . have been and continue to be insep-arably linked to several values, ideals, or simply inner urges which I would like to recall. Above all it is an elementary feeling of sharing responsibility for the state of the world and common matters. I do believe in the moral origins of politics as a service to our fellow beings. I do believe in the moral roots of any purposeful human coexistence on earth. I do believe in civic values and civic community. I do believe in human freedom. I do believe in democracy . . . This is me and I will not be changed.[16]

After he had resigned as federal president, Havel replied to a question about whether a politician can always abide by his high moral principles by stating:

If it were the basis of politics that he who devotes himself to it must automatically give up his moral principles, I would not devote myself to politics. I, however, consider the notion that politics is by its nature dirty to be immensely dangerous. In politics, a person simply has a somewhat different type of responsibility than an ordinary citizen. Often it happens, for example, that he must assert his principles not by the fact that he chooses the best solution but by the fact that he chooses the least harmful of the solutions that are available to him.[17]

Since 1989, there have been many who have criticized Havel for abandon-ing his moral principles on a variety of issues, ranging from his signing of the controversial law on the illegality of the communist era, and the citizenship law that in effect denies many Romanies the possibility of becoming Czech citizens, to his failure to challenge a law making it a crime to slander the president and other high officials.[18] Although Havel may be open to criticism on concrete issues, it is clear that his perception of the role of president and of his own actions as president has a consistent and deep moral dimension.

From the outset, Havel defined his role as non-partisan. Although he was one of the founders of Civic Forum, he disassociated himself from the group and all other parties and movements upon becoming president. As he argued in January 1992, "I try to be a president. I would not like to stay above the party, for that would look as though I were elevating myself above the rest. I would rather stay a nonparty president, or a president outside any party. This is not because the law or the constitution pre-scribes this for me, but because I have made such a decision." Havel also emphasized the integrating role of the president, who, being above political parties, could talk to all sides and create a scope for dialogue and consensus.[19]

Havel argued in a 29 June 1990 speech in parliament just prior to his reelection as Czechoslovak president after the June 1990 elections that the powers of the president were too extensive and should be curtailed in the new constitution to be adopted.[20] At the same time, despite his initial perceptions concerning the nature of the office and its constitutional limitations, Havel played an extremely important role in the day-to-day life of his country as Czechoslovak president. This role was particularly evident in the first year and a half after the revolution when Havel was clearly the dominant political figure. A good deal of Havel's ability to influence political developments appears to have happened by default. By far the most prominent public figure and the clear first among equals in the dissident community, Havel exerted more influence during this period than he would once the development of other political institutions, the growth in support for other politicians, and the resurgence of influence of certain groups and organizations from the old regime, constrained his actions to a greater extent. Trusted far more by the public than other political leaders, Havel had a decisive role in choosing the prime minister and members of the government as well as in most of the major decisions of the day.

Three of the most important members of the Czechoslovak government formed after the June 1990 elections, for example, Prime Minister Marián Čalfa and the ministers of the interior and defense, were not the choices of Civic Forum, the movement that won the election in the Czech lands, but of the president. A critic noted at the time that the operation of the parliamentary system was "impeded by the vagueness and – to be blunt – by the undefined nature of presidential authority. Although we define our system as a parliamentary system, the president has every right and opportunity to behave in the same way as in a presidential system, although he is elected by parliament alone and not by a universal vote. This is a remnant from the old communist constitution."[21]

Havel's influence was also evident in Czechoslovakia's economic policies in the first year and a half after the revolution. Havel's main economic advisers, Valtr Komarek, then deputy prime minister, and Václav Klaus, then finance minister, disagreed about the scope and speed of economic reform. Unsure about the best direction to take in the economic realm, Havel temporized for approximately six months after becoming president. The victory, in September 1990, of Klaus's conception of economic reform, which emphasized the importance of a radical, rapid move to recreate the market coupled with macro-economic stabilization policies, reflected Havel's growing conviction that the third way strategy espoused by Komarek would delay both market reform and the building of a stable base for democracy.

While serving as president of the Czechoslovak Federation, Havel made frequent use of his ability to introduce legislation for parliament's consideration. Many of these initiatives were related to his efforts to see that the country had a new constitution by the June 1992 parliamentary elections. The adoption of the new constitution was blocked by the inability of Czech and Slovak political leaders to agree despite repeated negotiations and several near misses at achieving an agreement on a power-sharing formula or the nature of the state. Havel sought to moderate the conflict between Czech and Slovak leaders in order to facilitate the adoption of a new constitution and avert the break-up of the federation. Havel was among the first to see the continued inability of leaders of the two regions to agree on a division of powers between the republic and federal governments as well as on economic policies as a threat to the stability and continuation of the common state, and he called for greater efforts on the part of political leaders in both parts of the country to compromise.[22] In a March 1991 effort to help resolve the crisis, he proposed a draft federal constitution. However, this constitution was not adopted by parliament.[23] Havel made further proposals to the federal parliament in late 1991 in the form of five draft bills to help facilitate a constitutional arrangement. Parliament rejected Havel's proposals in January 1992.[24]

Havel also advocated the use of a referendum to resolve the issue of the nature of the state. However, although the federal parliament adopted a law providing for a referendum on the future of the state in July 1991,[25] a referendum was never held. The law stipulated that the president must call a referendum at the request of either the Federal Assembly or the legislature of one republic. However, Havel's September 1991 call for the Federal Assembly to request a referendum was opposed by both the Christian Democratic Movement in Slovakia and Vladimír Mečiar's Movement for a Democratic Slovakia. Slovak opposition also prevented agreement on the questions to be included in the referendum in November 1991, which made it impossible to hold it.[26]

Fear that the federation would break up was the primary factor that led Havel, earlier an advocate of more limited powers for the president, to call in December 1991 for an expansion of the powers of the presidency. At that time, Havel asserted that the country faced a constitutional crisis as a result of the threat of Slovak leaders to disregard the decisions of the federal legislature if it did not adopt the Slovak proposal for a devolution of power to the republics.[27] In this situation, Havel noted, it was clearly his responsibility as president to take action to protect the constitution. In an interview during this period, Havel noted that, "At this serious moment, when the existence of our federative state is actually under threat, I cannot act the dead beetle."[28]

In his request for greater powers, which he presented as a necessary temporary measure to preserve the unity of the country until a new constitution could be adopted, Havel called for the president to be given the power to reject a law and return it to parliament for further discussion, as well as the power to rule by decree in the period between the dismissal of parliament and the establishment of a new legislature. He also proposed that the president be given the power, in crisis situations, to appoint a caretaker cabinet.[29] In addition, Havel asked parliament to establish a constitutional court that could settle disagreements concerning power-sharing. He also requested emergency legislation that would allow a referendum on the future of the state to be held.[30] Havel noted that Czechoslovakia's first president, Thomas G. Masaryk, wrote that, "states are sustained only through the ideals which brought them into being. This applies also to our young, fragile, and inexperienced democracy . . . The condition of our state as it appears today . . . on the International Day of Human Rights, does not reflect many of the ideals of the past year. We can easily find ourselves on the brink of a constitutional crisis, among other things, because many of us are forgetting the original ideals or fail to be guided by them."[31]

In justifying his call for emergency powers for the president, Havel referred to his own earlier attitudes toward the presidency and denied that he was interested in increasing his personal power: "I believe strongly that you have come to know me enough over the last year that you don't need to suspect that I am dreaming of increasing my personal power. For a long time I even believed that the powers of the president of the Republic should be reduced by the future constitution." Noting the danger to democracy as well as to the existence of the federation that the threat to declare a republic's laws sovereign posed, Havel argued that he would be unable to fulfill his presidential oath if his powers were not strengthened during the transition period.[32] He also linked his requests to the provisions of Czechoslovakia's 1920 constitution.

Most of Havel's December 1990 legislative initiatives were rejected by the federal parliament, largely as the result of the so-called Slovak bloc, i.e., members of nationalistic Slovak political parties in parliament. After the defeat of his first three proposals, Havel withdrew his proposal for a reorganization of the Federal Assembly.[33] Havel's other efforts to mediate the conflict between Czech and Slovak political leaders were also unsuccessful. After the failure of his efforts to create new mechanisms that the president could use to resolve the crisis resulting from Czech–Slovak disagreements, Havel became increasingly marginalized from discussion of the issue of the proper form of power-sharing between the republic and federal governments.

As noted above, Havel continued to enjoy very high levels of trust and popularity, particularly in the Czech lands throughout the period. He also enjoyed substantial popular support in Slovakia, although he was far less popular in Slovakia than in the Czech lands. Nonetheless, he was unable to bridge the gap that increasingly separated Czech and Slovak leaders on the matters of constitutional change and economic reform. A reflection of historical, economic, and political factors, including the legacy of communist rule in the two areas, and the particular characteristics of the politics of transition, the break-up of the Czechoslovak federation was also influenced by institutional factors.[34] These included the fact that the country continued to be organized along federal lines and the impact of the provisions of the constitution, which was the one that had existed during communism (with the exception of those clauses that dealt with the special position of the Communist Party and the working class). In effect this constitution allowed 38 deputies in one house of parliament, the House of Nations, to prevent the passage of a law, and 31 out of a total of 300 to prevent the passage of constitutional amendments.[35]

The victory in the June 1992 elections of Klaus's center-right Civic Democratic Party in the Czech lands and Mečiar's left of center Movement for a Democratic Slovakia in Slovakia, sealed the fate of the federation. Mečiar's victory in Slovakia also made it a certainty that Václav Havel would not be reelected president by the newly elected federal parliament. Opposed by the Movement for a Democratic Slovakia, the Party of the Democratic Left of Slovakia, and the Slovak National Party, Havel failed to receive the required three-fifths of the votes in the House of the People and the Slovak body of the House of Nations in the first round of voting. He failed to receive the required majority of votes in the second round in the Slovak part of the House of Nations.[36]

Scheduled to remain in office until 5 October if no one else succeeded in being elected president, on 17 July Havel announced his resignation, which took place on July 20, immediately after the Slovak National Council adopted a declaration of sovereignty. A final indication of the failure of efforts to save the federation, the declaration of sovereignty and Havel's subsequent resignation also reflected the limited impact even a political president could have in bridging the different perspectives on public issues and aspirations of Czechs and Slovaks by the summer of 1992.[37]

In explaining his resignation to the nation, Havel emphasized the fact that he did not feel able to fulfill the obligations of his oath of office in a way that would be compatible with his "nature, convictions, and conscience."[38] He noted:

Just as I do not wish to become an obstacle to this historical development (the attainment of Slovak sovereignty), neither do I want to be a mere clerk who knows his days are numbered and who waits a few more months for the moment when he will leave office for good and who, during that time, only passively watches further developments as they unfold before him, and who only formally fulfills his formal duty . . . The office of federal president no longer enables me to do creative and constructive work.[39]

Given the unusual nature of the issue involved, Havel's limited influence in stemming the trend toward the break-up of the Czechoslovak state cannot be taken alone as an indication of the waning power of his presidency. However, there are other indications that Havel's influence on political developments had decreased substantially by the end of his tenure as Czechoslovak president. Havel had very little part in the negotiations between Klaus and Mečiar that brought about the end of the federation, for example. He also appears to have had little influence on the composition of the new federal and republic governments formed after the June elections. After his resignation, Havel argued that his role was too ceremonial, and, in affirming his willingness to run for president of the Czech Republic, noted that he would not become merely a ceremonial leader.[40]

Constitutional limitations on the powers of the president prevented Havel from playing a more direct role in the resolution of the power-sharing crisis and also limited the role he could play in successfully influencing the legislative agenda of the federal parliament. Thus, although certain of Havel's legislative initiatives were passed by the parliament, many others were not. And, as the fate of the law on the referendum illustrates, the impact of ethnic politics and the ability of Slovak parties to block almost all legislation if they chose to do so, meant that even those areas in which Havel succeeded in persuading the federal parliament to pass legislation he proposed, these laws were subject to being vitiated by the inability or unwillingness of the federal parliament to act to implement them. The system of indirect election of the president by the legislature also weakened Havel's ability to influence political developments, as he had no direct mandate from the population to draw upon. In addition, under the decision rules inherited from the communist era, a small handful of deputies in the legislature was able to block his reelection as president in 1992.

The erosion of the president's influence on day-to-day political events also reflected the institutionalization of political life in Czechoslovakia between 1990 and 1992. Thus, in 1990, Havel was one of a very small handful of political figures, most of them former dissidents, who had the moral stature to gain public trust and respect. At a time when personalities rather than political institutions dominated political life, his reputation gave him political resources unmatched by other leaders. As the political system and political life became more routinized, and as the umbrella movements that led the revolution in both the Czech lands and Slovakia gave way to more highly structured parties and movements, the advantages these resources provided diminished and politicians skilled at building electoral bases and organizing support came to dominate the political arena.

Havel continued to have an impact on certain political decisions in the last months of the Czechoslovak Federation's existence. For example, his announcement on 17 November 1992, that he would be a candidate for the presidency of the Czech Republic increased the pressure on members of parliament to pass a law to formally end the Czechoslovak Federation. However, in this case, Havel's influence was due to his personal authority rather than that of the office he had vacated several months earlier.[41]

The Czech presidency: Havel as first incumbent

In his vision of the presidency of the new Czech Republic prior to its creation, Havel proposed that the president be elected directly. He noted that he was uninterested in merely being a "decorative" president, but he nonetheless accepted election to a post that had fewer formal powers than that of the Czechoslovak presidency.

As in the period when he was president of Czechoslovakia, Havel continued to define his role as Czech president in both symbolic, moral, and functional terms. Recognising that his role as Czech president would be much smaller than that as Czechoslovak president, immediately after his election to that office Havel defined his responsibility as an "inconspicuous guardian of a high standard of political etiquette and of the political standards of public life" in the Czech Republic.[42] He also emphasized his role as the guarantor of the longer term interests of the nation and of democracy and pledged to stay above the fray of day-to-day partisan political struggles.

In an article published just prior to his election as Czech president, Havel underscored that the main differences in the function of the Czechoslovak and Czech presidency arose from the fact that the function of the latter was defined differently in the constitution, and from the radical changes in the political situation in the Czech Republic. The central change Havel highlighted was the shift to "the phase in which parliamentary democracy was stabilizing itself, based, already very clearly, on the competition of political parties of different orientations, and on a clearly defined system of shares of political power."⁴³ Noting that the revolutionary era had ended, Havel argued that the president therefore would no longer need to fulfill the "curious role of some sort of 'leader of the nation' or symbol of a new era. Nor will he be forced – or be allowed – to intervene in every thing and be in that way responsible for everything."⁴⁴

The president, therefore, Havel argued, should not set forth his own political program. Rather, his main task was to "have an idea about the constitutional and political position of the presidency, and about the ways in which he would implement these ideas and the values he, as head of state, in exercising his powers and in his public activity would defend, protect, and promote."⁴⁵ Pointing to the five-year term of president, Havel argued that while governments might come and go, "the president will, however, stay in his office for his whole five-year term." Because of this fact, and the ability of the president to designate the government (as he did following the June 1996 parliamentary elections) and in certain circumstances to dissolve parliament, the president is to be a "guarantor of or a means of ensuring the continuity of state power, and also a representative of the identity and integrity of the state . . ." He should be a " 'fixed point, an institution of the last resort' – or the 'last solution' – and represent permanent security in the midst of the dynamics of democratic development."⁴⁶

According to this vision of the president's role, the president should focus on long-term matters that affect the "very existence and democratic substance of the state, the stability of its political system, values on which the state is established . . . He should not participate in mundane and ephemeral political disputes and quarrels as the political entities that compete among themselves on the political scene do."⁴⁷ The president, Havel continued, should be a moderator in political discussions who would seek to facilitate consensus; he should serve as an integrating factor and focus on the style of resolution of political disputes rather than their content. "Rather than 'playing' the game himself, he should make sure that the rules of the game are being observed."⁴⁸ Havel also outlined his belief that the president should be responsible for fostering a civic society and a "good political atmosphere" in the country by stressing the moral meaning of citizenship and morality in politics.⁴⁹

At the same time, Havel clearly saw a link between these symbolic, or moral tasks of the president and practical political life. He emphasized that the president, through his right to send legislation back to parliament and to co-sign legislation, had the opportunity to make sure that higher principles were not violated in the conduct of day-to-day decision-making. In this conception, the president should play the "role of guardian of those spiritual, moral and political values upon which the state has been established, and its long-term prospects and international prestige, and be capable of sacrificing at times temporary interests for the benefit of the greater general interest and that of future generations."[50] In conclusion, Havel stressed that the Czech president's "situation will not be at all easy; he decidedly will not have any automatic influence on public affairs and he will have to work hard for his place in the sun, and gain it through the authority of his personality and the credibility of his everyday work. However, I believe, that this is for the best."[51] Havel's perceptions of the role of president, then, reflect the impact of constitutional changes. In a continuation of the process that began during his last year as president of the Czechoslovak Federation, Havel's role and powers as president of the Czech Republic were constrained by the growing role of other political actors, including parliament and the prime minister.

Despite Havel's less active role as president of the Czech Republic, his relationship with the government and Prime Minister Klaus in the first few months after his election as Czech president reflected certain tensions. There were several instances in which the president made statements concerning the country's foreign policy that were at odds with the views of the prime minster and the Foreign Ministry. These included his statement calling for air strikes on Serbian positions in Bosnia during a visit to Washington, and his calling for multilateral military intervention in Bosnia. Havel's condemnation of the forced expulsion of the Sudeten Germans from Czechoslovakia at the end of World War II also differed from the government's stated position that this issue be closed.[52] Havel also openly criticized what he perceived to be a lack of coordination between the President's Office and the Foreign Ministry in March 1993.[53]

Relations between Havel and the Foreign Ministry had improved perceptibly by the time of President Clinton's visit to Prague in January 1994. In part this was due to the role which Alexander Vondra, former adviser to Havel and currently deputy foreign minister, played in mediating relations between Havel and Josef Zieleniec, the foreign minister. However, as the difference of opinion between Klaus and the president on the desirability of a visit to Prague of writer Salman Rushdie illustrated, tensions persisted in this area.[54]

Havel's relationship with parliament improved if only because the president was no longer able to present bills to parliament but only return them for reconsideration. Havel used the presidential veto sparingly. He also took more care than during his tenure as federal president to meet with deputies and cultivate relationships with a wide variety of political figures.[55] In May 1994, Havel indicated his desire to be in more frequent contact with members of the government. As he stated, "I have come to the conclusion that it will be useful for both sides if I change somewhat the method of my contact with the government as a whole, with the individual ministers, and with the Prime Minister. I think that it is in the interest of the stability of our state that these contacts be routine and frequent."[56] Havel also established a pattern of regular meetings with representatives of different groups of parliamentarians, and monthly dinners with the chair and deputy chair of parliament, as well as *ad hoc* meetings with deputies.

Although Havel emphasized the president's role as defender of the country's larger and long-term interests, he clearly regarded the role of president as critical. Thus, Havel continued to play an important role in the political debate on issues which he identified as central to the Czech state and the defense of democracy. As in the last years of his tenure as Czechoslovak president, his actions in this regard often brought him into conflict with Prime Minister Klaus.

Early in his term as Czech president, Havel pledged to cooperate closely with the prime minister and the government. In what many see as an attempt to increase his influence on policy-making, Havel instituted the practice of attending cabinet meetings and consulting with members of the government individually.

Nonetheless, there were persistent reports of tension between the president and the prime minister.[57] Although the two men generally refrained from commenting on each other's actions, they publicly espoused different views on numerous issues. A reflection of their differing personalities and general orientations as well as institutional perspectives, this conflict was evident in such areas as administrative reform and the establishment of the Czech Senate. It was also reflected in the differing perspectives the two men had on the nature of democracy and, particularly, the importance of civil society and the non-governmental sector to democratic political life.

One particular area in which Havel's disagreements with Klaus were evident was the question of the creation of regions. The old regional structure of the communist era was abolished in 1991, as were the district level governments. As a result, there was no intermediary level of government between the central government in Prague and individual local governments. The Czech constitution adopted in late 1992 in anticipation of the creation of an independent Czech state called for the establishment of regions. However, it did not specify their number, how they should be elected, or their functions. Nor was their relationship with the central government clarified. As a result, the issue became the subject of continuous political disputes.

Given the inability of Czech and Slovak leaders to agree on a division of powers between the federal and regional governments in the early post-communist period, the sensitivity of any discussion of new institutional forms inhibited serious discussion of new forms of regional government. Early efforts to propose a new system of regional organization thus were shelved.[58] In the Czech lands, the issue had added sensitivity given the strength after 1989 of support for the Movement for a Self-Governing Democracy – Association for Moravia-Silesia, in Moravia.

With the end of the federation, many of the barriers to considering the issue were removed. However, the Klaus government displayed little interest in moving ahead with plans to create a new regional structure. His reluctance was based on a variety of factors, including fear that a devolution of power from the center to the regions would threaten the unity necessary for further successful economic reform. Political considerations also played a role. Civic Democratic Party spokespersons argued that adopting a regional structure could foster disputes between the center and the regions that would be more threatening to a newly reestablished democracy, such as the Czech Republic, than to an older, more established democratic system. As a result, a resolution submitted to parliament by opposition deputies in November 1993 calling for a regional structure to be introduced as soon as possible was effectively shelved by the Civic Democratic Party, whose leaders decided to put the decision about a new regional structure off until after the fall 1994 local elections.[59]

Stalemate on this issue, coupled with his own strong view of regional governments as a necessary avenue for citizens to be involved in self-governance, led Havel to enter the debate in 1994. Noting that continued disagreement among the coalition partners could threaten political stability if it continued, Havel sent a letter in June 1993 to leaders of all four coalition parties calling for action to implement this provision of the constitution.[60] Three days later, the coalition agreed on a compromise proposal that would have created seventeen regions in the Czech Republic, but it did not pass.[61] On 24 August the Czech government approved a new draft for a regional system of government. However, Prime Minister Klaus required that it be passed by a three-fifths majority.[62] The constitutional amendment needed to approve regional reform had still not been passed by parliament by mid-April 1995, when Havel called once again for its passage before the 1996 parliamentary elections.[63]

Havel and Klaus have also locked horns on the issue of the Senate.

Another institution called for in the 1992 constitution that was yet to be established, the Senate was included in the constitution as a compromise measure in order to obtain enough votes to pass it. It was seen by many, including the prime minister, as an unnecessary body that would only complicate the legislative process. In an interview in September 1993, Klaus said that he could not identify a function for the Senate.[64] Klaus also cited the lack of enthusiasm for the Senate by the media as a symptom of the "factual uselessness" of the body. However, the Civic Democratic Party's deputies, along with other members of the government coalition, voted against an effort by left-wing deputies to amend the constitution to abolish the Senate in September 1994.[65]

Several proposals were set forth in 1993 and 1994 on the method of electing senators and the timing of their election. Here, too, disagreement between the ruling coalition and the opposition parties, and within the government coalition itself, prevented the adoption of measures to establish the Senate.[66] Similarly, a draft law on parliamentary elections, which would have allowed the holding of elections for the Senate in 1994, failed to pass the parliament in June 1994.[67] Public opinion polls indicated that there was little support among the population for the establishment of the Senate. Approximately 45 percent of those polled in late May 1994, for example, opposed the creation of the Senate, and another 37 percent did not have an opinion concerning the issue. Only 18 percent favored the creation of a second chamber of parliament.[68]

Supporters of the creation of the Senate, including the president, argued that it represents a necessary check on the power of the lower house of parliament. In calling for the establishment of the Senate, Havel argued that the lack of an upper house could create a major crisis as the president would not be able to dissolve parliament and call for new elections if the lower house could not agree on a government. He also argued that the president could not be expected to substitute for the Senate as monitor of the work of the lower house of parliament.[69] Finally, elections were held for an 81-seat Senate in November 1996. Not only did Havel's stand on this second chamber win out, his preference for chair of the Senate, Petr Pithart Cuch, premier between 1990–92, was chosen the following month over the objections of Klaus.

A final area in which Havel clashed with the prime minister was on the subject of civil society. A reflection to some degree of his emphasis on the importance of morality in politics, Havel's views reflected his perception of his role as defender of the long-term interests of democracy in the Czech Republic. Sometimes presented as a difference in world views, the president and the prime minister clearly held different views on the nature of civil society and the kinds of non-governmental institutions that were

necessary to sustain a democratic political system. In his public statements, Havel has repeatedly emphasized the importance of a strong,
diversified non-governmental sector in maintaining citizen participation
and input in a democratic society.[70] Calling for a "new vision" to guide
developments in the Czech Republic, Havel argued for the decentralization of the political system and increased citizen involvement in politics.
The difference in the perspectives of the president and prime minister
continued to be evident up to the 1996 elections, as Klaus argued that
advocates of civil society were trying to "create bureaucratic layers between the citizen and the state."[71] Klaus also adopted a skeptical stance
concerning the value of non-profit organizations.[72]

Havel restated his political vision in his address to parliament in March
1995. He focused on the importance of human rights as one of the central
elements of civil society and democracy. He called once again for the
creation of the Senate and regional administrative reform. And he reiterated his support for further development of the non-profit sector.
Klaus, who opposed the idea of a state of the nation address by Havel
when Havel proposed it, admitted to disagreeing with many parts of the
president's address.[73] He even contested the president's notion that the
Czech Republic needed a new vision and argued that most Czechs
already had a clear vision of what they wanted.

The results of the June 1996 parliamentary elections suggested that the
Czech public may have grown tired of the Havel–Klaus standoff and
chose to increase the number of important political actors on the national
stage. In what many observers found a surprising result, Klaus's Civic
Democratic Party and its two right-of-center coalition partners lost their
absolute majority in parliament. The biggest winner was the Social
Democratic Party (CSSD), a successor to the former ruling Communist
Party, which became the second largest party (after the Civic Democratic
Party) in parliament. Adding seats won by the CSSD, unreconstructed
communists, and the right-wing Republican Party, these now commanded a majority that, if acting in concert, would be sufficient hypo-
thetically to form a government and certainly to control legislation.

Havel was presented with the dilemma of asking one of the party
leaders to try to form a government. In conventional parliamentary
practice, he turned to the leader of the largest party, Klaus, even though
at first the Social Democrats asserted they would bring down any Klaus-
led government. Clearly, negotiations that would bring in CSSD leader
Milos Zeman were required if Klaus was to succeed in forming a viable
minority government. President Havel played a pivotal role in July 1996
in brokering a deal whereby Klaus's minority government would present
its draft program for discussion with the CSSD before introducing it in

the legislature. This arrangement, together with the appointment of Zeman as parliamentary chair, seemed enough to persuade the CSSD to refrain from voting no-confidence in Klaus. But it was obvious that no amount of diplomacy by Havel could secure a long-term *modus vivendi* between the two largest parties and new elections to resolve the impasse were likely.

Another challenge for Havel in 1996 was to overcome the difference in views on the desirability of the Czech Republic's membership in NATO. Havel was an eager supporter of NATO membership as was Klaus. Even the Social Democrats were prepared to accept membership if certain conditions were met, such as the holding of a general referendum on the subject. But in 1996 Czech public opinion was divided on NATO, with only one-third firmly in favor and the rest opposed or undecided. A test of his effectiveness as president was, therefore, for Havel to persuade the public of the advantages of membership in the Western alliance. Helping shape the country's government and determining its long-term security policy were issues as fundamental as any president could face. In 1996 Havel, the philosopher-king and a constitutionally restricted president, seemed at the crossroads of how the Czech political system and its presidency would evolve for some time to come.

Conclusion

The changed role of Václav Havel as president of the Czechoslovak Federation and the Czech Republic, like the fate of the Czechoslovak Federation itself, illustrates the important role other institutions, political contingencies, and the impact of individual personalities play in defining the office of president in political systems in transition. What has determined the strength of the presidency in the Czech Republic? As I have argued, the formal powers of the office were limited prior to the end of the Czechoslovak Federation. Havel was able to exert a great deal of influence on political developments in Czechoslovakia immediately after the revolution largely because he had very little competition and faced few institutional constraints. In the months immediately after the fall of communism, parliament was weak and disorganized. As there were still many deputies who had been elected during the communist period, it was also a somewhat discredited institution. Those legislators chosen to sit in parliament after the expulsion of some of the most compromised deputies were inexperienced and, because they had not been chosen in popular elections, had little base for challenging Havel and his actions. The newly created or resurrected political parties were very weak organizationally and had both poorly defined and differentiated platforms, and a small and fluctuating base of supporters. In this situation, the political capital Havel had earned as the result of his position of uncompromising opponent of the old regime gave him a significant advantage. Havel also benefited during this period from the general consensus concerning the major goals of the day, often expressed in the slogans that came to dominate the 1990 legislative elections: democracy, the market, and a return to Europe.

As the postcommunist period progressed, several elements of this situation changed. After the elections of 1990, parliament began playing a more influential role. In addition, politicians such as the then finance minister, Klaus, who was instrumental in breaking up the non-partisan Civic Forum, began creating mass-based hierarchically organized political parties that provided them with a power base separate from that of their association with the president. In Slovakia, Mečiar's Movement for a Democratic Slovakia provided him with a similar base of power.

This process continued after the June 1992 elections. After emerging as leaders of the most popular political forces in their respective republics, Klaus and Mečiar in effect negotiated the end of the federation. The federal presidency as well as the federal parliament were marginalized as it became clear that the federation's days were limited.

The decline in the fortunes of the presidency continued in the Czech Republic that came into being on 1 January 1993. Now holding the office of prime minister, Klaus emerged as the dominant politician in day-to-day decision-making in the Czech Republic. Havel, as Czech president, became confined increasingly to ceremonial or symbolic roles. However, despite the formal limits on his power and efforts to isolate him from daily politics, his moral authority and popularity were still important political resources that allowed him to exert greater influence than his office alone would provide.

From a broader perspective, the fate of the Czechoslovak Federation and political developments in Czechoslovakia since the end of communism illustrate the complexity of political life in postcommunist states. Havel is sometimes criticized for failing to hold the federation together. However, responsibility is more properly placed at the door of parliament and the parliamentary system. Despite the fact that Czechoslovakia had a parliamentary system, it failed to pass the most basic test of effectiveness: the federal state broke up.

As Jana Reschová has argued in an analysis of the actions of the federal parliament between 1989 and 1993, the Federal Assembly played a minor role in the negotiations that brought about the dissolution of the federation after the June 1992 elections. After the elections, the discussions that mattered moved from the Federal Assembly to the much smaller circle of top Czech and Slovak officials, particularly Klaus and Mečiar.

The results of extraparliamentary negotiations between the two, who also led the strongest parties in the two regions, were in many instances merely ratified afterwards by parliament.[74] Thus, although the Federal Assembly passed twenty-eight constitutional laws between December 1989 and December 1991,[75] it lost its dominant role in the process of changing the constitution after the June 1992 elections. This pattern was reminiscent of the pattern of informal consultations among party leaders in Czechoslovakia during the interwar period. However, in contrast to that period, when such consultations contributed to the stability of coalitions and thus to overall political stability, in the postcommunist period, they led to the break-up of the state itself.

In short, the inability of parliamentary leaders from the two regions to agree to a power-sharing formula and the negative perceptions of parliament and of the federation their behavior created were factors that fed separatist tendencies in Slovakia and increased readiness on the part of the Czech public, particularly after the June 1992 elections, to agree to a break-up.

At the same time, both presidential and parliamentary systems carry risks. As Valerie Bunce has noted, in a transitional period in which so much, including political institutions themselves, is in flux, it is difficult to trace political outcomes to particular institutional patterns.[76] The dissolution of the Czechoslovak Federation illustrates this point. One could argue that a more powerful presidential system, which would have allowed Havel to move more quickly to break the deadlock in the Federal Assembly over the power-sharing issue or gain approval of a referendum, might have saved the federation, or at least have bought enough time for the public, which did not favor the split, to assert itself. However, it is uncertain that a presidential system or a mixed presidential-paraliamentary system would have saved the federation. Havel himself was not a popular figure in Slovakia, and giving him greater power might well have increased the alienation of Slovaks and provoked a more nationalistic reaction in Slovakia. It is also difficult to see how the very different perspectives of Czechs and Slovaks on a variety of important public issues, as well as Slovak aspirations for a position of parity within the federation, supported by even those who did not favor complete independence, could have been accommodated except under a parliamentary system.

Similarly, a different institutional structure might have made it more difficult for a minority of parliamentary deputies to block progress toward a power-sharing agreement and for top political leaders to by-pass both the president and parliament. But it would not have solved the underlying problems that gave rise to different perspectives and aspirations in the Czech lands and Slovakia.

The Czechoslovak and Czech experiences, then, caution against linking political instability or, conversely, political effectiveness, to a particular kind of system. In divided societies undergoing radical transformations in which significant portions of the population have grievances against the current institutional framework, the very parliamentary system required to take diversity into account can also produce political instability or even the dissolution of the state.

NOTES

1 See Alfred Stepan and Cindy Skach, "Constitutional Frameworks and Democratic Consolidation: Parliamentarianism versus Presidentialism," *World Politics*, 46 (October 1993), pp. 1–22; Juan J. Linz, "The Perils of Presidentialism," *Journal of Democracy*, 1, 1 (June 1990) pp. 51–69; Donald L. Horowitz, "Comparing Democratic Systems," *Journal of Democracy*, 1, 4 (Fall 1990); Seymour Martin Lipset, "The Centrality of Political Culture," *Journal of Democracy* 1, 4 (Fall 1990); Arend Lijphart, "Double-Checking the Evidence," in L. Diamond and M. Plattner (eds.), *The Global Resurgence of Democracy* (Baltimore, MD: Johns Hopkins University Press, 1993), pp. 171–177.

2 See Valerie J. Bunce, "Presidential Systems and Postcommunist Transitions," in Kurt Von Mettenheim (ed.), *Presidents in Democratic Transitions* (Baltimore: Johns Hopkins University Press, forthcoming) for an evaluation of the importance of this factor on the performance of institutions in postcommunist Central and East Europe and for a discussion of the relative merits of presidential and parliamentary systems in the region.

3 See Katarina Mathernova, "Czecho? Slovakia: Constitutional Disappointments," *The American University Journal of International Law and Policy*, 7 (1992), p. 495, and *The Constitutional Foundations of the Czechoslovak Federation* (Prague: Orbis Press Agency, 1978).

4 Ibid.

5 "Constitution of the Czech Republic Adopted by the Czech National Council December 16, 1992," Prague, MS, pp. 10–13.

6 "Constitution of the Czech Republic," Article 58, pp. 10–11.

7 See Jana Reschová, "Parliaments and Constitutional Change: The Czechoslovak Experience," in Attila Agh (ed.), *The Emergence of East Central European Parliaments: The First Steps* (Budapest: The Hungarian Center of Democracy Studies, 1994), p. 5.

8 See James McGregor, "The Presidency in East Central Europe," *RFE/RL Research Report*, 3, 2 (14 January 1994), pp. 23–31.

9 In December 1989, 73 percent of respondents surveyed in the Czech Republic favored the election of Havel as president. See "Poll on Havel, Government Popularity Reported," FBIS-EEU-89-248, 28 December 1989, p. 18.

10 "Čalfa Nominates Havel," FBIS-EEU-89-249, 29 December 1989, p. 22.

11 See "Havel Leads Poll as Popular Choice for President," FBIS-EEU-009-93, 14 January 1993, p. 18.

12 Research conducted by STEM, the Center for Empirical Research, as reported in "More and More Czechs Trust President Havel," *Carolina*, no. 156, 21 April 1995.

13 Jindrich Lion, "Guarantor of Free Elections, Symbol of Understanding," *Der Standard*, 28 December 1989, p. 4 as reported in "Havel Discusses Future Tasks as President," FBIS-EEU-89-248, 28 December 1989, p. 19.

14 Ibid., p. 19.

15 Václav Havel, Prague Castle, 15 March 1990.

16 "President Addresses Federal Parliament," FBIS-EEU-92-124, 26 June 1992, pp. 7–8.

17 Jitka Götzová, "Nechci být zbožňovaným vųdcem národa," *Rudé Právo*, 11 September 1993, pp. 1, 4.

18 See above article for criticism of Havel's action in regard to the law on the illegality of communism by Professor Zdenek Jicinsky.

19 Stanislava Dufkova, "Conversations at Lany," as reported in "Havel Discusses Political Contacts, Constitution," FBIS-EEU-92-008, 13 January 1992, p. 10.

20 CTK, 5 July 1990 as reported in "Further on Election," FBIS-EEU-90-129, 5 July 1990, p. 22.

21 Jiri Hanak, "A Government of Considerable Compromise," *Lidové Noviny*, 2 July 1990, p. 1, as reported in "New Government Seen As Compromise," FBIS-EEU-90-132, 10 July 1990.

22 Prague Domestic Service as reported in "Havel Outlines Proposals to Solve Crisis," FBIS-EEU-90-238, 11 December, p. 10.

23 "Prezidentův návrh ústavy jen podkladem," *Rudé Právo*, 26 March 1991, p. 2.

24 See "Ústavě a referendu – ne," *Hospodářské noviny*, 22 January 1992, p. 1, and "Stop pravomocím prezidenta," *Hospodárske noviny*, 29 January 1992, pp. 1, 2.

25 Jiri Pehe, "The Referendum Controversy in Czechoslovakia," *RFE/RL Research Report*, 1, 43 (30 October 1992), p. 35.

26 Ibid., p. 36.

27 Burton Bollag, "Havel Asserts Nation Faces Breakup," *New York Times*, 11 December 1990, p. A12. See also, "Boj proti dobrodruhům," *Lidové noviny*, 4 December 1991, pp. 1, 5.

28 Jiri Vejvoda, "Conversations at Lany," 8 December 1990, as reported in "Havel Radio Address Views Constitutional Crisis," 9 December 1990. FBIS-EEU-90-240, 13 December 1990, p. 13.

29 "Boj proti dobrodruhům," *Lidové noviny*, 4 December 1991, pp. 1, 5.

30 Ibid.

31 "Ještě máme šanci," *Lidové Noviny*, 11 December 1990, pp. 1, 8.

32 Ibid., p. 12.

33 See Mathernova, "Czecho? Slovakia," pp. 495–497.

34 See Jiří Musil, "Czech and Slovak Society," in Jiří Musil (ed.), *The End of Czechoslovakia* (Budapest: CEU Press, 1995), pp. 77–96; Fedor Gal, *Dnešni krize česko-slovenských vztahů* (Prague: 1993); Sharon Wolchik, "The Politics of Ethnicity in Post-Communist Czechoslovakia," *East European Politics and Societies*, 8, 1 (Winter 1994), pp. 153–188; and Sharon Wolchik, "Institu-

tional and Political Factors in the Break-Up of the Czechoslovak Federation," MS, Prague, June 1996, p. 28.

35 See Katarina Mathernova, "Federalism that Failed: Reflections on the Disintegration of Czechoslovakia," *New Europe Law Review*, 1, 2 (Spring 1993), pp. 477–488.

36 See Jiri Pehe, "Václav Havel Defeated in Bid to be Reelected President," *RFE/RL Research Report*, 1, 29 (17 July 1992), p. 2. See also, "Václav Havel Nezvolen," *Lidové Noviny*, 4 July 1992.

37 See Jan Obrman, "Slovakia Declares Sovereignty; President Havel Resigns," *RFE/RL Research Report*, 1, 31 (31 July 1992), pp. 25–29.

38 "ČSFR Bez Prezidenta," *Lidové noviny*, 18 July 1992, pp. 1, 8.

39 Ibid.

40 Obrman, "Slovakia Declares Sovereignty," p. 26.

41 See Jiri Pehe, "Czechoslovak Parliament Votes to Dissolve Federation" *RFE/RL Research Report*, 1, 48 (4 December 1992), pp. 1–5.

42 "Havel Holds News Conference," FBIS-EEU-93-016, 27 January 1993, p. 13.

43 Václav Havel, "Role českého prezidenta," *Mlada fronta dnes*, 19 January 1993, p. 7.

44 Ibid.

45 Ibid.

46 Ibid.

47 Ibid.

48 Ibid.

49 Ibid.

50 Ibid., p. 18.

51 Ibid.

52 See "Foreign Minister on Havel's Criticism of Ministry," FBIS-EEU-93-062, 2 April 1993, p. 5.

53 Ibid.

54 See Jiří Leschtina and Petr Nováček, "Havlův první rok: politická veličina v záloze," *Mlada fronta dnes*, 26 January 1994, p. 7; see also, Evy Martínkova, "Nemyslím, že se každá návštěva musí konzultovat," *Lidové noviny*, 8 July 1994, pp. 1, 23, for the dispute that arose concerning the visit by the Iraqi foreign minister in the summer of 1994. Klaus indicated in the course of this interview that he did not think that the visit of all foreign ministers must be discussed between the Foreign Ministry and the president.

55 Leschtina and Novacek, "Havlův první rok," p. 6.

56 "Prezident chce udržovat těsnější styky s vládou," *Mlada fronta dnes*, 19 May 1994, p. 2.

57 See for example, "Přetřásejte si dál, řekl Klaus o své údajné aroganci k Hradu," *Rudé právo*, 19 May 1994, p. 2.

58 See Jan Obrman and Pavel Mates, "Subdividing the Czech Republic: The Controversy Continues, *RFE/RL Research Report*, 3, 9 (4 March 1994), pp. 27–32 for a discussion of the commission formed to examine this issue and its proposals.

59 *RFE/RL Daily Report*, no. 217, p. 3.

60 *RFE/RL Daily Report*, 121, 28 June 1994.

61 *RFE/RL Daily Report*, 123, 30 June 1994, p. 4.
62 *RFE/RL Daily Report*, 161, 25 August 1994, p. 4.
63 *RFE/RL Daily Report*, 13 April 1995, p. 4.
64 See "Removal of Senate 'Not Under Consideration,'" FBIS-EEU-93-173, 9 September 1993, p. 6.
65 "Czech Deputies Reject Plan to Eliminate Senate," *RFE/RL Daily Report*, 185, 28 September 1994, p. 4.
66 Jiri Pehe, "Czech Senate Election Stirs Controversy," *RFE/RL Research Report*, 3, 14 (8 April 1994), pp. 7–12.
67 "Parliament Votes Down Draft Law on Elections," *RFE/RL Daily Report*, 104 (3 June 1994), p. 3.
68 Ibid.
69 "Havel on Slovak Elections, Role of Senate," as reported in FBIS-EEU-94-104, 31 May 1994, pp. 13–15.
70 See "Transformace ekonomiky je nezvratná, prohlásil prezident Václav Havel," *Hospodářské noviny*, 3 January 1994, pp. 1, 2.
71 Jiri Pehe, "A Leader in Political Stability and Economic Growth," *Transition*, 1, 1 (30 January 1995), p. 2.
72 See Jiři Weigl, Chief Adviser of Václav Klaus, "Havel versus Klaus čili mantení pojmů," *Mlada Fronta Dnes*, 24 January 1994, p. 6.
73 See Eva Martínková, "V prezidentově projevu je celá řada tezí, se kterými nemohu souhlasit," *Lidové noviny*, 17 March 1995, pp. 1, 3.
74 Reschová, "Parliaments and Constitutional Change," p. 60.
75 Ibid., p. 59.
76 Bunce, "Presidential Systems," pp. 26–29.

7 Hungary: political transition and executive conflict: the balance or fragmentation of power?

Patrick H. O'Neil

One of the greatest challenges that has confronted Eastern Europe since the end of socialism has been the need to build new political institutions to replace the discredited structures of the old order. In some sense tearing down the previous "party-state" system was an easier task; how democracy can now be constructed on the ruins of state socialism remains a more complicated and fractious issue. Indeed, within politics this has become one of the central issues of the postcommunist period: what is the proper configuration of political institutions to stabilize an uncertain political system, withstanding the numerous crises that plague the region? How to "craft democracies"?[1]

Transitions from authoritarianism, like many other periods of political crisis, are inevitably problematic. The end of authoritarian rule, with its unipolar system of political activity, often threatens the fragmentation or polarization of domestic politics; long-suppressed interests and groups (re-)appear on the scene, demanding access to resources and the ability to shape the new political system in order to guarantee the institutionalization of their own political preferences. Party structures tend to be weak and lacking organizational skills, and thus more narrow sectoral interests may dominate the post-authoritarian order. In addition, post-authoritarian political systems are often dominated by large-scale crises – those very catalysts which weakened the old regime live on as their unwelcome legacy. These kinds of intractable problems demand a coherent set of integrated policies, but the very nature of the post-authoritarian system, where political uncertainty, fragmentation, and paralysis predominates, only threatens to worsen the situation through inaction caused by both a lack of accord and a weak central authority.

As the other cases in this volume have indicated, this tension inherent in the move from a monist system of political control to one where no single actor may be able to control political outcomes inevitably stems from one basic issue, the level of centralization of political power within state institutions. Who should be able to do what, and under what circumstances? Or, to be more specific, who should rule, and with what restrictions?

The conflict over the locus of political power ranges over a number of state institutions, but as events in Eastern Europe and the former USSR have shown, one key political institutional issue is that of executive power – the core of political decision-making, leadership, and policy formulation. Should executive power be vested in a parliamentary based prime minister and cabinet, or would stability be better served by the construction of a "strong presidency" or "semi-presidential" office?[2] Initially, one would expect that the West European norm of cabinet-based executive power would have been quickly adopted in the former Soviet Union and Eastern Europe, given the large degree to which other political reforms in the region have been modelled after continental institutions (such as electoral systems).

However, despite the West European example of cabinet governments, in the postcommunist countries of Europe and Central Asia we find a distinct movement toward stronger presidencies, semi-presidential systems where the head of state wields real executive power over the prime minister and cabinet, often creating confusion and conflict over the functional division of political power. Why do we find such a deviation in executive power from the majority of European cases? What are the implications of this institutional dualism for political change and stability in the region as a whole? An examination of the sources of presidentialism and how the debate over this office has shaped political developments in Hungary indicates that the very nature of the collapse of communism has created a political vacuum in which presidencies have arisen, an institution whose very attractions can serve to destabilize the political system as a whole.

Presidentialism and political stability: an unstable mix?

Presidencies can be risky institutions. This conclusion is being accepted by an increasing number of scholars within political science, thanks largely to research on the subject begun by Juan Linz.[3] In his studies Linz has noted that the specific institutional characteristics of strong presidential systems – among them, the autonomy of presidential offices, their fixed terms, as well as their zero-sum and non-collegial nature – can serve to polarize political groups in a weak democracy, increasing the potential for political deadlock and conflict. In conclusion, Linz argues that a powerful presidential office is not a wise choice in terms of democratic stability, especially in cases of political transitions where the new democratic order is fragile and the separation of political powers within the state is still weak. Since the collapse of communism this debate quickly surfaced in Eastern Europe and the former Soviet Union, as the construction of new executive institutions became for those countries a very real and critical issue.[4]

If strong presidential offices are likely to increase rather than mitigate political conflict by preventing coalitional political arrangements, one would think that this alone would be enough to eliminate support for the creation of such institutions. However, as events in Eastern Europe and the former Soviet Union have shown, what is paradoxical about the institution of the presidency is that those very factors which make presidencies a destabilizing force are precisely what precipitate the creation of the office in a powerful format. During periods of intense political crisis where extant institutional arrangements are in flux, various political forces often respond by pressing for the creation of new governmental structures that will better serve their own political objectives.

Presidencies, by virtue of their relative autonomy and singularity, offer the ability to consolidate political power, to rule without dependence on any other political group or institution. The danger of a presidency is the flip side of its attraction: to rule without compromise or consensus, a single leader as opposed to rule by cabinet where the executive power of a prime minister is limited to *primus inter pares*. This promise of singular power thus appeals to actors at various levels.

As a result, the creation of a powerful presidency is often one outcome of periods of political instability, as can be seen in the West European examples of France, where a presidency emerged from a serious political crisis in 1958, and Portugal, where a strong presidency was created following the 1974 revolution. Similarly, in Eastern Europe and the former Soviet Union, as we have been reminded in the previous chapters, the decline of one-party socialism led to a massive destabilization of political institutions, a crisis in authority that has prompted many to view presidentialism as a way to reassert control over the political situation. In a number of cases, the specific construction of these presidencies has been strongly influenced by tactical considerations on the part of political actors. These inevitably center around the specific future powers of the president, the method of election (direct or indirect), and its timing (before first multiparty parliamentary elections or after).

Sources of presidentialism in Eastern Europe and the former Soviet Union

Before turning to the study of the Hungarian presidency, let me summarize some of the general processes affecting institution building in states shedding their communist structures. During the transitions from one-party socialism, Communist Party leaders often sought the creation of a strong presidential structure as a way to recast their power at the state level. Traditionally, under socialism state executive institutions have not been viewed as the real locus of political power, given the dominance of the party over the state structure as a whole. In addition, state executive structures have tended to be collective rather than singular; a council of ministers, headed by a prime minister or premier, and a presidium or state council whose chairman nominally functioned as the head of state but held few real powers.[5]

Once the Communist Party's monopoly on power was called into question, however, there arose the threat that the party would be disengaged from the state, its vanguard role written out of the constitution, and it would be reduced to the level of a "mere" political party, competing with others for political power. Since this prospect held little appeal for communist elites, their response was to seek out a political base within the state in which power could be reconsolidated – some governmental institution which would provide a high degree of centralized political control.

Presidencies represent the ideal structure for political retrenchment, due to their potentially high levels of executive power and their autonomy from parliament – unlike prime ministers, who in comparison can be more easily recalled if there is sufficient parliamentary support. Consequently, during many of the early stages of transition events in Eastern Europe and the former Soviet Union, communist leaders attempted to build strong presidencies for themselves, as a means to retain political control over the system in transition – what Bartlomiej Kaminski terms an attempt to "constitutionalize communism."[6]

In a number of these cases, particularly in the former Soviet Union, the specific objective was the creation of a presidency that would at least initially be indirectly elected by the legislature prior to fully free elections, a move to ensure that the leadership could simply elect one of its own to the office. Directly elected presidencies were in many cases initially assumed to be too risky, as there was always the possibility that an opposition candidate might win.[7] The creation of a powerful Soviet presidency in 1990 can be viewed in this manner, as a means by which Gorbachev could vest his power within the emerging state structure and thereby continue to dominate the reform process. While some members of the Congress of Peoples' Deputies wished to make the office directly elected, Gorbachev refused, threatening to resign before he would face a popular election.[8]

Shortly thereafter, many of the Soviet republics followed suit, creating powerful, indirectly elected presidencies prior to any kind of unrestricted parliamentary elections. In almost all of these cases, republic first party secretaries were then elected to the new office by the communist-dominated local legislatures. This was particularly the case in Soviet Central Asia, where opposition forces have been relatively weak and unable to block such actions or extract a promise of multiparty elections prior to such constitutional changes.[9]

Interestingly, however, by 1991 all of the Central Asian presidencies had become directly elected offices, and it is clear from subsequent results that in these cases former communist leaders supported such an action because they expected to (and did) defeat weak opposition even in open elections. Similarly, in Eastern Europe communist leaders in a number of cases also sought to create strong presidencies prior to open parliamentary elections, and whether communist leaders wanted the office to be directly or indirectly elected depended on how they viewed their chances at the ballot box.

As we have mentioned, in some cases opposition forces in the early stages of the transition process lacked the ability to block actions by communist leaders to reconsolidate their power. However, even in those situations where non-regime forces have held relatively greater power, strong presidencies have also often emerged. For example, in Poland the roundtable negotiations between the ruling Polish United Workers' Party (PUWP) and Solidarity produced a strong presidency through an electoral compromise – the office would initially be elected by the two houses of the legislature, following elections which had been structured to assure the PUWP a majority control over the legislature. However, the next set of elections for the presidency was to be held by direct vote, which Solidarity was certain to win.[10]

Opposition groups or leaders have in fact often been less concerned about the specific powers of the presidential office than the actual manner of its election, in many cases supporting a presidency that is directly elected and therefore more likely to be won by an opposition candidate. A strong presidency appeals not only to political incumbents, for if the opposition could win the post itself the powers of the office could then be used to marginalize the Communist Party and facilitate the takeover of the state apparatus. In addition, where non-regime forces are divided and in conflict, some dominant opposition groups appear to have sought a strong presidency as a means by which they can consolidate their own power not only relative to the communists, but other opposition forces as well. The logic of these strategies is not much different from that of the communist leadership, and it derives from the zero-sum characteristics of the office.

In Romania, the provisional National Salvation Front quickly enacted a set of constitutional amendments following the revolution, establishing a powerful, directly elected presidency, which the NSF's own candidate, Ion Iliescu, then won. A similar process followed in Georgia: following the October 1990 elections, in which Zviad Gamsakhurdia's political coalition swept parliamentary elections, a powerful presidency was established that April and direct elections held in May, producing a victory for Gamsakhurdia. It was this executive base which Gamsakhurdia then utilized in his attempt to eliminate other opposition forces, eventually precipitating civil war.

However, it should not be concluded from the above discussion that the move toward presidentialism in Eastern Europe and the former Soviet Union has come about only through the tactical maneuvers of shrewd political figures. Support for a strong presidency reflects the central contradication of post-authoritarianism – the tension between the desire for direct democracy and the legacy of paternalist and authoritarian rule.[11] This can be seen in the earlier debate over Soviet academician A. Migranyan's argument that during the Soviet Union's political and economic transition a new authoritarian system should be established, in the form of a powerful presidency that could carry out the necessary reforms to pave the way for the later establishment of liberal democracy.[12]

While there may exist broad support for the right of the people to choose their own leaders, this often coexists alongside a commonly held conviction that a single leader, ruling with a "strong hand," should preside over the nation to provide the strength and guidance necessary to overcome domestic crises – despite the threat that this could eventually facilitate the restoration of authoritarianism. The idea of a powerful presidency, particularly one that is directly elected, may therefore attract support as an uneasy fusion of these clashing sentiments; a "strong democracy" vested in a single elected ruler, to stand above petty political squabbles and bring strong, coherent leadership to the country in its current time of troubles.[13]

In Czechoslovakia, while a last-ditch attempt by the communists to hinder the transition with the proposal of a directly elected president was denounced by the Civic Forum as an attempt to create a "presidential republic" and eventually blocked, one survey indicated that four-fifths of those polled favored the proposal.[14] The March 1991 referendum in the Russian Republic on the creation of a powerful presidency, elected by universal suffrage, succeeded by almost 70 percent of the vote. Similarly, a May 1992 referendum on a strong presidency in Lithuania was favored by approximately the same figure.[15] In Estonia as well, the powers of the presidency became a central issue in the framing of the 1992 constitution. These last two cases are particularly interesting given the historical lessons of Baltic presidencies in the interwar period. In Estonia and Latvia in the 1930s, presidential institutions in those nations were eventually utilized to bring an end to democratic rule.[16]

A strong presidency as a transition outcome may thus be the product of different forces functioning at different political levels, depending on how the process of institutional change unfolds, the actors it involves, and the resources they bring to bear in this conflict.[17] This is further complicated by situations where the balance of power has been less certain and more transient, and where as a result no one set of political actors has been able to dominate the transition process. In such cases institutional reform has proceeded through negotiation, threat, and compromise, with results not reflecting the ideal preference of any one side, but rather the default and unintended outcomes that arise from this political bargaining.[18] Under such conditions the presidency clearly shows its divisive and fragmenting nature, for no one side is assured of the office, yet the presidency holds the promise that whoever acquires it may be able to exert a disproportionate amount of power over the political arena. Subsequently, these unintended institutional outcomes which result from such struggles may "freeze" or "lock in," leaving countries with executive structures determined more by the exigencies of the transition than by objective considerations.[19]

Political change and the presidency in Hungary

The process of political transition and executive reform in Hungary stands apart as a case where political power was the most widely defused within and between the Communist Party and the opposition. With the inability of any one side to dominate the transition combined with the shifting fortunes of regime and opposition, institutional change occurred simultaneously with the political transition itself rather than subsequent to it, as in the case of most other communist states.[20]

Within this battle over the course of political change, the issue of the powers of the head of state became a central point of contestation, severely fragmenting the opposition as well as weakening the regime. No one political preference was able to prevail over the construction of the presidency, resulting in an office built by piecemeal arrangements rather than clear institutional crafting. And although by the standards of some scholars this indirectly elected office would not qualify as being semi-presidential, for all practical purposes dual executive powers have in fact clearly emerged.[21] The lack of clarity regarding the presidential powers as a result of the splintering of political authority during the transition process has created an office with an ambiguous role in politics, increasing parliamentary and intra-executive conflict in the post-authoritarian period.

The executive in Hungary: previous variants

While the role and powers of the presidency became one of the most important issues in the transition from authoritarianism, as in most of Western Europe Hungary has had little history of an actual presidential office, though there has been a tradition of splitting executive functions between a head of government and a head of state, whereby the latter was dominant. Under the Habsburg monarchy, the position was held by the emperor; from 1919–44, Admiral Horthy ruled Hungary from his position as regent, representing in effect a monarchy without a monarch. Following the end of World War II, Law No. 1 of 1946 created the first office of president of the republic, as a head of state elected by parliament and vested with quite limited powers – an essentially ceremonial office.

Through the constitutional imposition of socialism in Hungary in 1949 the position of president of the republic was eliminated. The council of ministers (the equivalent of a cabinet) technically became the highest executive organ, with a premier at its head, and the entire body in theory responsible to parliament. In addition there was established a collective presidential council, whose chairman acted as head of state. The presidential council's scope of responsibility was to function in place of parliament when it was out of session, which soon came to be most of the time, as the average number of days in which the legislature was in session fell from seventy per year from 1945 to 1949 to less than six days per year during the period 1981 to 1986.[22]

In reality, however, these two executive structures did not comprise the apex of political power, which effectively flowed from the Communist Party leadership. An indication of the weakness of both executive positions can be illustrated by the fact that first secretary of the Hungarian Socialist Workers' Party (MSZMP), János Kádár, only twice held top state positions – that of premier of the Council of Ministers from 1956 to 1958, and again from 1961 to 1965.[23] Power was exercised at the Politburo level of the MSZMP, of which Kádár was the head until 1988.[24]

The transition to democracy and the development of the presidency

With the process of reform in Hungary in the late 1980s the issue of state powers independent of the party reemerged. As in the roundtable negotiations in Poland, constitutional reform was seen by many inside and outside the MSZMP as a necessary step toward recasting power within the framework of a new semi-democratic governmental structure, re-legitimizing support for the regime while avoiding too radical a political change. Within the context of a new constitutional order, the party could create the political institutions necessary to allow limited pluralism while retaining control over key sectors of power.

Anticipating Migranyan's argument, central to these discussions was the idea of a powerful presidential office from which to direct reform. These ideas initially appeared at the margin of political debate, raised by academics rather than politicians; however, it soon became clear that the party leadership had also taken an interest, particularly after the ouster of Kádár in May 1988 and his replacement by the more reform-oriented Károly Grósz. Already in June 1988 political scientist Mihály Bihari (who had been expelled from the MSZMP that April precisely for his views on political reform) had drawn up a "Program Basket for Democracy," which among other things called for the creation of a potentially powerful president of the republic. This program was signed by fifteen independent parliamentarians and submitted to parliament by deputy Zoltán Király (who had also been purged alongside Bihari). Rather than being rejected outright as many had expected, the proposal was sent to committee for further discussion, indicating that the party was considering institutional reform to reshape (if not reduce) its political power.[25]

The possibility that the MSZMP could unilaterally fashion a new set of political institutions to its own liking began to fade as rifts within the party and popular opposition steadily increased. Internal power struggles within the MSZMP intensified among the party leadership, particularly between General Secretary Grósz and the more radical and outspoken Politburo figure Imre Pozsgay. These conflicts in turn began to undermine party power, discrediting the MSZMP and mobilizing opposition within state and society.[26]

Due to this slow unravelling of one-party rule, by the beginning of 1989 numerous alternative organizations had coalesced within society and the MSZMP itself, pressuring the fragmenting regime for ever-greater reform and the opening of a dialogue with the opposition. Yet the opposition was no more unified than the ruling party. Though their forces were united in their desire to bring an end to authoritarianism, they were unable to agree on how this political change should come about, or what should replace the old order.

These differences reflected the widely varied ideological views held by opposition forces. Most prominent among them were the urban-liberal Free Democrats (SZDSZ) and the populist-nationalist Hungarian Democratic Forum (MDF), representing the traditional urbanist-populist rift that had divided the Hungarian intelligentsia at least since the

1930s. Other forces included the Young Democrats (FIDESZ), which initially rose as a challenge to the youth organization of the MSZMP, as well as pre-communist era parties such as the Independent Smallholders (FKGP), Christian Democrats (KDNP), and Social Democrats (MSZDP). The opposition thus in no way represented a "mass front" like Solidarity or the Civic Forum, but rather an uneasy coalition of forces, fully aware that eventual multiparty elections would pit them against one another.[27]

A temporary alliance was eventually formed among the opposition, but only after the regime attempted to negotiate with several opposition groups on an individual basis – something which smacked of the classic communist "salami tactics" of dividing the opposition so that the regime could then destroy them one by one. This attempt backfired; the most prominent groups reacted by forming a single umbrella organization known as the Opposition Roundtable (EKA), eventually accepting a regime offer to enter into power-sharing negotiations. Negotiations officially began on 10 June 1989.[28]

Early in the talks the opposition agreed that constitutional amendments should include the creation of a presidency, though its future powers remained unresolved, and groups within the EKA were not in agreement as to the electoral mechanism for the office. Aware of the MSZMP's desire to reconsolidate its power through a presidential office, however, in their first position statement during negotiations the EKA made it clear that a presidential election of any kind should not precede free elections for parliament.[29]

Despite this initial resolution, during the negotiation process several EKA members, most prominent among them the KDNP, FKGP, and the MDF, began to support the idea that a president should be *directly elected* by year's end – and thus before free parliamentary elections. This sudden change in opinion represented a direct contravention of the previous stance of the EKA as a whole. Why these groups chose to support the MSZMP objective remains unclear – it may have been a risk-minimizing strategy to ensure that the regime did not pull out of negotiations, or the product of a back-door arrangement with the communist leadership. Certainly none of these opposition groups had at that point a single figure who was especially likely to win the presidency in direct elections, particularly given the high levels of popularity for outspoken party reformer Pozsgay.[30]

Since most of the EKA generally favored a presidency elected by parliament, with real executive powers vested in a prime minister, the direct election of a president was presented as a one-time compromise. It was assumed that later constitutional amendments would eventually designate the office as being elected by parliament.[31] In September a preliminary agreement between MSZMP and EKA representatives was drafted, stating that "in the interest of political stability" it was desirable to have the first election of the president occur before the end of 1989, presumably by popular vote. Negotiations were then to continue on the final form of eventual constitutional amendments, including the power and status of the presidency.

For several of the participants in the EKA – in particular, the SZDSZ and FIDESZ – early, direct presidential elections represented a blatant betrayal of their previous commitment to parliamentary elections first. The actual powers of the office still remained undefined, and an election at this early stage was likely to provide a victory for an MSZMP over the little-known opposition. Four members of the EKA subsequently objected to this part of the EKA–MSZMP roundtable accord – FIDESZ, SZDSZ, and the League of Independent Trade Unions refused to sign, while the Social Democrats attached a statement to its signature criticizing the concession.[32]

FIDESZ and the SZDSZ did not take this setback lightly. Following the roundtable accord these two parties set about collecting signatures in support of a referendum which would block the presidential election and limit the financial, organizational, and paramilitary powers of the MSZMP.[33] The FIDESZ–SZDSZ referendum proposal, among other things, asked voters if presidential elections should be held before that of parliament (the actual manner of the election itself not being included in the question). By mid-October the petition drive had collected over 140,000 signatures where only 100,000 were required. Accusations by the still communist-dominated parliament and some hopeful opposition candidates for president that the signatures had been collected by means of deception brought about a popular backlash; in a mere three days an additional 60,000 signatures were collected from a population that sensed trickery.[34]

Simultaneous with the petition drive, the first set of constitutional amendments hammered out by regime and opposition was enacted by parliament. On 23 October 1989 (the anniversary of the 1956 revolution) Hungary was declared a non-socialist republic. The presidential council was eliminated, replaced by the office of president of the republic and the head of parliament as interim president.

New constitutional amendments concerning the presidency gave the office a potentially powerful role in government, though many of these provisions were vague and open to interpretation, reflecting the continued lack of agreement between the regime and opposition negotiators over the future role of the office within the political arena. The head of state was described as "expressing the unity of the nation" and "watching over the democratic functioning of the state structure" as representative of the Hungarian state. The president was also listed as head of the armed forces. More specific powers included the ability to confirm high appointments to the military, national bank, and various other state positions, to set national and local elections, to send legislation back to parliament for a second reading, to convene special sessions of parliament as well as to dissolve the body and call new elections if it withdrew support from the government four times within the space of a year.[35] According to the new constitution, in future the president would in fact be selected by parliament. However, a supplementary law provided for the first presidential elections to be decided by direct popular vote.[36]

By this time the MSZMP had been transformed at its October party congress, spearheaded by delegates who saw that their party could survive in a pluralistic Hungary only if it decisively rejected its authoritarian past. Out of this internal revolt arose the new Hungarian Socialist Party (MSZP), without its old Marxist–Leninist platform as well as much of its conservative leadership. With this dramatic transformation of the ruling party, Pozsgay seemed well positioned in the upcoming presidential elections, set for 25 November. It was widely assumed among both the opposition and the regime that given the short period of time until the election, as well as the monopolistic position that the MSZP still held over the state and media, Pozsgay would easily win. However, once parliament reluctantly accepted the validity of the FIDESZ–SZDSZ petition, the election for president had to be delayed until the referendum took place, which was scheduled by parliament to occur instead of the planned presidential elections.

In response, the MSZP tried to discredit the referendum, arguing that the FIDESZ–SZDSZ in fact sought to deny the people their right to choose their own head of state. This tactic was further reinforced by actions in parliament. While the referendum question explicitly asked whether the election of the president of the republic should take place only after parliamentary elections, the explanation affixed by parliament to the ballot explained that the vote would determine the *manner*, not the *timing*, of presidential elections – whether by the people or by parliament. This attempt to confuse the ballot led to accusations that parliament had illegally intervened in the referendum process.[37] The MSZP campaigned for a "no" vote on the presidential election delay, while the MDF urged a complete boycott of the referendum, apparently hoping that a low turnout would invalidate the outcome and serve its objectives without having to side openly with the regime.

In the end these tactics failed – though just barely. On 26 November,

58 percent of eligible voters turned out to approve all four of the questions put forth. Though the three questions regarding the powers and assets of the old MSZMP were overwhelmingly supported (approximately 95 percent in favor on each), the motion to delay the election of the president won by an incredibly slim margin: 50.07 percent in favor, 49.93 percent against, a difference of little more than 6,000 votes out of the 4.5 million cast.[38]

While one might expect that this narrow victory would have ended the controversy over the presidency once and for all, in reality it was only the beginning of conflict. In accordance with agreements reached by the MSZP and the opposition, national parliamentary elections were held on 25 March and 8 April, 1990. Of the 386 seats in parliament, the MDF and SZDSZ were the big winners, the former gaining 164 and the latter 92 – these two parties alone comprising two-thirds of the total seats in the legislature.

Yet shortly before the two rounds of parliamentary elections and in direct contravention of the roundtable agreements, the incumbent MSZP-dominated parliament passed an amendment to the constitution redesignating the office of president as being *permanently* elected by the populace. Ironically, this action was initiated not by the MSZP but rather by independent deputy Zoltán Király. Long nursing presidential aspirations, Király was able to push his amendment through parliament, which was eager not to oppose anyone associated with the opposition and more than happy to pass legislation that potentially could lead to the election of an MSZP candidate as well.[39]

Consequently, while it has been argued that one major achievement of the transition was that Hungary created "a governmental structure with a weak presidency and strong parliament," very little regarding the presidency had in fact been resolved.[40] The new democratic parliament was to begin its first session in early May with no certainty as to the electoral status of eventual political powers of the presidency relative to the parliament and cabinet. The idea that after one national referendum and two rounds of parliamentary elections a new set of presidential elections should be held was unacceptable to most political leaders, as it might not generate enough voter turnout for a valid result, or worse, lead to an MSZP victory – whose leadership still remained popular despite their overall poor showing in the national elections.

As a result, as the two largest parties in parliament the MDF and SZDSZ leadership entered into negotiations in late April to reach an accord on a number of constitutional revisions, including the structure of government and the presidency. The resulting MDF–SZDSZ pact agreed to eliminate the old Council of Ministers and replace it with a cabinet headed by a relatively strong prime minister, being modelled after the German "constructive vote of no confidence," whereby such an action against the prime minister must be simultaneously accompanied by the nomination and election of a new head of government. As for the presidency, the two sides agreed to redefine the office "in accordance with the restoration of Law No. 1/1946 to its original status" – in other words, to return it to its previous limited role as an indirectly elected head of state. The power of the president to dissolve parliament was also to be limited to periods of "absolute necessity."

Despite these revisions, few other changes were made in the murkier powers of the president, leaving the office much as it had been constructed during the earlier roundtable negotiations.[41] Assumptions seem to have been similar to those of many Western political scientists on this issue – that the manner of presidential election was the key component in determining the strength of the office, and with this issue resolved the actual constitutional powers were of little concern. In order to gain SZDSZ support for these constitutional changes (particularly those which would weaken the parliamentary opposition's power over the new cabinet, as it was clear that the SZDSZ would not be a part of the MDF ruling coalition), the MDF leadership agreed to back the election of SZDSZ parliamentary deputy Árpád Göncz for the office of president.[42]

Consistent with the understanding of the pact, on 3 May the new democratic parliament elected Göncz president of parliament – and thus pro tempore president of the republic – until the provisions of the MDF–SZDSZ pact could be enacted as formal constitutional amendments, and the power to elect the president of the republic thus reinvested in parliament. In late May parliament endorsed the new cabinet, a coalition of the smaller KDNP and FKGP alongside the dominant MDF, with MDF party leader József Antall as prime minister. The MDF– SZDSZ provisions were successfully amended to the constitution on 19 June.

Some members of the opposition – specifically, the MSZP and presidential hopeful Király – were less than pleased with the decision to redesignate the presidency as an indirectly elected office. Even before the MDF–SZDSZ amendments had passed, Király and the MSZP began another petition drive calling for yet another referendum, this time specifically on the manner of the presidential election itself. Enough signatures were collected to render the petition valid, and the new government scheduled the vote for 29 July. Despite Király's and the MSZP's hopes that this new referendum would provide each of them with a shot at the presidency through popular elections, nothing of the sort occurred. Earlier speculation had been correct; the populace was exhausted by eight months of voting, and consequently only 14 percent of registered voters turned out (though 85 per cent of those votes cast supported a presidency directly elected by the people).[43] As a result of the low turnout the referendum was declared invalid; the notion of a directly elected president was dead. On 3 August 1990, Göncz was formally and overwhelmingly elected president of the republic by parliament for a five-year term.[44]

The consolidation of state power and intra-executive struggles

As the new president, the 68-year-old Göncz was distinguished through his participation in the resistance movement during World War II, as well as his role in the 1956 revolution, for which he was imprisoned and served six years of a life sentence. Since then he had worked as a writer and literary translator, and had helped found both the Network of Free Initiatives, the predecessor to the SZDSZ, as well as the Committee on Historical Justice.[45] Expectations were that Göncz would play the "grandfatherly" role as president, leaving the real tasks of government to the cabinet and Prime Minister Antall. Göncz stated early on that his intentions as president were to "put the nation's interests before the interest of any party," yet this was not tantamount to saying that he would not pursue the powers at his disposal.[46] Göncz soon made it clear that since the actual powers of the office had not yet been tested, he did not view the presidency as politically ineffectual or merely ceremonial, nor would he treat the office in this manner.[47] Indeed, the ambiguous political powers of the presidency were soon put to the test by Göncz himself.

In October 1990 the new cabinet under Prime Minister Antall came to the decision that gasoline prices would have to be increased drastically to reflect the decline in Soviet deliveries and the rise in oil prices due to the Gulf crisis. Without warning, on 25 October the government announced that gas prices would increase the following day by 65 percent, a move which angered in particular taxi and truck drivers who saw their livelihood threatened by this action. In an immediate and dramatic response, these drivers chose to indicate their displeasure by blockading most roads and many rail lines within Hungary, including border crossings with Austria and Yugoslavia. Virtually all automobile traffic in Budapest came to a halt; international and domestic road and rail transportation throughout the country became difficult to impossible. As Prime Minister Antall was in hospital at the time, Interior Minister Balázs Horváth found himself in charge of the government and thus responsible for resolving the crisis. Deepening the tension in the country, Horváth responded that the government would "restore order with every legal means necessary" – implying the possible use of military force.[48]

In the midst of this tense standoff, President Göncz asserted the authority of his position. Employing his constitutional powers as commander-in-chief of the armed forces, Göncz gave the order that the army should remain in its barracks and stated that the military could not be used to intervene in the blockade. Also consistent with his powers, Göncz proposed convening an extraordinary session of parliament. The president called upon the government to rescind the price increases and enter into negotiations with the drivers.[49] Through these actions Göncz asserted his power over the armed forces and his right to convene parliament, and defined his position as one of arbiter between the government and society. The drivers appealed to Göncz to mediate between themselves and the government. For its own part, the government refused to give in on the price increases, while MDF members of parliament accused Göncz of overstepping his authority, as well as of siding with the drivers and thus prolonging the blockade.[50]

With criticism mounting over its handling of the price increases and the crisis itself, the government eventually agreed to a compromise with the drivers on 28 October, but not without first staging a pro-government rally where protestors called for the president's resignation.[51] The resolution of the drivers' strike greatly increased the prominence and popularity of Göncz. By December one opinion poll found him to be the most trusted man in the country, and a survey conducted after the drivers' strike showed that more people believed Göncz was better suited to resolve the crisis than parliament itself.[52] While the strike may have strengthened the position of Göncz, it also set the stage for a formal struggle for power between the prime minister and the president.

Throughout the course of 1991 Göncz continued to test the limits of his authority, utilizing those vague provisions of the constitution which accorded him powers over the military, foreign affairs, and state appointments. For example, prior to the Visegrád Summit of the leaders of Hungary, Czechoslovakia, and Poland, Göncz argued that he too should be included in the meeting, since the constitution gave him the power to conclude international agreements. In this dispute the government grudgingly acquiesced. In addition, the conflict over control of the armed forces intensified as Göncz moved to block a reorganization of the army command structure by the cabinet, a clash which led the commander of the army to tender his resignation – which Göncz then refused.

In these struggles, several factors worked to the president's advantage. The separation of powers between the head of state and the head of government remained unclear, further blurred by the activist stance which Göncz took in the pursuit of his office. Second, by virtue of the fact that the president did not come from a party in the cabinet in addition to the widespread popularity he enjoyed, Göncz was able to assert his role as separate from – and in some ways above – the government.[53] Third, the lack of a constitutional mechanism to replace the president during his term (other than impeachment for criminal or unconstitutional activity) insulated him from any retaliatory government action.

As the president's assertion of power came increasingly into conflict with the cabinet, support for his activities began to emanate from some segments of parliament. Perhaps not surprisingly, the opposition SZDSZ, which had through their earlier compromise with the MDF agreed to the idea of a weak presidency, increasingly began to offer the opinion that more power should be exercised at the presidential level in order to act as a check on the cabinet. The SZDSZ now realized that the "chancellor democracy" system had substantially reduced its power to influence policy-making, leading many to view greater presidential powers as a means to weaken the MDF-dominated government.

But it was not only the SZDSZ which contended that an activist president "is a needed barrier around the dangerously great power of the government."[54] In fact, some MDF members of parliament also began to take up this argument – for example, the so-called "rebelling 52" who accused the party of developing anti-democratic tendencies, intolerant of those individuals or groups who opposed the party's policies.[55] Realizing this threat to their control over executive power, the dominant block of the MDF argued that it was the growth of authority in the presidency that would in fact create an "unchecked power" with an anti-democratic potential, and accused those who supported a strong presidency of Stalinist inclinations.[56] Although it remained in opposition, FIDESZ sided with the MDF in opposing the strengthening of the presidency. As one writer in a FIDESZ-affiliated paper astutely noted, "the SZDSZ leaders had forgotten to consider the fact that they might not love every president of the republic in the same way as they liked this one."[57]

The conflict between the president, the prime minister, and their partisan supporters could not be resolved by means of compromise and dialogue – the specific powers of the presidency would somehow have to be amended or explicitly defined. The government chose the latter path, asking the Constitutional Court to consider a number of issues regarding the president's scope of authority as set out in the current constitution.

In September 1991 the Constitutional Court ruled on three petitions regarding the powers of the president as head of the armed forces, his authority over state appointments, and his inviolability under the law. The court ruled that the president was not accountable to parliament; however, it also ruled that the president was the "overseer" and not the leader of the armed forces, and that the constitutional authority over the armed forces rested with the cabinet. Finally, the court ruled that the president could not refuse to countersign state appointments from the cabinet except in cases where such appointments had not met certain statutory provisions or "would gravely disturb the democratic functioning of the state."[58]

Although this ruling would appear to have effectively curbed the power of the presidency, Göncz instead took it as an affirmation of his power, which could be exercised in the protection of democracy. The president thus continued to function independent of the will of the cabinet, leading to even more serious clashes between the head of government and the head of state. The most intense struggle emerged during the course of late 1991 and 1992, as government and opposition forces came into conflict with regard to government power over the state-run media.[59]

Since 1990, relations between the government and the interim presidents of state-run Hungarian radio and television had been steadily eroding, as the ruling parties grew convinced that national media institutions retained a communist orientation that translated into an anti-government bias. The government responded by trying to increase its influence over the media, to which opposition forces reacted by accusing the government of seeking to dominate the media in order to shape public opinion. Controversy came to a head when Prime Minister Antall finally sought to sack the president of state-run radio, in order to replace him with a pro-government candidate.

President Göncz, however, refused to countersign the dismissal, arguing that such action endangered the democratic system (thus giving him the right to block government actions as determined by the Constitutional Court). While opposition groups in parliament supported the president, the government again turned to the Constitutional Court to determine if Göncz had by his actions broken the law – the only reason for which the president can be impeached (though the MDF denied that it sought to remove Göncz from office).[60] The court ruled that the president could not in fact refuse to dismiss state officials if requested by cabinet, but also confused matters by reaffirming the president's "limiting and balancing role" *vis-à-vis* the cabinet as a democratic safeguard, and his right to reject appointments or dismissals should they disturb the democratic functioning of the state.[61]

The court decision, as ambiguous as its earlier 1991 ruling, did little to resolve the conflict. Both the government and president hailed the ruling as a victory for their position, and the cabinet resubmitted its dismissal of the president of state-run radio, this time adding to it the head of television as well. Göncz again argued that in keeping with the court's ruling on his constitutional powers, the dismissals were unconstitutional and undemocratic due to the pending media law, and refused to accede to the government's demands. The court, meanwhile, refused to become more entangled in this battle.[62] The conflict subsided only when the radio and television presidents themselves stepped down in early 1993, though Göncz remained adamant, refusing to countersign even their resignations. With the failure of the constitutional court ruling to effectively resolve this issue, the underlying struggle over the division of power between the president and prime minister was never truly resolved, thus threatening to resurface in the future.[63]

Political change and the future of the presidency

The most important changes in the relationship between the presidential and prime ministerial office since 1992 have been in terms of personnel rather than in the resolution of institutional power. In December 1993, Prime Minister Antall died after a long struggle with cancer. Under his replacement, Péter Boross (also of the MDF), the struggle over the media continued; many now saw this as a desperate attempt by an increasingly unpopular government to influence media content prior to the upcoming elections.[64] This only increased support for the president's prior actions, and enhanced his image as the defender of the fragile democratic order. Even as public support for the coalition eroded, the president maintained the highest level of popular support of any Hungarian political figure.[65]

And, indeed, parliamentary elections in 1994 witnessed a complete reversal of fortunes for a number of parties. The MDF was completely routed at the polls, losing most of its seats. In contrast, the MSZP enjoyed a stunning political resurrection, gaining a majority of seats in parliament by redefining itself as a moderate and technocratic party, able to solve the nation's economic problems while maintaining a strong social welfare system. Following elections the MSZP formed a ruling coalition with the liberal SZDSZ, President Göncz's original party, with MSZP party leader Gyula Horn as prime minister. This coalition gave the new cabinet control over two-thirds of the seats in parliament.[66]

As opposed to the previous coalition, relations between the new government and the president were more congenial – too much so, for many now in parliamentary opposition. For example, one of the first actions of the new government in late 1994 was to propose new candidates to head national television and radio, even as consultations were underway with other parties on the subject. Although the opposition petitioned the president to reject these nominations as he had consistently done in the past, due to the still-pending nature of the new media law, Göncz countersigned the appointments. To many observers, this action called into question Göncz' willingness to act as a check on cabinet now that his former party, the SZDSZ, shared power.[67]

In fact, in light of these changes in the Hungarian government one might argue that the clash between the heads of government and state was not an institutional problem but a political one, due simply to the temporary need for provisional power-sharing between the first postcommunist government and the opposition. Consequently, such "cohabitation" along the lines of the French model might be avoided in future. This, however, ignores the obvious problem that presidents have a fixed five-year term, whereas the cabinet must call elections within four years, and may fall from power much earlier. A cabinet and president from the same party may thus change suddenly through shifts in parliamentary power – as has occurred in France. Moreover, even the alignment of a president with government does not preclude power struggles over the office.

As evidence of this last point, with the end of Göncz's term in 1995 tension soon mounted within the MSZP–SZDSZ coalition over whether Göncz could seek a second term with the backing of both parties, or if the MSZP would seek to acquire the office for one of its own, consolidating power to an even greater degree. While most of the MSZP party leadership supported Göncz, some argued that the party should elect one of its own to the office and thus reduce the power of the SZDSZ within the executive branch. Not surprisingly, many of those within the MSZP who advocated this action sought the office for themselves. This created a degree of tension within the socialists' ranks, not only because it risked destroying the MSZP–SZDSZ coalition, but also because Prime Minister Horn and others feared an MSZP presidency as an alternative locus of power, linked to the party yet beyond its organizational control. This concern was in fact nothing new; some had previously surmised that Prime Minister Antall originally agreed to the election of Göncz precisely because he feared that if someone from his own party were made president, the office could have served as a power base from which to launch a political challenge against him.[68]

This conflict over the reelection of Göncz was further complicated by the new parliamentary opposition. The KDNP, FIDESZ, and MDF quickly seized upon the old rhetoric of the SZDSZ, arguing that the presidential office belonged in the hands of the opposition, a check against the clearly overwhelming parliamentary power of the MSZP–SZDSZ coalition. The new ruling coalition chose to ignore this argument. The FKGP went further, garnering over 200,000 signatures in support of a new referendum which in part sought to make the presidency a directly elected office with increased executive powers. This too was rejected by the government and the constitutional court, which ruled that changes to the constitution could not be enacted through popular referendum.[69] These attempts having failed, several of the opposition parties (the KDNP, FIDESZ, and MDF) chose to present a joint candidate, the legal scholar Ferenc Madl, against Göncz. This effort, largely symbolic, sought to make clear that the opposition did not support the reelection of the president. On 19 June, Göncz was reelected by parliament to his second (and final) term with 258 votes. Madl, in contrast, received only 76.[70]

The 1995 presidential election demonstrates that the presidency still remains controversial and a source of political conflict in Hungary, and that pressures to alter the institutional framework of the office remain strong. Moreover, with Göncz's reelection to a second five-year term, it remains to be seen how his long-term presence in the office may shape the institutionalization of formal and informal presidential power, setting the stage for presidential influence in the future.

Conclusion

Has Hungary developed into a semi-presidential system? Despite the elaboration above, this remains a difficult question to answer. Presidential power in Hungary, while in many aspects strong, is still in transition, a reflection of the incremental and shifting process of political change in 1989–90. Lacking a dominant set of state or societal actors to clearly empower or constrain the presidency, the office has emerged as a piecemeal arrangement, shorn of its original intended powers but retaining enough residual influence to stymie cabinet government and seize the initiative in some areas of policy. This ambiguity has allowed an active political figure like Göncz to use the office to its full effect; in turn, this may have set a precedent for the consolidation and expansion of presidential power in the future, creating a clearly semi-presidential system. For now, however, the powers of the presidency continue to be institutionalized.

Despite this lack of clarity, one can make some generalizations from the actual struggle over the office itself. Presidencies in Eastern Europe and the successor states of the Soviet Union have the power to threaten political stability in two distinct ways. First, since all presidential structures in the region exist alongside a prime ministerial office and cabinet, there is the danger that the problem of the functional division of power between the head of government and head of state will increase conflict within both the executive and legislature, fostering political polarization and paralysis. In Hungary, for some members of parliament the presidency is seen as a second executive power base from which to check executive activity, and attempts to strengthen the president so as to weaken the cabinet intensified political rifts within and among political parties in the legislature, creating deadlock on a number of issues.

While these conflicts have so far been resolved in a positive manner, primarily through the use of judicial mechanisms, this has also generated a good deal of hostility within parliament, hindering the policy-making and legislative process. The danger from these struggles is that dual bases of conflicting executive power can become institutionalized over time, intensifying cleavages within the political system and slowing down the reform process and the resolution of domestic issues.[71]

A second concern is whether power will continue to gravitate toward presidencies, via constitutional amendments or the informal expansion of power. In such cases, the office could provide the means for the reestablishment and/or consolidation of authoritarian rule. Without sufficient executive mechanisms to allow for consensus-building and coalition formation, political power becomes highly centralized, deepening political cleavages by clearly delineating who is in power and who is out. For those who dominate a strong executive, authoritarian actions can be taken with less threat of political sanction, and consequently this becomes a more attractive option. For those excluded from power under such circumstances, actions to paralyze the government become options of last resort.

However, beyond these admonitions, presidential structures can also be seen in a positive light. There is the chance that if properly balanced, presidential offices in the region could serve a positive role, helping to overcome political crises and providing a sense of national leadership, as occurred in France under De Gaulle. Indeed, Linz and others do note that while powerful presidencies are a source of danger, more restricted variants can have an important function as an arbiter between conflicting forces, creating stability in times of political crisis.[72] For the moment we will have to wait until future political developments provide us with more data. In general, it seems obvious that throughout the region presidencies will continue to serve as a pivotal institution in the new political systems. They may act variously as forces for democratic breakthrough (Wałęsa in Poland), political continuity (Yeltsin in Russia), constitutional reform (Kuchma in Ukraine), political legitimacy (exemplified best by Havel in the Czech Republic), stability and moderation (Göncz in Hungary), or strong leadership (Nazarbaev in Kazakstan). In carrying out these different functions, presidents may be contributing to democratic consolidation – though not invariably. On occasion they have themselves been regarded as agents of democratic destabilization, *inter alia* Yeltsin during the 1993 confrontation with the Russian parliament, Lukashenko in Belarus, Shevardnadze in Georgia, and even Wałęsa in his final years in power. Predictably, however, institutional checks on presidents have served to promote democracy in postcommunist states more constructively than expanding their powers has. But as we will see in chapter 8, such checks may be more the result of bargaining among vested interests than of thoughtful and far-sighted design.

NOTES

This chapter is a revised and extended version of an earlier work, entitled "Presidential Power in Post-Communist Europe: The Hungarian Case in Comparative Perspective," *Journal of Communist Studies*, 9, 3 (September 1993), pp. 177–201. My thanks to Richard Hall and James B. Christoph for their comments on previous versions of this article.

1 I borrow this term from Giuseppe DiPalma's work *To Craft Democracies* (Berkeley: University of California, 1990).

2 I use the term "semi-presidential" or "strong" presidentialism to refer to those executive systems where (1) executive power is divided between a prime minister as head of government and a president as head of state; (2) the office is largely independent of the legislature; (3) the office is vested with its own base of domestic legitimacy; and (4) the president is able to formulate a significant portion of state policy. Maurice Duverger and others argue that the election of the president through universal suffrage is also necessary. However, while it is commonly thought that a directly elected presidential office will be powerful due to its popular mandate, while an indirectly elected president will be weak, it appears that direct election is neither a necessary nor sufficient condition for strong presidencies: Austria, Iceland, and Ireland all possess directly elected presidents, yet they remain largely ceremonial posts without significant executive power; in contrast, the Czech, Slovak, Albanian, and Hungarian presidents are elected by their respective legislatures, yet wield a substantial amount of political authority. Many political actors in Eastern Europe and the Soviet Union have, however, viewed direct presidential election as a distinct source of presidential power, and this consideration has affected events in the region. For discussion of semi-presidential systems and their powers see Maurice Duverger, "A New Political System Model: Semi-Presidential Government," in Arend Lijphart (ed.), *Parliamentary Versus Presidential Government* (Oxford: Oxford University Press, 1992), pp. 142–149; also Matthew Soberg Shugart and John M. Carey, *Presidents and Assemblies: Constitutional Design and Electoral Dynamics* (Cambridge: Cambridge University Press, 1992), as well as the various contributions in Juan J. Linz and Arturo Valenzuela (ed.), *The Failure of Presidential Democracy* (Baltimore: Johns Hopkins University Press, 1994).

3 Linz's work on this topic can be found in his book *The Breakdown of Democratic Regimes, Volume 1: Crisis, Breakdown, and Reequilibration* (Baltimore: Johns Hopkins University Press, 1978), pp. 71–74; "Transitions to Democracy," *The Washington Quarterly*, 13, 3 (Summer 1990), pp. 143–164; "The Perils of Presidentialism," *Journal of Democracy*, 1, 1 (Fall 1990), pp. 51–69, and more recently, "Presidential or Parliamentary Democracy: Does it Make a Differ-

ence?," in Linz and Valenzuela, *The Failure of Presidential Democracy*, pp. 3–90. For a contrasting view which emphasizes that presidencies can also be crafted so as to resolve rather than generate conflict, see Shugart and Carey, *Presidents and Assemblies*.

4 For example, the work of Linz and others on presidentialism has been published and widely debated among scholars in Hungary since the early stages of the transition from socialism; for example, Arend Lijphart, "Presidentialism and Majoritarian Democracy: Theoretical Observations," in György Szoboszlai (ed.), *Democracy and Political Transformations: Theories and East-Central European Realities* (Budapest: Hungarian Political Science Association, 1991), pp. 75–93. Lijphart's paper was originally presented at the US–Hungarian Roundtable in Political Science in 1990. Other examples include Scott Mainwaring, "Presidentialism, Multipartism and Democracy: The Difficult Combination," in György Szoboszlai (ed.), *Flying Blind: Emerging Democracies in East-Central Europe* (Budapest: Hungarian Political Science Association, 1992), pp. 59–85, and Thomas A. Baylis, "Presidents Versus Prime Ministers: Shaping Executive Authority in Eastern Europe," *World Politics*, 48, 3 (April 1996), pp. 297–323. See also the critique of Linz's work by Hungarian scholars István Kukorelli, "Melyik kormányforma veszélyebb as Elbatól Keletre?," *Politikatudományi Szemle*, 2 (1992), pp. 161–165, and Péter Paczolay, "Prezidenciális vagy parlamentáris demokrácia – választhat-e Közép-Europa?," *Politikatudományi Szemle*, 2 (1992), pp. 167–176.

5 The only major exception to this structure could be found in Czechoslovakia and Romania. In the case of Czechoslovakia, the singular presidential structure which had existed prior to the communist take-over was retained, though substantially weakened by the 1960 constitution; this was the office which Vaclav Havel inherited from the party first secretary, Gustav Husak. In contrast, in Romania a singular head of state was a relatively new development, instituted in 1974 and reflecting Ceausescu's consolidation of personal power.

6 Bartlomiej Kaminski, "Systemic Underpinnings of the Transition in Poland: The Shadow of the Round-table Agreement," *Studies in Comparative Communism*, 24, 2 (June 1991), p. 181.

7 One variation on this pattern can be found in Turkmenistan; there, where the communists faced few opposition challenges, the republic's Supreme Soviet designated the new executive presidency as directly elected, and simply avoided the threat of an opposition victory by allowing only one candidate for the post – republican first secretary, Saparmurad Niyazov. Charles Carlson, "Inching Towards Democratization," *Radio Liberty Report on the USSR* (hereafter *RL Report*), 4 January 1991, p. 35.

8 Aurel Braun and Richard B. Day, "Gorbachevian Contradictions," *Problems of Communism*, 39, 3 (May–June 1990), p. 43.

9 As, for example, in Uzbekistan, Kazakstan, Azerbaijan, and Tajikistan.

10 Kaminski, "Systemic Underpinnings," pp. 181–183.

11 I do not wish to stray too far into the controversial and often murky discussion of whether some societies are more "prone" to democracy than others, or whether some nations or cultures exhibit anti-democratic tendencies. The currently dominant school of thought on this subject posits that successful

transitions to democracy are not influenced by any generic set of "conditions" or "preconditions" that are conducive to such political changes. However, other scholars continue to argue that macro-level forces such as economic development, social, and cultural structure do in fact make a difference. See, for example, Samuel Huntington, "Will More Countries Become Democratic?," *Political Science Quarterly*, 99, 2 (Summer 1984), pp. 193–218.

12 "The Long Road to a European Home," *Novy Mir*, 7 (July 1989), pp. 166–184; translated in *Current Digest of the Soviet Press*, 41, 42 (1989), pp. 6–9, 32.

13 To some extent this resembles the idea of the "Just Tsar." Stephen White contends that in tsarist Russia, "[o]ne consequence of the weak articulation of representative institutions was a highly personalized attachment to political authority," and the belief in an all-powerful ruler to preserve the country and act in the people's best interest. This legacy, White believes, continues up to the present. "The USSR: Patterns of Autocracy and Industrialism," in Archie Brown and Jack Gray (eds.), *Political Culture and Political Change in Communist States* (London: Macmillan, 1979), p. 34.

14 Pehe, "The Election of the President," p. 2.

15 The referendum in Lithuania failed, however, since it did not command a majority of support from *all* eligible voters, whether they voted or not. See *Radio Free Europe/Radio Liberty Daily Report* (hereafter *RFE/RL Daily Report*), 99, 25 May 1992; For details on the referendum in the Russian Republic see *RL Report*, 29 March 1991, p. 31.

16 Linz, *The Breakdown of Democratic Regimes*, p. 70; in the case of Estonia in particular see Tönu Parming, "The Collapse of Liberal Democracy and the Rise of Authoritarianism in Estonia," Sage Professional Papers in Contemporary Political Sociology, no. 06–010, 1975.

17 Jon Elster, "Constitution-Making in Eastern Europe: Rebuilding the Boat in the Open Sea," *Public Administration*, 71 (Spring/Summer 1993), pp. 169–217.

18 Jon Elster, "Bargaining over the Presidency," *East European Constitutional Review*, 2–3, 4–1 (Fall 1993–Winter 1994), pp. 95–98. The implication is therefore that even if presidential offices can be crafted in such a way that they can resolve rather than generate conflict (as Shugart and Carey argue), the fact that new political structures in a period of transition often emerge through default outcomes or as the expression of currently dominant interests means that objective institution-building in this area may be doubtful at best.

19 Arend Lijphart, "Democratization and Constitutional Choices in Czecho-Slovakia, Hungary, and Poland 1989–1991," in Szoboszlai, *Flying Blind*, pp. 99–113; for more on the process of institutionalization and its effects see Walter W. Powell and Paul D. DiMaggio (eds.), *The New Institutionalism in Organizational Analysis* (Chicago: University of Chicago Press, 1991).

20 Péter Paczolay, "Constitutional Transition and Legal Continuity," *Connecticut Journal of International Law*, 8, 2 (Spring 1993), p. 565.

21 Alfred Stepan and Cindy Skach, for example, define Hungary as one of the few examples in Eastern Europe and the former Soviet Union where there exists a "pure parliamentary" as opposed to a semi- or pure presidential system, solely on the basis of its electoral mechanism. However, in practice,

presidential powers have been much more prominent than this structural definition implies, undermining the credibility of such conclusions based on the method of election alone. "Presidentialism and Parliamentarism in Comparative Perspective," in Linz and Valenzuela, *The Failure of Presidential Democracy*, p. 120. Baylis, who notes the power of the Hungarian presidency, similarly criticizes this approach, arguing that "the significance of direct election in Eastern Europe is not yet proved," given that the office itself, regardless of election method, provides the opportunity for presidents to "convert their assets of prestige into 'real' power over policy." "Presidents versus Prime Ministers," pp. 303, 306.

22 Elemér Hankiss, *East European Alternatives* (Oxford: Oxford University Press, 1990), p. 19.

23 The office of president of the council was always held by a member of the Politburo, however. József Bölöny, *Magyarország Kormányai 1848–1987* (Budapest: Akadémiai Kiadó, 1987), pp. 204–205, 311–312.

24 However, one interesting fact indicates the large degree of overlap between the MSZMP leadership and the government: as of 1988, thirteen of twenty-one members of the Council of Ministers were also members of the MSZMP Central Committee and three of them served additionally in the Politburo. See Lajos Ficzere, "The Council of Ministers as Government Committees," in Géza Kilényi and Vanda Lamm (eds.), *Parliamentarism and Government in a One-Party System* (Budapest: Akadémiai Kiadó, 1988), p. 150.

25 Hankiss, *East European Alternatives*, pp. 226–229. For a discussion of this reform package and the potential implications for a parliamentary versus presidential form of government, see Péter Szalay, "Mi van a 'demokrácia csomagterv'-ben?" in Sándor Kurtán, Péter Sándor, and László Vass (eds.), *Magyarország Politikai Évkönyve 1988* (Budapest: Reform, 1989), pp. 254–264. The interest of the party leadership in recasting its political power within new state structures is evident in Central Committee documents and transcripts from 1988 and 1989; for further details see Patrick H. O'Neil, "Revolution from Within: The Hungarian Socialist Workers' Party 'Reform Circles' and the Transition from Socialism" (Ph.D. diss., Indiana University, 1994).

26 Much has been written on the process of political change in Hungary over the course of the late 1980s, including Hankiss, *East European Alternatives*; László Bruszt and David Stark, "Remaking the Political Field in Hungary: From the Politics of Compromise to the Politics of Competition," in Ivo Banac (ed.), *Eastern Europe in Revolution* (Ithaca: Cornell University Press, 1992), pp. 13–55; András Bozóki, András Körösényi, and George Schöpflin (eds.), *Post-Communist Transition: Emerging Pluralism in Hungary* (London: Pinter, 1992).

27 For a discussion of the differing political ideologies among the various opposition forces, see András Körösényi, "Revival of the Past or a New Beginning? The Nature of Post-Communist Politics," in Bozóki, Körösényi and Schöpflin, *Post-Communist Transition*, pp. 111–131, and also László Bihari (ed.), *A többpártrendszer kialakulása Magyarországon 1985–1991* (Budapest: Kossuth, 1992).

28 A detailed discussion of the EKA can be found in Károly Vigh, "Az Ellenzéki

Kerekasztaltól a Nemzeti Kerekasztalig," in Sándor Kurtán, Péter Sándor, and László Vass (eds.), *Magyarország Politikai Évkönyve 1990* (Budapest: Aula-Omikk, 1990), pp. 232–234; see also Anna Richter, *Ellenzéki Kerekasztal* (Budapest: Ötlet, 1990), pp. 287–293, and András Bozóki, "Hungary's Road to Systemic Change: The Opposition Roundtable," *East European Politics and Society*, 7, 2 (Spring 1993), pp. 276–308.

29 Richter, *Ellenzéki Kerekasztal*, p. 303.

30 Popularity and familiarity polls showed that in mid-October only 28 percent of those surveyed were familiar with József Antall, at that time president of the Hungarian Democratic Forum, and that on a popularity rating of 0 to 100 he received a 58 (other opposition figures scored even lower); in contrast, Pozsgay's numbers were 92 percent familiar and a 69 in popularity. Only independent deputy, Zoltán Király, had a familiarity and popularity rating close to that of Pozsgay. "A Közvélemény 1989-ben," in Kúrtan, Sándor, and Vass, *Magyarország Politikai Évkönyve 1990*, p. 451.

31 For details see András Bozóki, "Political Transition and Constitutional Change in Hungary," in Bózoki, Körösényi, and Schöpflin, *Post-Communist Transition*, pp. 66–67.

32 Edith Oltay, "HSWP and Six Opposition Groups Agree on First Steps Toward Multiparty Elections," *Radio Free Europe Research* (hereafter *RFE Research*), 4 October 1989, pp. 37–40.

33 Bruszt and Stark view the FIDESZ–SZDSZ move as a calculated attempt to prevent their marginalization in the eventual parliamentary elections by publicly attacking the EKA agreement as a "deal" with the communists, thus drawing attention to themselves as "the authentic anti-communists" and casting doubt on those groups that had signed the accord. This interpretation seems overly cynical. While the referendum did bolster SZDSZ and FIDESZ recognition and popularity, Bruszt and Stark ignore the fact that the EKA had originally agreed *not* to compromise on the issue of the presidential elections so desired by the MSZMP, and only later reneged on this agreement for unclear – and thus suspicious – reasons. "Remaking the Political Field in Hungary," pp. 48–50.

34 Endre Babus, "Népszavazás – 1989," in Kurtán, Sándor, and Vass, *Magyarország Politikai Évkönyve 1990*, p. 210; see also Steven W. Popper, "Slouching Towards Budapest: A Trip Report" (Rand Report P-7613, January 1990), p. 7.

35 Law No. 31/1989; *Magyar Közlöny*, no. 74, 23 October 1989, pp. 1219–1243.

36 Law No. 35/1989; *Magyar Közlöny*, no. 78, 1 November 1989, pp. 1331–1333.

37 Edith Oltay, "Preparations for Hungary's First National Referendum Marked by Controversy," *RFE Research*, 22 December 1989, pp. 1–5. In reality, the SZDSZ and FIDESZ were divided on the future status of the presidency, with the former originally in favor of eventual direct elections for the office and the latter opposed.

38 Vigh, "Az Ellenzéki Kerekasztaltól," in Kurtán, Sándor, and Vass, *Magyarország Politikai Évkönyve 1990*, pp. 231–234.

39 Law No. 16/1990; *Magyar Közlöny*, no. 21, 12 March 1990, pp. 412–425. An

explanation of the circumstances surrounding this amendment can be found in Péter Szalay, "Rendszerváltozás és alkotmánymódosítás – 1990," in Kurtán, Sándor, and Vass, *Magyarország Politikai Évokönyve 1991* (Budapest: Ökonómia Alpítvány-Economix, 1991), p. 431.

40 Bruszt and Stark, "Remaking the Political Field in Hungary," p. 51. It is particularly ironic that Bruszt and Stark make this claim as a positive result of the transition, for the SZDSZ–FIDESZ referendum can largely be credited for this, which the authors viewed as little more than an act of self-interest.

41 Law No. 40/1990; *Magyar Közlöny*, no. 59, 25 June 1990, pp. 1269–1279.

42 "A paktum," in Kurtán, Sándor, and Vass, *Magyarország Politikai Évkönyve 1991*, pp. 428–429; a complete version of the pact's constitutional provisions can be found in *Magyar Hirlap*, 3 May 1990; translated in Foreign Broadcast Information Service, *Daily Report: East Europe* (hereafter *FBIS*), 14 June 1990, pp. 26–30. While this change in conviction by the SZDSZ with regard to the election of the president may seem a self-serving act on the part of the party leadership, in reality the SZDSZ had for some time been backing away from its support for a directly elected presidency, which was apparently reinforced by the close outcome of the FIDESZ–SZDSZ referendum. See Babus, "Népszavazás – 1989," in Kurtán, Sándor, and Vass, *Magyarország Politikai Évkönyve 1990*, p. 212.

43 "Tizenkét hónap krónikája," in Kurtán, Sándor and Vass, *Magyarország Politikai Évkönyve 1991*, pp. 476–477; an earlier opinion poll showed that 58 percent of those surveyed supported a direct election of the president. See "A politikai közvélemény 1990-ben," in ibid., pp. 589–590.

44 310 votes were cast: 295 were in favor of Göncz, 13 against, and two were invalid. For a thorough discussion of the motivations and events surrounding the 29 June referendum, see Judith Pataki, "Public Shows Little Interest in Referendum on Presidency," *RFE Report*, 10 August 1990, pp. 20–22.

45 MTI (Budapest), 3 August 1990; *FBIS*, 6 August 1990, pp. 26–27.

46 Budapest Domestic Service, 4 August 1990; *FBIS*, 6 August 1990, p. 24.

47 *Magyar Hirlap*, 18 August 1990, pp. 1, 3; *FBIS*, 29 August 1990, pp. 34–38.

48 "Tizenkét hónap krónikája," in Kurtán, Sándor, and Vass, *Magyarország Politikai Évkönyve 1991*, p. 486. Later reports suggest that the government had in fact actually discussed the use of the military against the drivers; see Budapest Television, 22 February 1991; *FBIS*, 4 March 1991, p. 19, and Máté Szabó, "The Taxi Driver Demonstration in Hungary: Social Protest in Policy Change," in Szoboszlai, *Flying Blind*, 358–359.

49 MTI (Budapest) and Budapest Domestic Service, 26 October 1990; *FBIS*, 29 October 1990, p. 37; see also "A Taxisblokád," in Kurtán, Sándor, and Vass, *Magyarország Politikai Évkönyve 1991*, p. 692, and Szabó, "Taxi Driver Demonstration," pp. 358–360.

50 Budapest Domestic Service, 28 October 1990; *FBIS*, 29 October 1990, p. 37; "A Taxisblokád," in Kurtán, Sándor, and Vass, *Magyarország Politikai Évkönyve 1991*, p. 694.

51 "Tizenkét hónap krónikája," in Kurtán, Sándor, and Vass, *Magyarország Politikai Évkönyve 1991*, p. 487.

52 *Népszabadság*, 28 December 1990; translated in Joint Publications Research Service *Eastern Europe* (hereafter *JPRS*) 1 February 1991, p. 10; see also "A

Politikai Közvélemény 1990-ben," in Kurtán, Sándor, and Vass, *Magyarország Politikai Évkönyve 1991*, p. 598.

53 László Kéri, *Összeomlás után* (Budapest: Kossuth, 1991), 100.

54 SZDSZ member of parliament, Miklós Szabó, "President and Government in the Era of Peaceful Transition," *Kritika* (July 1991), pp. 10–11; *JPRS*, 27 August 1991, pp. 9–12.

55 *Népszabadság*, 10 September 1991, p. 5; *JPRS*, 8 October 1991, pp. 19–20.

56 MDF Member of Parliament József Debreczeni, "Toward a Constitutional Crisis?" *Magyar Hirlap*, 3 September 1991, p. 7; *JPRS*, 3 October 1991, pp. 20–21.

57 *Magyar Narancs*, 9 October 1991, p. 3; *JPRS*, 25 November 1991, pp. 19–20.

58 Constitutional Court decision No. 48; *Magyar Közlöny*, no. 103, 26 September 1991, pp. 2111–2125; see also Judith Pataki and John W. Schiemann, "Constitutional Court Limits Presidential Powers," *RFE Report*, 18 October 1991, pp. 5–9.

59 A good review of these events from differing perspectives can be found in Edith Oltay, "Hungarian Radio and Television Under Fire," *Radio Free Europe/Radio Liberty Research Report*, 24 September 1993, pp. 40–44, Judith Pataki, "Hungarian Radio Staff Cuts Cause Uproar," *Radio Free Europe/Radio Liberty Research Report*, 13 May 1994, pp. 38–43, and Robert Bonte-Friedheim, "Journalists Still Treated as Cannon-Fodder," *IPI Report*, August 1993, pp. 16–19.

60 *RFE/RL Daily Report*, no. 100, May 26, 1992; *ibid*, no. 102, 29 May 1992. The constitution stipulates that a motion for impeachment may only proceed if the president has violated the constitution or some other law; the motion can be initiated by as little as one-fifth of the members of parliament, although the actual vote on impeachment requires a two-thirds vote to pass. The Constitutional Court is empowered to rule on the legality of presidential actions.

61 Budapest Kossuth Radio Network, 8 June 1992; *FBIS*, 9 June 1992, p. 21; for the text of the constitutional court ruling see "Médiavita: a levelezések éve," in Sándor Kurtán, Péter Sándor, and László Vass (eds.), *Magyarország politikai évkönyve 1993* (Budapest: Demokrácia Kutatások Magyar Központja Alapítvány, 1994), pp. 187–188.

62 "Médiavita: a levelezések éve," pp. 189–205.

63 András Mink, "Hungary," *East European Constitutional Review*, 2–3, 4–1 (Fall 1993–Winter 1994), p. 71.

64 One example was the 1994 firing of over 100 editors and journalists at Hungarian Radio for reasons that to many appeared to be more political than fiscal in nature, Pataki, "Hungarian Radio Staff Cuts Cause Uproar," pp. 41–43; also Peter Elam, "Hoist by its Own Media," *Index On Censorship*, 23, 3 (July–August 1994), pp. 20–22.

65 László Bruszt and János Simon, "Az Antall-korszak után, a választások előtt," in Sándor Kurtán, Péter Sándor, and László Vass (eds.), *Magyarország politikai évkönyve 1994* (Budapest: Demokrácia Kutatások Magyar Központja Alapítvány, 1994), p. 802.

66 For details on recent political change in Hungary see Patrick H. O'Neil, "Hungary's Hesitant Transition," *Current History* (March 1996), pp. 135–139.

67 Judith Pataki, "Controversy over Hungary's New Media Heads," *Radio Free Europe/Radio Liberty Research Report*, 12 August 1994, pp. 14–17.

68 *Magyar Narancs*, 9 October 1991, p. 3; *JPRS*, 25 November 1991, p. 19. Such a conflict is not mere speculation. Intense clashes in Romania between President Ion Iliescu and former Prime Minister Petre Roman, both of the ruling National Salvation Front, contributed to the fragmentation of the NSF; similar rifts between Lech Wałęsa and former Prime Minister Tadeusz Mazowiecki helped bring an end to Solidarity, and Slovakia has witnessed serious conflict soon after independence between President Michal Kovac and Prime Minister Vladimir Meciar, who initially were close political allies and co-founders of the Movement for a Democratic Slovakia.

69 Rick E. Bruner, "Constitutional Court Nixes Presidential Referendum," *Hungary Report* 〈www.isys.hu/hrep/archive.html〉, 7 May 1995.

70 On the 1995 presidential election see *Hirmondo* hun@cs.uchicago.edu 12 April–22 June 1995, and Sarah Roe, "Göncz Re-Elected President by One Vote," *Hungary Report* 〈www.isys.hu/hrep/archive.html〉, 26 June 1995.

71 Baylis, "Presidents Versus Prime Ministers," pp. 321–322.

72 Linz, *The Breakdown of Democratic Regimes*, p. 74; see also Baylis, "Presidents Versus Prime Ministers," pp. 320–322.

8   Afterword: the making of postcommunist presidencies

Jon Elster

The study of the presidency and its relations to other political institutions can be carried out in (at least) three perspectives. First, there is the *factual* study of the presidency and its powers. On this point, the recent treatments by Shugart and Carey[1] and Linz,[2] as well as the articles collected in Lijphart,[3] offer a fairly complete picture of the varieties of presidential regimes, together with a discussion of their downstream properties (see below). They can be supplemented by McGregor[4] and Lucky,[5] which survey the presidencies in fifteen postcommunist countries with regard to forty-three and thirty-eight variables respectively. Secondly, there is the *upstream* study of the making of the presidency in new constitutions. Thirdly, there is the *downstream* analysis of the effects of the presidency once the new institutions begin to work. The two latter, more theoretical tasks are of course related to each other. The effect of a constitution depends among other things on its perceived legitimacy, which in turn is related to the way it came into being. Conversely, constitution-makers obviously have to take account of probable downstream consequences of the various alternative arrangements they are choosing among. Yet to a first approximation the approaches are distinct and may be discussed separately.

In my own work on constitution-making in Eastern Europe I have focused on upstream analysis.[6] In these writings I have tried to identify individual and institutional actors in the constitution-making processes, and their motives and constraints; as well as the arguing and bargaining that took place before the new constitutions became adopted. I have also studied constitution-making in other times and places. In one article,[7] I compare the making of the American constitution of 1787 and the French constitution of 1791; in another,[8] I compare executive-legislative relations in the making of the French constitutions of 1791, 1848, and 1958. Because I know something about these upstream processes, and much less about what happens downstream, my comments here are limited to the former aspect.

Also, it is fair to say that in the postcommunist countries it may be too

225

early for downstream analysis. First, political practices are generally underdetermined by the written constitution. A presidency that looks powerful on paper may be quite weak in reality; and vice versa. Only the slow emergence of constitutional conventions will settle the textual ambiguities or gaps. In the French constitution of 1958, for instance, it is not clear whether the president can revoke the prime' minister. When challenged on this point during the process of elaborating the constitution, de Gaulle answered that the president "ne peut pas revoquer le premier ministre."[9] Nevertheless, a custom developed that the president can revoke a prime minister *from his own side*, as happened with de Gaulle and Debré, with Pompidou and Chaban-Delmas, and with Mitterand and Rocard. Second, a robust downstream analysis must await until the dust has settled, i.e., until the political system has found some kind of equilibrium state. In most postcommunist countries the party system and electoral legislation have probably not found their definitive form. Thirdly, it is difficult to distinguish the powers of the presidential office from the impact of exceptional personalities that emerged in the transition process.

In discussing the adoption of specific presidential regimes in (some of) the postcommunist states, I focus on the following issues: (i) design of the presidency as part of the "negotiated transition to democracy"; and (ii) design of the presidency to fit (or to constrain) a particular presidential contender. First, however, I consider the concept of presidential powers.

Powers of the presidency

Shugart and Carey[10] and McGregor[11] offer indices of overall presidential power, as weighted sums of numerous individual powers. By the nature of the case, these constructions are somewhat arbitrary. Let me first focus on one weakness that is common to both indices: they do not reflect the important power difference between directly and indirectly elected presidents. In his chapter in this volume Stephen White observes that, "Yeltsin owed much of his dominance to the fact that he had been directly elected, unlike Gorbachev." O'Neil, in his chapter, writes that the Hungarian bargaining over the presidency took place under the assumption "that the manner of presidential election was the key component in determining the strength of the office." Going beyond the East European context, it is widely recognized that the powers of the French presidency under the Fifth Republic were strongly enhanced with the introduction in 1962 of direct elections of the president.

Shugart and Carey cannot really be flawed on this point, as they explicitly limit themselves to regimes with directly elected presidents.

McGregor's "constitutional power score," however, is applied to countries both with directly and indirectly elected presidents. In constructing his score solely on the basis of formal attributes of the presidency he then overlooks the fact that the power *conferred by* the constitution goes beyond the powers *listed in* the constitution. Because the mode of election of the president is stipulated in the constitution, the power it confers ought to be a component, and an important one, of any index of constitutional power. The neglect of this source of presidential power probably explains the surprising fact that the Hungarian presidency receives the highest score of all fourteen countries covered in McGregor's survey, just ahead of the Polish one. One cannot, of course, refute the construction simply by observing that Wałęsa was much more powerful than Göncz. That difference might also be due to the greater prestige and charisma of Wałęsa. Yet there are many general reasons, not linked to personalities, why popular election confers more power on the presidency than election by parliament. Let me mention some of them.

Following the maxim "Let the king beware of the kingmaker," one may argue that an indirectly elected president lacks power because he is the creature of the parliament that has made him. As stated, the argument is not persuasive. In fact, the opposite maxim might seem more appropriate: "Let the kingmaker beware of the king." Once the president has been elected by the assembly, he owes it nothing. The first maxim is apt, nevertheless, if the president can and does seek reelection, for then he continues to depend on the assembly that has put him into power. Another argument is that faced with a choice between a strong and a weak presidential contender, an assembly will elect the latter from whom it has less to fear. (Below I argue that a constituent assembly may have an incentive to design a weak *presidency*, especially if the front-runner is a forceful personality.) These arguments are merely negative. There are also positive reasons why a popularly elected president can use his stronger democratic legitimacy to get his way in a conflict with parliament. He may be able to stage a direct confrontation by mobilizing masses or crowds on his side. He may also be able to mobilize the press and other media and, through them, to put pressure on the parliamentarians.

Even when we disregard the problem of arbitrariness, these indices may not measure all relevant aspects of presidential power. Suppose that we want to test an hypothesis to the effect that under specific circumstances constitutions tend to be made so as to favor the president at the expense of the government. In that case, the dependent variable is the power of the president *relative to that of the government* rather than the power relative to the power (as measured by the power indices) of the presidency in other countries. The former variable cannot be constructed on the basis of the latter. Suppose we compare three countries. In country A, the president has extensive emergency powers. In country B, the government has the same powers. In country C, these powers are not vested in any institution. On the presidential power indices, B and C would be ranked as equal on that dimension, and both would be inferior to A. Yet it is clear that compared to the government the presidency is weaker in B than in C. Also, the right to call referenda or to bring legislation before the Constitutional Court might belong to the president, to the government, to both, or to neither. Similar problems would arise if one wanted to test the hypothesis, further discussed below, that if the sole author of the constitution is an assembly that also serves as an ordinary legislature, it will tend to write large powers for the legislature into the constitution at the expense of the president. For instance, the right to appoint the governor of the central bank may belong to the president, to parliament – or to neither.

To summarize, the notion of presidential powers, as measured by the formal powers of the office, is fragile. It harbors problems both of reliability and of validity. First, there is the fact that political practice may go beyond the constitutional text. Secondly, the weights assigned to the different powers are irremediably arbitrary. I can see no reason to expect the conclusions in chapter 8 of Shugart and Carey to be invariant under (plausible) positive monotonic transformations of the weights; the claim that their method "is preferable to a purely nonquantitative impressionistic ranking,"[12] remains to be proven. Third, the power measure is deficient in that it does not take account of the mode of election of the president. Finally, the power indices do not measure the powers of the presidency relative to other institutions. I am not saying that assessments of presidential powers are impossible, only that they are best left to *judgment* (a term I prefer to "impressionistic ranking") rather than to a mechanical procedure.

The presidency as transition compromise

Arend Lijphart has argued that the political dynamics in Eastern Europe can be explained by a generalization of the "Rokkan hypothesis." Rokkan had claimed that countries in the transition to democracy will adopt a system of proportional representation "through a convergence of pressures from below and from above. The rising working class wanted to lower the threshold of representation in order to gain access to the legislatures, and the most threatened of the old-established parties demanded PR to protect their position against the new waves of mobilized voters created by universal suffrage."[13] Extending this reasoning, Lijphart suggests that three of the arrangements that emerged from the

Round Table Talks (RTT) in Eastern Europe were intended to guarantee a political presence for the communist nomenklatura as well as for the new opposition. First, there were compromises over the electoral system. Second, the bi-cameral system can be engineered so that the old regime will do well in elections to one house and the new forces in elections to the other. Finally, because the communists feared that they would be in a minority in parliament, they demanded and got the presidency for their candidate. Here I shall focus on the last claim. I limit myself to Bulgaria, Hungary, and Poland, which are the countries I know something about.

In the process of bargaining over the presidency in these countries we find a few recurrent themes. One is that constitutional arguments about the proper role of the presidency in a system of checks and balances played a very minor role. Instead, the presidency was designed to fit a particular candidate for the office (see also the following section). Another finding is that the design of the presidency was part of a larger bargaining process, in which the powers of that office were traded off against other political demands. Finally, we find that the calculations and expectations that went into the bargaining and logrolling were regularly proven wrong by later events. In all three countries, a presidency designed for the communist candidate was eventually occupied by a member of the opposition.

Poland introduced the institution of the presidency as part of the deal struck in the Round Table Talks in the spring of 1989. The government negotiators offered to have free elections to some of the seats in the Sejm (lower house). In exchange, they demanded the introduction of the office of the president to replace the Council of State, a sort of collective presidency created by the 1952 constitution. It was understood from the beginning that the president would be General Jaruzelski, the central figure of the communist apparatus. Vested with large powers, he would be elected by the Sejm together with various other bodies that could be counted on to vote with the communists. In this way, any democratic procedures initiated by the new Sejm could be thwarted, if necessary. When the negotiators from the opposition refused this proposal – Bronisław Geremek, the chief Solidarity negotiator, said that he could accept to see democracy raped once, but not twice – deadlock set in. As described by Wiktor Osiatyński,[14] the stalemate was broken by a government negotiator and future Polish president, Aleksander Kwaśniewski, who launched a new idea: "How about electing the president by the Sejm and the Senate, which, in turn, would be elected freely?" "This is worth thinking about," said Geremek.

Although duly elected to the presidency, Jaruzelski correctly perceived that he did not have the legitimacy to use the vast powers of his office.

These powers became more important with the election of Wałęsa to the presidency in December 1990. It then became clear that the powers were not only extensive, but vaguely defined. According to one commentator, they had been "left deliberately vague on the assumption, current early in 1989, that a communist president would use whatever prerogatives he saw fit, since he could rely on the backing of the army, security forces and his Soviet sponsors."[15] According to another, it was the other way around: "Opposition negotiators have since admitted also to having deliberately designed the 'presidential clauses' of the round-table agreement to be as confusing as possible, with an eye to reduce Jaruzelski's room for maneuver."[16] According to a centrally placed participant in the RTT, who will have to remain anonymous, the powers of the presidency have a different origin. Stanisław Ciosek (Politburo member and one of the two main party negotiators) is reported to have said: "The Politburo will never accept anything short of a strong presidency, designed for Jaruzelski. But without a president it will not be possible to destroy the Party."

In *Hungary*, the Round Table Talks in the summer and fall of 1989 similarly included bargaining over the presidency (see O'Neil's chapter in this volume). In fact, two different bargaining processes centered on this issue, within the opposition and between the opposition and the Communist Party. Formally, three issues were at stake: the mode of election of the president (direct or indirect), the timing of the presidential election (before or after the election of a new parliament), and the powers of the presidency. In reality, the main issue was whether, and on what terms, the opposition would accept Imre Pozsgay, a reformist communist leader, as president. Because of the extreme fluidity of the political situation, the questions were never definitely settled during the RTT, and the eventual outcome differed from what had been expected by most participants.

From the point of view of the communists, the alternatives were assessed as follows. If the president was elected by the obedient parliament then in session, their candidacy was a certain winner – but his legitimacy might suffer. If he was elected by popular vote before the elections to the new parliament, Pozsgay's visibility and popularity made it likely that he would win. Although slightly more risky, this option offered the advantage of greater legitimacy. The opposition's main demand was to delay the election of the president until after the election of the new parliament. A secondary demand, based on the assumption that Pozsgay was in fact likely to be elected, was for a strict limitation of the powers of the presidency.

In the course of negotiations, the communists made several concessions aimed at creating a consensus for Pozsgay. In August, they offered that in exchange for the acceptance of his candidacy, they would dissolve the Workers' Defense, a paramilitary communist organization. In September, they also offered to have the new president elected by popular vote. This was presented as a concession, as they could easily have elected the president by the parliament then in session. Yet, as mentioned, this course also offered the advantage of greater legitimacy. The communists also agreed to limit the powers of the presidency. Faced with these proposals, the opposition was unable to reach internal agreement. At least three oppositional groups favored a presidential election before the parliamentary elections, thus in effect accepting Pozsgay as president. Others, notably the Free Democrats under the leadership of Janos Kiś, insisted that the presidency be offered to the communists, but only after the parliamentary elections, so that it could be used as a bargaining chip. Although the former got their way, the latter kept their options open by refusing to sign the final agreement on 18 September 1989.

At that time, the general expectation was that there would be an early election of Pozsgay. The calculations were upset by a major unforeseen event. When the Communist Party dissolved itself and created a new Socialist Party to take its place, a majority of the members failed to join the new party. Not even a majority of members of parliament – selected for their blind loyalty – joined up. Moreover, the expected election of Pozsgay as president of the new party also failed to materialize. These events created a severe demoralization in the regime. In the ensuing power vacuum, the government was able to be a surprisingly active force, and to push through a number of constitutional amendments with minimal resistance in parliament. The Free Democrats and their allies called for a referendum on the timing of the presidential elections and obtained, by a narrow margin, that the president be elected after parliament. When a later referendum (called by the ex-communists) for direct elections of the president failed to get the necessary quorum, the final result was the very opposite of the implicit deal of the RTT agreement. Instead of a communist candidate chosen in direct elections before the election of a new parliament, the presidency went to a politician from the opposition elected by the new parliament.

In *Bulgaria*, the presidency was also a major bargaining issue in the Round Table Talks that took place in the winter of 1990, between the Communist Party and the Union of Democratic Forces (UDF), a "forum organization" of oppositional groups. These talks differed from those in Poland and Hungary in one important respect. The Communist Party had started to reform itself before the talks began, by expelling its long-time leader, Todor Zhivkov, from power. Because they changed their ways by preemption rather than concession, the party had a much stronger legitimacy than its counterparts elsewhere in Eastern Europe. Also, because Bulgaria did not harbor the virulent anti-Soviet feelings that characterized most of the other countries, the communist leaders were never seen as traitors.

The communists began by demanding a constitutional amendment for the introduction of a president who would be directly elected within a five-year or six-year mandate and enjoy strong powers. Both sides knew that the communist candidate, the current head of state, Peter Mladenov would be chosen as president if there were direct elections. He had been the leading figure in the ousting of Zhivkov from power, and public opinion surveys showed that he had overwhelming popular support. The UDF insisted on a president elected by the currently acting National Assembly with a one-year mandate and limited functions of the presidential institution. This preference, too, was based on an assumption (or agreement) that Mladenov would be the new president. In the end, the UDF solution was chosen, partly because of pressure from the agrarian party, which had been allied with the communists but now turned against them.

Mladenov was duly elected president by the assembly, as part of a package solution that also included an agreement on elections to a Constituent Assembly. The first act of the latter body, however, was to depose Mladenov from power, when it turned out that during demonstrations in Sofia on 16 December 1989 he had said, on camera, "Let the tanks come." Meanwhile, mass protest has spread in the form of "towns of truth" – tent camps in the centers of about twenty big towns. Parliament voted for a president in conditions of expanding mass peaceful protest. Day-by-day the National Assembly building was besieged by a crowd demanding the election of a president from the opposition. After four unsuccessful rounds of voting (neither side was able to control the two-thirds of the votes needed for the election of a new president), the leader of the opposition Zheliu Zhelev was elected to the presidency.

Both sides miscalculated. The opposition demanded a weak presidency because they assumed that it would be occupied by the communist candidate. Then, more or less by accident, it acceded to a presidency that, on its own insistence, had been shorn of strong powers. The communists had insisted on a strong presidency because they feared they might become a minority in the new parliament. As it turned out, they gained a majority in the Constituent Assembly.

Tailor-made presidencies?

Ideally, constitutions ought to be written under a veil of ignorance, and not with specific circumstances, individuals, or parties in mind. As

Pierre-Henri Teitgen said in the debate over the French constitution of 1958 "une bonne constitution, c'est une constitution qui n'est pas faite 'sur mesure', c'est une constitution 'de confection', parce qu'elle est appelée à durer généralement longtemps."[17] In the same debate, Alfred Bour asserted "Nous ne faisons la Constitution ni pour un homme ni pour des circonstances données."[18] To implement this idea, one might decide that the constitution should not take effect until, say, ten years after it has been adopted.

It does not take much knowledge of constitutional history to know that, and why, things do not work like this in practice. Constitutions are written in times of crisis that do not allow for the luxury of waiting.[19] Also, they are written by individuals who are very likely to be involved in running the new regime and who cannot in general be expected to ignore that fact. First, most constitutions are written by assemblies that at the same time serve as ordinary legislatures. They have an incentive, therefore, to write a strong role for the legislature into the constitution. (A rare exception is the first French Assemblée Constituante of 1789–91, which declared its members ineligible to the first ordinary legislature.) Secondly, presidential candidates, including in some cases the current occupant of the office, may try to design the constitution to enhance their likelihood of attaining or retaining that office, and/or to increase its powers. Conversely, their opponents, including in many cases the legislature or parts of it, may try to design the constitution to reduce that likelihood, and/or to reduce the powers of the office.

This second tendency can be captured in the idea of "tailor-made" presidencies. Sometimes, the presidency is made *by the tailor for the tailor*. The outstanding case is the making of the 1958 French constitution, written by de Gaulle and for him. In other cases, the constitution is written *against the front-runner by his opponents*, in order to reduce the powers of his office as much as possible. Classical cases are the design of the Polish constitution of 1921 (written against Piłsudski) and of the French constitution of 1946 (written against de Gaulle). In both cases, the supposed candidates refused the straitjacket their opponents had designed for them; and in both cases they came back later, with a vengeance.

As noted earlier, the overall power of the presidency is determined both by the formal powers of the office and by the power associated with a particular mode of election. Tailor-making for the purpose of strengthening or weakening a particular candidate who seems likely to be elected can be concerned with both aspects. In addition, the choice of a mode of election can be motivated by the desire to render the victory of a particular candidate more or less probable. This was, for instance, very much a concern of the framers of the French constitution of 1848, many of whom strongly argued for election of the president by parliament to prevent Louis-Napoleon from being chosen. This second effect of the mode of election might well enter into conflict with the first effect (affecting the power of the office). The supporters of a given candidate will obviously want to maximize both his chances of being elected and the powers he will have once elected. In general, the second objective is best realized by direct elections. Sometimes, however, the first is best realized by indirect elections. As noted earlier, the Hungarian communists faced a trade-off of this kind in 1989.

Constituent assemblies that also serve as ordinary parliaments have, as noted, an incentive to create weak presidencies, a tendency that is reinforced if the most likely contender is a strong personality. The most effective procedure, however, obviously to create a presidency with few formal powers, is to have the president elected by parliament, and then proceed to elect a weak personality as president (if the strong candidates have not already taken themselves out of the race for the emasculated office).

In considering now some of the postcommunist presidencies, I began with Poland, where at least three stages in the evolution of the presidency can be understood in the light of these general arguments. In the spring of 1989, the RTT agreement on the mode of electing the president was clearly designed to ensure the choice of Jaruzelski. In the fall of 1990, as observed by Krzysztof Jasiewicz in his chapter, "The idea of electing the president by a popular vote rather than by a vote of the National Assembly originated in Mazowiecki's camp. Although Mazowiecki's public opinion ratings were still quite high, Wałęsa and his supporters realized that the prime minister's popularity was fading, and consequently accepted the challenge." In the fall of 1992, the making of the "little constitution" focused on the powers of the presidency rather than on the mode of election.[20] The central issue concerned the relative powers of the president and parliament in the appointment of the prime minister. President Wałęsa offered a very "presidential" draft, which gave strong powers to the presidency in the appointment process. His main opponent (and former ally), Jarosław Kaczyński, leader of the Center Alliance (a center-right split-off from Solidarity) and member of the extraordinary commission of the Sejm to examine the little constitution, had a consistently anti-presidential attitude. In principle, he was for a strong presidency – as long as it was not occupied by Wałęsa, towards whom he had developed violently hostile feelings. In the constitution-making process, therefore, he pushed for a predominant role for the Sejm in the formation of the government. The final document was a very complicated compromise formula, in which the president and the

Sejm take turns in proposing candidates for the position of prime minister.

I need not say more about the role of personalities in the shaping of the Bulgarian and Hungarian presidencies. Instead, I conclude with some comments on the design of the presidency in the Czechoslovak Federation and the Czech Republic.[21]

Václav Havel tried, with little success, to strengthen the powers of the two presidential offices he has occupied. One reason for his failure may, perhaps, be found in his very special conception of politics. Many close observers explained his behavior in terms of his background as a playwright. According to one, Havel lived in "dramatic time," not understanding that parliamentary politics takes place in "epic time." He wanted long periods to be condensed into short, dramatic moments. According to another, Havel saw himself as an actor, acting in a play written by himself. He had no feeling of being subject to constraints. By the time he understood how normal politics worked, valuable time had been lost. But his failure to shape constitutional politics in the Czechoslovak Federation may also have a more mundane explanation. As explained in Sharon Wolchik's chapter, he repeatedly asked parliament to increase the powers of the presidency. His constitutional draft of 5 March 1991, for instance, gave the president the right to declare a state of emergency, to dissolve parliament, and to call referendums. It is not surprising that these proposals, coming from the very office whose powers were to be enhanced, met with great resistance. I am confident that Havel was motivated by the best interests of the country; in fact, I think his proposals probably were in the best interest of the country. Yet the fact that they could be presented as self-serving made it possible for parliament to turn them down. Perhaps he should have emulated the French *constituants* of 1789 and announced that he would step down from the presidency once its enhanced powers had been voted.

After Havel's resignation from the federal presidency, it was reported that he might accept the presidency of the Czech republic if that office was vested with more than symbolic powers. In addition to direct election of the president, he reportedly wanted a strong presidential veto and no requirement of a countersignature. None of these wishes were fulfilled. More generally, in the Czech constitution, the presidency is not a strong institution.[22] The main explanation is probably that Havel had lost his power base. The parties that had originated in Havel's Civic Forum had been wiped out in the 1992 elections, and Václav Klaus had emerged as the dominant politician in the Czech Republic. Nevertheless, Havel's *de facto* powers go well beyond those that can be read off from the constitution. The tradition from the First Republic according to which "the

Castle" – i.e., the president – is heavily involved with foreign policy is still alive. Also, Havel's personal stature probably enhances his influence. It would follow, though, from the arguments presented earlier that one reason why the formal powers of the presidency are relatively weak is that the framers anticipated and tried to reduce the effect of Havel's personal stature. To some extent, the constitution may have been written against him. This remains conjectural, however.

Summary

The design of the postcommunist presidencies owes much to general mechanisms that operate in other constitution-making contexts. Similar power play among politicians – parliamentarians and presidential contenders – has been observed over and over again in the last 150 years. At the same time, the process also owes much to the highly specific features of the transition from communism to democracy.

Three important forces in the shaping of the postcommunist presidencies are individual interest, group interest, and institutional interest. Individual interests are those of occupants of the office or pretenders to it, who try to design the attributes of the office to make it as powerful as possible and the mode of election to maximize their chances of attaining it. Group interests are the interests of the communists and postcommunists in retaining (some) power and that of the oppositional forces in excluding them. Institutional interest is the interest of constituent assemblies in enhancing the power of the legislature at the expense of the executive and judiciary.

To my knowledge, no postcommunist constitution-makers have engaged in genuinely impartial discussion to choose the regime that would best serve the interests of the country. Bargaining rather than arguing has been the predominant mode of reaching agreement. Reason has been crowded out by interest and passion.

NOTES

1 Matthew Shugart and John Carey, *Presidents and Assemblies* (Cambridge: Cambridge University Press, 1992).
2 Juan Linz, "Presidential or Parliamentary Democracy: Does It Make a Difference?" in Juan Linz and Arturo Valenzuela (eds.), *The Failure of Presidential Democracy*, vol. I (Baltimore, MD: Johns Hopkins University Press, 1994), pp. 3–87.
3 Arend Lijphart (ed.), *Parliamentary Versus Presidential Government* (New York: Oxford University Press, 1992).
4 James McGregor, "The Presidency in East Central Europe," *RFE/RL Re-*

search Report, 14 January 1994.

5 Christian Lucky, "Table of Presidential Powers in Eastern Europe," *East European Constitutional Review*, Fall 1993/Winter 1994, pp. 81–94.

6 Jon Elster, "Constitutionalism in Eastern Europe An Introduction," *University of Chicago Law Review*, 58 (1991), pp. 447–482; Jon Elster, "Rebuilding the Boat in the Open Sea: Constitution-Making in Eastern Europe," *Public Administration*, 71 (1993), pp. 169–217; Jon Elster, "Bargaining Over the Presidency," *East European Constitutional Review*, Fall 1993/Winter 1994, pp. 95–98: Jon Elster, "Transition, Constitution-Making and Separation in Czechoslovakia," *Archives Européennes de Sociologie*, 36 (1995), pp. 105–134.

7 Jon Elster, "Argumenter et négocier dans deux assemblées constituantes," *Revue Française de Science Politique*, 44 (1994), pp. 187–256.

8 Jon Elster, "Executive-Legislative Relations in Three French Constitution-Making Episodes" (forthcoming).

9 *Documents pour servir à l'histoire de l'élaboration de la constitution du 4 octobre 1958*, vol. II (Paris: La Documentation Française, 1988), p. 300.

10 Shugart and Carey, *Presidents and Assemblies*.

11 McGregor, "The Presidency in East Central Europe."

12 Shugart and Carey, *Presidents and Assemblies*, p. 149.

13 Cited after Lijphart, *Parliamentary Versus Presidential Government*, p. 108.

14 Wiktor Osiatyński, "The Roundtable Negotiations in Poland," in Jon Elster (ed.), *The Round Table Talks and the Breakdown of Communism (Constitutionalism in Eastern Europe)* (Chicago: University of Chicago Press, 1996).

15 Anna Sabbat-Swidlicka, "Poland," *RFE/RL Research Report*, 3 July 1992. This was a special issue on the rule of law in Eastern Europe.

16 Marcin Król, cited in Louisa Vinton, "Poland's 'Little Constitution' Clarifies Wałęsa's Powers," *RFE/RL Research Report*, 4 September 1992.

17 *Documents*, vol. II, p. 218.

18 Ibid., p. 89.

19 Jon Elster, "Forces and Mechanisms in the Constitution-Making Process," *Duke Law Review*, 1995.

20 For details, see Elster, "Rebuilding the Boat in the Open Sea."

21 See Elster, "Transition, Constitution-Making and Separation in Czechoslovakia."

22 Vojtech Cepl and Mark Gillis, "Survey of the Presidency in the Czech Republic," *East European Constitutional Review*, Fall 1993/Winter 1994, pp. 64–68.

Select bibliography

Agh, Attila (ed.), *The Emergence of East Central European Parliaments: The First Steps* (Budapest: Hungarian Center of Democracy Studies, 1994).

Baylis, Thomas A., "Presidents Versus Prime Ministers: Shaping Executive Authority in Eastern Europe," *World Politics*, 48, 3 (April 1996), 297–323.

Colton, Timothy J. and Robert C. Tucker (eds.), *Patterns in Post-Soviet Leadership* (Boulder, CO: Westview Press, 1995).

Duverger, Maurice, "A New Political System Model: Semi-Presidential Government," *European Journal of Political Research*, 8, 2 (June 1980), 165–187.

Easter, Gerald M., "Preference for Presidentialism: Postcommunist Regime Change in Russia and the NIS," *World Politics* 49, 2 (January 1997), 184–211.

East European Constitutional Review, "The Postcommunist Presidency," 2, (Fall 1993), and 3, 1 (Winter 1994).

Elster, Jon (ed.), *The Roundtable Talks and the Breakdown of Communism (Constitutionalism in Eastern Europe)* (Chicago: University of Chicago Press, 1996).

Fabbrini, Sergio, "Presidents, Parliaments, and Good Government," *Journal of Democracy*, 6, 3 (July 1995), 128–138.

Gwyn, William B., "The Separation of Powers and Modern Forms of Democratic Government," in Robert A. Goldwin and Art Kaufman (eds.), *Separation of Powers – Does It Still Work?* (Washington, DC: American Enterprise Institute for Public Policy Research, 1986), pp. 65–89.

Higley, John, Judith Kullberg, and Jan Pakulski, "The Persistence of Postcommunist Elites," *Journal of Democracy*, 7, 2 (April 1996), 133–147.

Horowitz, Donald L., "Comparing Democratic Systems," *Journal of Democracy*, 1, 4 (Fall 1990).

Huskey, Eugene (ed.), *Executive Power and Soviet Politics: The Rise and Decline of the Soviet State* (Armonk, NY: M. E. Sharpe, 1992).

King, Anthony, "Executives," in Fred I. Greenstein and Nelson W. Polsby (eds.), *Handbook of Political Science: Governmental Institutions and Processes*, vol. 5 (Menlo Park, CA: Addison-Wesley, 1975), 173–256.

Laski, Harold J., "The Parliamentary and Presidential Systems," *Public Administration Review*, 4, 4 (Autumn 1944), 347–359.

Laver, Michael and Kenneth A. Shepsie, *Cabinet Ministers and Parliamentary Government* (Cambridge: Cambridge University Press, 1994).

Lijphart, Arend, "Constitutional Choices for New Democracies," *Journal of Democracy*, 2, 1 (Winter 1991).

Lijphart, Arend, "Presidentialism and Majoritarian Democracy: Theoretical Observations," in Gyorgy Szoboszlai (ed.), *Democracy and Political Transformation: Theories and East-Central European Realities* (Budapest: Hungarian Political Science Association, 1991), 75–93.

Lijphart, Arend (ed.), *Parliamentary Versus Presidential Government* (New York: Oxford University Press, 1992).

Lijphart, Arend and Carlos Waisman (eds.), *Institutional Design in New Democracies: Eastern Europe and Latin America* (Boulder, CO: Westview Press, 1996).

Linz, Juan, "The Perils of Presidentialism," *Journal of Democracy*, 1, 1 (Winter 1990).

"The Virtues of Parliamentarism," *Journal of Democracy*, 1, 4 (Fall 1990).

Linz, Juan, and Alfred Stepan, *Problems of Democratic Transition and Consolidation: Southern Europe, South America, and Postcommunist Europe* (Baltimore, MD: Johns Hopkins University Press, 1996).

Linz, Juan and Arturo Valenzuela (eds.), *The Failure of Presidential Democracy: Comparative Perspectives*, vols. I–II (Baltimore, MD: Johns Hopkins University Press, 1994).

Linz, Juan, and Arturo Valenzuela, *Presidential or Parliamentary Democracy: Does It Make a Difference?* (Baltimore, MD: Johns Hopkins University Press 1992).

Mainwaring, Scott, and Matthew Shugart (eds.), *Presidentialism and Democracy in Latin America* (Cambridge: Cambridge University Press, 1997).

McGregor, James, "The Presidency in East Central Europe," *RFE/RL Research Report*, 3, 2 (14 January 1994), 23–31.

O'Neil, Patrick H., "Revolution From Within: Institutional Analysis, Transitions from Authoritarianism, and the Case of Hungary," *World Politics* 48, 4 (July 1996), 579–603.

Olson, David M. and Philip Norton (eds.), *The New Parliaments of Central and Eastern Europe* (London: Frank Cass, 1996).

Price, Don K., "The Parliamentary and Presidential Systems," *Public Administration Review*, 3, 1 (Winter 1943), 317–334.

Remington, Thomas (ed.), *Parliaments in Transition: The New Legislative Politics in the Former USSR and Eastern Europe* (Boulder, CO: Westview Press, 1994).

Sartori, Giovanni, *Comparative Constitutional Engineering: An Inquiry Into Structures, Incentives and Outcomes* (New York: New York University Press, 1994).

Shugart, Matthew, and John M. Carey, *Presidents and Assemblies* (Cambridge: Cambridge University Press, 1992).

Stepan, Alfred and Cindy Skach, "Constitutional Frameworks and Democratic Consolidation: Parliamentarianism versus Presidentialism," *World Politics*, 46, 1 (October 1993), 1–22.

Vile, M. J. C., *Constitutionalism and the Separation of Powers* (Oxford: Clarendon Press, 1967).

Von Mettenheim, Kurt, *Presidential institutions and democratic politics: comparing regional and national contexts* (Baltimore, MD: Johns Hopkins University Press, 1997).

Von Mettenheim, Kurt (ed.), *Presidents in Democratic Transitions* (Baltimore, MD: Johns Hopkins University Press, forthcoming).

White, Stephen, *Gorbachev and After* (Cambridge: Cambridge University Press, 1994).

Index